T0248082

LEAD!

LEAD!

BOOK ONE

Finding Your Leadership Identity

GREGORY H. GARRISON

PEAKPOINT
— PRESS —

Peakpoint Press books may be purchased in bulk at special discounts for sales promotion, corporate gifts, fund-raising, or educational purposes. Special editions can also be created to specifications. For details, contact the Special Sales Department, Skyhorse Publishing, 307 West 36th Street, 11th Floor, New York, NY 10018 or info@skyhorsepublishing.com.

Peakpoint® and Peakpoint Press® are registered trademarks of Skyhorse Publishing, Inc.®, a Delaware corporation.

Visit our website at www.skyhorsepublishing.com.

10 9 8 7 6 5 4 3 2 1

Library of Congress Cataloging-in-Publication Data is available on file.

Cover design by Tom Lau and David Ter-Avanesyan

ISBN: 978-1-5107-8009-5
Ebook ISBN: 978-1-5107-8023-1

Printed in the United States of America

Dedicated to my sons Matthew and Christopher

Contents

Preface

As I carefully consider my own leadership journey and what learning I might impart through this work, I am reminded of Warren Bennis, who is widely considered the founding father of modern leadership. As a consequence of his harrowing experiences in World War II, in leadership discussions, he often cites examples of transformative traumatic experiences in leaders' lives. He characterizes these events that dramatically shaped and honed their leadership abilities as "crucibles of leadership."

Through trying or tragic experiences, one examines their life, values, and principles to emerge changed, stronger, and surer of oneself and their purpose as a leader. Bennis further states that we all have crucibles. However, when a leader deals decisively with and overcomes these devastating negative experiences, they transform into something constructive and beneficial that creates, reveals, or enhances the leader's character and ability to influence and inspire.

These are the thoughts that I reflect upon as I sit writing this in my garden in the Tramuntana mountains of Mallorca in the spring of 2020, far from my US family during the COVID-19 pandemic. The pandemic we all lived through is an event of historical significance that we all survived and coped with. In our own ways, we all have been transformed in some way by this experience. Now, as we exit this crisis, how can we mold this experience into something formative and constructive for our future, perhaps even as a testament to those who did not survive this trauma?

In those pre-vaccine days of March 2020, I collected my British family from their home in the UK to securely isolate in the mountains of a

Mediterranean island to sit out the pandemic for as long as it would take. I try not to be fatalistic; however, in dedicating this essay to my sons and grandchildren, who were far away in California, one naturally considers their heritage. What will our legacy be as we devote a substantial portion of our waking hours and, therefore, our lives to work and career? What will the quality of our work-life and work-life balance be? What will our contribution be? How do we want to be remembered, and how will we be remembered? Those were the musings that propelled me to start this book on day one of the first COVID-19 lockdown.

However, the origins of this work had been many years in the making. Still, I'd never anticipated writing about it until early 2017, during a long Sunday morning walk with a friend in Castle Bellver Park in Palma Mallorca. However, it took the 2020 pandemic lockdowns to provide the time and space to embark on this journey.

In February 2017, I had just been asked by my company, TUI, the European Travel Group,[1] where I was a chief technology officer, to deliver a presentation on my "Leadership Secrets" to the 250 global leadership at the annual conference in Berlin. Considering the conference presentation led me to ponder why I was being asked and what to say. All TUI staff had recently been tasked with completing a comprehensive leadership questionnaire, and my 96 percent satisfaction rating across my global teams turned out to be the highest in the company. Naturally, I was pleased and honored, but it immediately left me with many questions about my leadership style, capabilities, and teams.

At that time, I didn't really know, or at least was not consciously aware of, the precise nature of my leadership modus operandi. In carrying out my mission-critical duties, I'd not stopped long enough to reflect on what I was doing and to determine if there was anything unique about my leadership style, let alone if there was any special "secret sauce"!

So, to prepare for the leadership talk, I began to purposefully ponder what I had only previously subliminally sensed in an attempt to discern, crystallize, and then articulate my experiences as a leader. At that time, I was intensely focused on the major merger transformation I was running and creating new organizations, so I was on a roll, and perhaps, as Mihaly Csikszentmihalyi states, "in flow." Hopefully, as well, as I had read in Heidegger, "unconsciously competent" instead of being fully conscious

and cautious in my leadership style. But, initially, what I intuitively rec-
ollected was that something exciting and special had happened each time
in the past when I was in a position to create and build my own team.

My role at TUI was one of the happiest, most productive, and rewarding times of my career. I had an outstanding, high-performing team that
was a delight to know and lead, which I review later in a detailed case
study. Then, I recalled other memorable experiences I'd had as a leader.
In addition to TUI, there was a small but creative Innovation Team at
Hotelbeds, a tumultuous dot-com episode for my team at Worldsport
Networks, and a fantastic Training Team at Reuters in Singapore. Finally,
there was the challenging but marvelous experience of the five-year transformation program at the Usability Group and Design Labs at Reuters in
London. Interestingly, that group's Virtual Team organizational design
caught Tom Peters's attention, and he wrote a series of favorable articles on our team in his *On Achieving Excellence* newsletter[2] and for the
London *Financial Times*. This also gave me pause for reflection on the
leadership question.

These five separate occasions running large teams were each extraordinary experiences in distinct ways. Additionally, the TUI leadership
survey and Tom Peters's recognition led me to consider other experiences
I'd had as a leader, causing me to ponder further and analyze what had
happened and why.

That moment on the walk in the park, preparing for the presentation,
was perhaps the initial epiphany where I began to mark and capture
the moments, events, and people who had comprised those teams and
occurrences. Then, reflecting on these topics with my friend during that
springtime walk, she suggested delving into these topics more deeply and
perhaps to consider writing a book to share these experiences.

As I reconstructed those special moments, I began to piece together
and analyze the fragments of what and why those situations had been so
special. Naturally, I had an important role as the leader, but it was more
than that. It was the relationship and interaction I had with the directors
and managers, plus each and every staff member, contractor, and partner,
who were an integral part of the culture and chemistry we created.

After some soul-searching and a good deal of analysis, I identified
and crystallized the fundamental factors and critical behaviors that

catalyzed and shaped these circumstances. This led me to recognize what had happened and why they were distinctive and unique.

This all led to the following leadership messages and enduring lessons from these experiences and crucibles. First, there is an element of heartfelt, soulful management, or servant leadership, that is manifest as a type of devoted, caring, and mentoring motivation or drive. This is where the association between a mentor and a protégé is somewhat analogous to a healthy familial parenting relationship. It is an affiliation where the mentor has a deep concern and commitment to invest emotionally in and bond with the mentee. Consequently, the protégé consciously or even subliminally recognizes the mentor's caring and trustful commitment and investment in their well-being. In this bonded relationship, a high level of mutual trust and dedication is created that is deeper and stronger than the typical manager/staff relationship. When and where appropriate, this benevolent mentoring association has a beneficial synergetic impact on both the mentor and protégé.

Not to diminish the altruistic nature of this relationship; additionally, this also resonates with research on "social exchange theory," into which we will do a deep dive when we discuss the leadership characteristics of trust and authenticity. In brief, as it is not rocket science nor deep psychology, everyone wants to be loved and likes to be liked. Clearly, the only way that occurs genuinely is within a reciprocal, symbiotic trusting association, whether within a family, a marriage, a partnership, or a unique and special work relationship.

Many of you will remember the inspiring movie *Pay It Forward*,[3] based on the novel by Catherine Ryan Hyde.[4] The book and movie's inspirational theme is of acting altruistically in a way where one's actions create a future chain of benevolent "increasing returns" events. Extending this theme, one can see their own legacy, not just in a self-serving, not to be anonymously forgotten way. But as a way to make a difference and contribute to an endless ripple effect of positive reinforcing actions spreading forward through time. One hopes that their life and work life are not just happy and successful but also meaningful.

Critically, I realized that these experiences and the associated leadership behaviors were not some inherited or divinely imparted gift but that they are learnable and repeatable and that anyone can develop them.

I didn't start my career as a natural-born leader; it was a continuous evolution of education, effort, and experience. The awareness that these behaviors could be learned and developed became one of the primary impetuses for my motivation to share my experience and write this book. All my efforts, trials and tribulations, successes, and learnings had residual value and could be passed on to others to accelerate and enrich their leadership journey.

Therefore, I've captured these more than forty years of frontline professional experiences and learnings as leadership models, methods, and case studies in this book. Further, I'll share detailed reviews and analyses of the brightest and the best leadership gurus and assessment tools I've studied over the years. These are the things that I've explored, examined, and learned throughout my career that helped me develop from a novice trainee to a successful leader. These wide-ranging experiences and formal leadership studies provide an exceptional foundation and actionable guide for aspiring leaders on their leadership path.

My fervent hope is that these experiences, lessons, and learnings will help someone solve a problem, increase their confidence, create a constructive relationship, enhance their leadership skills, and accelerate their career. Therefore, along with the dedication to my sons and their children, I trust this work will also be beneficial to those former colleagues who came along with me on our journeys, as well as hopefully scores of others whom I will never personally know.

Life is a journey, not a destination.

—Ralph Waldo Emerson[5]

—Greg Garrison, Valldemossa, Spain, Spring 2020

Introduction

In the complex and diverse business ecosystem we work in today, enlightened and capable leadership has never been more imperative, in such critical demand, but also in such short supply.

Since its formal beginnings over the past five decades, the scope of the evolution of the leadership and management field is enormous. This work is envisioned as an overarching access bridge across this vast landscape of leadership knowledge. It is designed to capture essential learnings of the past, explore best practice experiences of today, and provide a foundation of knowledge and tools to prepare for and apply in the future.

The times constantly change, obsoleting antiquated ideas such as rigid command-and-control management approaches like Taylorism; nevertheless, the vast majority of the body of leadership learning is fundamental to human nature in the work context. These practical lessons and deep learning are both timely and timeless based on the pressing challenges leaders face today. Moreover, it may be even more crucial in the future, as the need for enlightened, ethical, and visionary leadership has never been so intense and pressing.

This book provides extensive knowledge, tried and proven frontline experience, and learnings to guide readers through the complexity and challenges of effectively leading teams today.

LEAD! is designed to address the critical need of aspiring top leaders to have one-touch access to an extensive and exhaustive overview of the leadership field. It provides a single "go-to" place where a leader can access, amass, and assimilate an awareness and overview of virtually the entire field of leadership.

This book will be invaluable for middle managers aspiring to develop to the C-suite, functional managers growing into a general manager position, consultants pivoting to line management, or trainers, mentors, and academics developing leadership program offerings for students or clients. It also comprises a fascinating amalgam of the management MBA, corporate training programs, organizational design psychology, business literature, and especially the language and tools of day-to-day, plus on-the-job practical experience.

We systematically examine the successful behaviors and methods of the preeminent leadership gurus and management thinkers of the past fifty years, surveying the most important leadership models plus an insightful array of authoritative psychological and psychometric tools.

All this learning and research is synthesized into a powerful proprietary model of the 20 Pillars of Leadership Character designed to guide aspiring leaders to find their unique leadership identity.

The comprehensive coverage and valuable synopsis of the leadership field capture the essence of this vast body of knowledge and apply it to an immediately actionable blueprint and road map for mastering the skills and practice of leadership.

This leadership treatise is a study and synopsis of my experience and learning gained leading teams over the past forty years. It is not intended as an academic or theoretical report. However, my twelve years in management development training, time working in consultancies, psychometric testing, and extensive executive education will impart an integral dimension of thought leadership, analytical overlay, and rigor to my decades of on-the-job experience.

I grew up in business in the heyday of the development of modern management and leadership philosophy. I lived it daily, role by role, book by book, as the field advanced to today. In other words, figuratively, I was there "in the room" while it all happened.

Therefore, one can view this book as a continuous leadership development case study in practice throughout these decades. Many academic and consulting leadership books study leadership from the outside in, and while this can have significant value, *LEAD!* looks at the field of leadership from the inside out! As in any good case study, I experienced, studied, tested, rejected, or validated everything contained in this book as a frontline leadership manager.

To personalize the leadership discussion and bring it closer to home, let's start with the perennial leadership question. Can a leader and leadership be developed, or is leadership an innate characteristic, and are leaders just born? Undoubtedly, as in my case, leadership skills can be learned, and leaders can be developed!

However, was my leadership path a straight-line case of leadership increasing returns, where I leaped deftly from one career stepping stone to the next, from one success to even greater success? Not remotely, it was a complicated and convoluted journey, fraught with challenges, one notable failure which we will dissect, and thankfully numerous successes, but all invaluable lessons, both the bad and good. I will recall, recite, and share my leadership journey with all its twists and turns, hurdles, stumbles, and accomplishments. Even the difficulties were formative and are an integral part of the learning, just as night defines the day, and the pauses between musical notes are compulsory components of a musical score.

I have compiled these learnings and experiences into two complementary companion books.

LEAD! Book 1, Finding Your Leadership Identity, considers the "Intrinsic Characteristics" of leadership by building a powerful leadership model elaborating on the twenty preeminent leadership characteristics. We study the psychology of leadership, its assessment, technologies, and tools. Finally, we review the philosophies and lessons of the top leadership gurus, thinkers, and academics.

We examine what it is to be a leader, setting a vision, finding your mission and purpose, and identifying your unique leadership identity, exploring leadership concepts such as the alchemy of leadership, servant leadership, and emotional intelligence.

The corresponding, interrelated *Book 2, Developing Your Leadership Style*, provides deep insight and expertise on effective "extrinsic operational behaviors," actions, methods, and processes. It comprises the latest cutting-edge leadership research and best practice management techniques, tips, and tools. In addition, we impart extensive on-the-ground, real-world experience and detailed case studies on the practice and performance of leadership.

In addition to the extensive review of management methods and research, we provide an in-depth study of creativity and innovation based on my experience running three corporate innovation initiatives and labs. We present insightful and applicable approaches, techniques, tools, and case studies for outsourcing, managing external teams, virtual teaming, and remote working. Finally, we look at leadership strategies and cutting-edge organizational design methodologies.

These essential intrinsic leadership characteristics in Book 1 and proven extrinsic behaviors in Book 2 provide the requisite array of knowledge, tools, and techniques vital to becoming an exceptional leader. Along with today's emerging digital technologies, evolutionary new-media business models, and evolving remote working challenges, leaders must develop exceptional leadership people skills to maximize their capabilities and impact in the world of work during their career working years. These leader strategies and behaviors will ensure you don't just "put in your hours" but devote the work portion of your lives to being more valuable and profitable, as well as more meaningful and fulfilling.

We will explore how to create ways of working that nurture the spirit, reinforce a culture of integrity and trust, encourage authenticity and confidence, and evoke passion and enthusiasm for work. All of these will result in more enjoyable and worthwhile experiences with staff and colleagues throughout your career. Life and work are exciting journeys in which we all must strive to live to the fullest and finest we can.

CHAPTER 1

Building Cathedrals: Visioning— The Art of the Long View

Vision Infused with Purpose

The ancient philosopher, in a bygone age, wove his way through the rubble of a vast building site in an old medieval square. Among the glare of the Mediterranean midday sun, clouds of dust, and the clamor of bustling activity, he happens upon two stonemasons diligently chipping away at large limestone blocks. Admiring the fine craftsmanship of the first, he asks, "What are you doing?" "I'm squaring this cornerstone" was the proud reply. "Very well done," he commended. The philosopher continued to the next mason, chipping away, seemingly exactly the same as the first. "And what are you doing?" he asks the second. The mason stops and looks up, beaming and gesturing with pride to the rising edifice: "We're building a cathedral!"

> A rock pile ceases to be a rock pile the moment a single man contemplates it, bearing within him the image of a cathedral.
> —Antoine de Saint-Exupéry[1]

This old allegory perfectly personifies one of the critical leadership challenges today. How to infuse work, any work, with a sense of purpose? Employees today are increasingly demanding and simultaneously disillusioned with the state of work. Especially during this period of post-pandemic reflections on career aspirations relative to enhanced work-life balance. Even if a worker becomes a master of their craft or trade, unless there is a more profound sense of purpose and consequently commitment embedded in the work, it remains soulless labor rather than a "labor of love" infused with passion that inspires and motivates the worker.

This should not depreciate the importance of disciplined dedication to your work, developing and training yourself to master your profession or craft to achieve high proficiency and realize pride of workmanship. However, in this context, I'm not yet explicitly alluding to how you perform your work but rather to why you are doing it.

Here, I'm inferring to virtually any work, not just altruistic endeavors such as solving world hunger, refugee relief, researching cancer, or being a teacher or a nurse. Indeed, many careers such as these we all recognize as having a higher calling. However, for the countless rest of us, who spend a major portion of our lives working day in and day out, perhaps in corporate life, retail, or services to provide for our families, it pertains to finding meaning and, thus, purpose in our labors.

Whether you are building a mobile app, creating a PowerPoint presentation or Excel spreadsheet, conducting a call center conversation, managing a shopping center, or writing a line of code, what is the final product, ultimate goal, USP, output, or deliverable? What is your product or service's real purpose, and how can you, as a leader, help build an emotional link between your employee's, colleague's, or contractor's work to the final product and, further, its use or outcome?

Let's, therefore, examine a task's essential function and purpose and how it contributes to the ultimate objective. How can we make people feel an integral part of the bigger picture and purpose to take psychological benefit or emotional solace from their efforts and the fruits of their labors? How to help them feel that whatever they do, no matter how seemingly trivial, contributes to something worthwhile or meaningful?

I'm reminded of a regrettably painful Thoreau quote from Walden my father frequently recited: "The mass of men lead lives of quiet desperation."[2] I, and no doubt many of you, have felt like this at one time or another, especially relative to work; however, this experience or sentiment need not be universally or individually true.

Many of us, or at least our staff, spend our days eking out our work lives doing what we perceive to be relatively menial tasks that do not in and of themselves initially appear to have great redeeming value. Spending eight to ten hours a day at a soul-stealing, mindless job is one of the great tragedies of modern society and "work" today. This is the dilemma that the hard stop of the COVID-19 lockdowns and its temporary respite from the corporate treadmill has thrust upon us.

Unfortunately, many people cannot see any connection between their perceived tedious tasks and labor and the ultimate fruit of their or the company's product or service. Peter Senge in *The Fifth Discipline* provides a poignant Robert Fritz quote, "In the presence of greatness, pettiness disappears." In the absence of a great dream, pettiness prevails.[3]

Hence, the dearth of satisfaction inherent in performing these repetitive tasks may not "feed our souls" sufficiently to deliver much in the way of self-satisfaction or self-actualization from our work and labors.

We as leaders must actively combat this melancholic perspective and positively change our emotional experience and that of our colleagues and workers by infusing our work and that of our associates and staff with meaningful purpose.

Let's return to the stonemasons for a moment. The first mason, even though a master craftsperson taking pride in the quality of his work, the sharpness of the angle, and the smoothness of the surface, this self-satisfaction or gratification, especially for repetitive tasks, is short-lived without it being instilled with some additional higher purpose.

The wholly self-satisfied person who works purely for the love of the task is rare, except perhaps in the case of mathematicians, artists, and musicians. In a business context, without a striving for a higher purpose, this worker may end up being just a high-caliber but fickle hired hand. This mercenary can quickly disappear to a competitor for a paltry 15 percent salary increase.

Conversely, the second mason is a dedicated devotee with a higher purpose who is willing to commit to a mission that can take months or even years to complete. It may even be a task that may not be accomplished in their own, their children's, or even grandchildren's lifetimes.

For example, the Palma Mallorca Cathedral, near where I live, took over 350 years to build. A modern multi-decade comparable might be the search for a cancer cure. A poignant example is Katalin Karikó, the visionary mRNA biochemist who persevered through thirty years of skepticism and rejection until, ultimately, her collaboration with Drew Weissman resulted in breakthroughs leading to the rapid development of the COVID-19 vaccines, saving millions of lives. Dedication to this type of undertaking, mission, or purpose transcends daily tasks and trivia. This passionate devotee with a higher purpose will not abandon their mission and jump ship to leave to build another building, product, or artifact with a lesser purpose, even for a sizable salary increase.

Consequently, our critical leadership mission is to create and crystallize a "vision with purpose" that is meaningful, convincing, challenging, and achievable. An exciting shared vision gives work purpose, motivates staff, and creates a common mission and cohesive camaraderie with colleagues. How, then, in practical terms, can we imbue our work and workers with that loftier sense of purpose? How do we conceive a clear, inspiring vision and articulate it in a personal and meaningful way?

To achieve a powerful and inspiring vision, the leader must think creatively, holistically, and expansively to visualize an objective and its outcomes and how it benefits the company, staff, and the end customer. With that vision and visualization in your mind's eye, a leader can create a vivid mental model or picture of the overall activity, product, and desired future state. Then, they can crystallize the objectives and associated challenges down to a concise and compelling image and depiction of the future.

To inspire your colleagues to buy into and personally own the vision, passionately communicate that vision with its purpose, and demonstrate how it contributes to their, your, and the company's objectives and deliverables. This helps build a rational and direct connection from the task assignment to the deliverable through meaningful outcomes that extend beyond annual targets or profit.

It may sound complicated, but with the right mindset, it's quite simple and powerful; let's deconstruct how to construct that meaningful purpose. First of all, "setting a vision with a purpose" should begin with aligning your overall personal aspirations and purpose. It is not just about what we do; rather, more critically, why and how we do it.

As Harvard Business School Professor and former Medtronic CEO Bill George says, discovering, creating, or crystalizing our Inner Purpose is our "true north"[4] or our "North Star" ("Southern Cross" for our friends down under). This is a fundamental character attribute that is part of the essence of our identity as a leader. Our North Star beacon or GPS provides a high-quality strategy for navigating the continuously evolving complexity of the world in which we live, work, and lead. It also lays a solid, unwavering cornerstone to build upon and a moral compass to guide any professional vision, purpose, or action we set or aspire to.

To find your personal purpose, you must deeply understand who you are, who you want to be, what motivates you, and what your values, aspirations, and passions are. It is a compass that helps us establish who we are personally and professionally to ensure they are both perpetually aligned. It reflects and infuses our ideals into our work activities and behaviors, guiding us to conduct our actions benevolently and constructively with colleagues, partners, and staff. This sets the model for our organization's overall cultural ethos and personal conduct that colleagues instinctively recognize, respect, and emulate as a benchmark for organizational behavior.

Having created, clarified, and internalized your personal and professional purpose, as a leader you can then look at the organization, the team, and the departmental goals to mature and translate your vision into the organizational objectives and outcomes. The critical factor here is that the leader's vision must contain an obvious benefit or opportunity for the staff and team in conjunction with delivering the corporate objectives. This may be an intrinsic value and purpose for the activity, plus perhaps provide the employees with learning, growth, and career opportunities. People need some raison d'être, literally some purpose for their being and being there, beyond their paycheck, to inspire them toward action and encourage them, especially in adversity. If you can win your staff's hearts and minds, a significant measure of your leadership challenge will already be accomplished.

There is significant evidence that creating and delivering inspiring leadership visions can have a powerful motivational impact on staff, thereby achieving the desired results, realizing goals, and ultimately, in increased productivity and profitability. Reinforcing these visions with leadership intention and organizational attention can dramatically improve the probability of success in achieving the planned outcome.

In summary, among a leader's most important responsibilities are divining and setting a vision, creating a sense of purpose, and communicating that vision to help staff appreciate how their role and actions are important and worthwhile and contribute to achieving that vision and goal. Terry Leahy in *Management in Ten Words*[5] cites architect Daniel Burnham's brilliant quote, *"Make no little plans. They have no magic to stir men's blood."*[6]

Divining a Leadership Vision

Visionary leadership is an enormously powerful skill set and strength to cultivate and enhance your leadership capabilities and repertoire. However, not everyone is a natural-born visionary, nor in the same measure. But that does not necessarily disadvantage anyone from developing effective visionary leadership capabilities.

Everyone in business will be distinctly aware of prominent and remarkable present-day visionaries, particularly in the high-tech arena, such as Steve Jobs, Bill Gates, and Elon Musk. But moreover, there are scores of other illustrious visionaries and countless unnamed others working diligently throughout business. Every organization needs leaders with vision at all levels to create new products and markets, inspire staff, and transform businesses for the future.

We can't all be world-renowned visionaries. However, regardless of your natural visionary aptitude and ability, every person in a leadership position can enhance or develop a visionary capability through the proper training, practice, and a leadership tool kit. Many of these renowned visionaries do these things naturally and instinctively; however, you can learn and apply the same skills and methods in a conscious, creative, and effective manner.

Let's explore this perennial question of natural-born versus self-made leaders.

Leaders—Born or Made?

The most dangerous leadership myth is that leaders are born—nonsense; the opposite is true. Leaders are made rather than born.
— Warren Bennis, the founding father of leadership[7]

Throughout history, and in particular business theorists, there has been lively speculation, debate, and research regarding the emotive issue of whether leaders are born or can be developed or made. This key leadership question brings us back to the fundamental issue of leadership: nature versus nurture.

It may well be that certain fortuitous genetic combinations of good parental gene stock may predispose certain individuals with superior intelligence and strength, thus instilling within them the exceptional characteristics that help enable them to develop into "natural-born" leaders. The English philosopher Thomas Carlyle put this view forward in his great man theory. However, that also presumes that the environmental conditions of their upbringing are favorable to the optimal development of those skills into exceptional leadership characteristics. Subsequently, the great man theory, which postulates that leaders are naturally born and predisposed to leadership, has been largely dismissed by the trait theory of leadership. Trait theory proposes that managers with an advantageous composition of personal and professional traits develop through challenge and experience that hone their talents until they become successful and exceptional leaders.

We've already briefly commented that leaders can definitely be developed. However, this is a fascinating topic that warrants deeper examination. Let's start with the arguments for nature versus nurture. There are many prominent examples, but Bill Gates is a great one. His father was William Gates, a renowned American attorney, author, and philanthropist. His mother, Mary Maxwell Gates, also renowned, was an American businesswoman who served for eighteen years on the University of Washington Board of Regents. Consequently, Bill benefited from an exceptional gene stock, but additionally, he had a phenomenally rich intellectual and privileged upbringing. Clearly, his inherited nature and stimulating nurture conspired to create an extremely successful entrepreneur, businessperson, and philanthropist.

Perhaps the best example of a fortuitous combination of nature and nurture is the extraordinary story of the three Wojcicki sisters. To start the story with genes, their father is a particle physics professor at Stanford University, where they were brought up. Their mother is a journalist and acclaimed author of the bestselling book "How to Raise Successful People." So, nature and nurture both get a big tick in the box, but to rule out any suggestion of luck, all three sisters have each been hugely successful in their own right. Anne Wojcicki is the co-founder of the DNA genetic testing company 23andMe. Susan Wojcicki is the chief executive of YouTube. Finally, Janet Wojcicki is a professor of epidemiology at the University of California, San Francisco.[8]

Bill Gates and the Wojcicki sisters provide clear evidence of the advantages of a positive combination of good genes and a highly favorable environment. But what about the rest of us who may not have had a particle physicist for a father or a university regent for a mother?

Seeming strong exceptions to this situation would be Steve Jobs, Bill Clinton, Ronald Reagan, and Barack Obama. By all accounts, they do not appear to have had prominent genetic advantages or exceptional upbringing at first.

Bill Clinton's father was a traveling heavy equipment salesperson who died in a car crash three months before Bill was born, plus his stepfather was an abusive alcoholic. His mother was one of nine children of a poor Texas farmer. Yet, he rose from these humble beginnings to become a Rhodes Scholar, exceptional orator, governor, and twice US president.

Ronald Reagan similarly was from a very small town in Northern Illinois, a little over an hour from where I grew up. His unpretentious beginnings from a low-income family and modest education would not presage his meteoric rise from radio sports broadcaster to Hollywood actor and then on to become the governor of California for eight years and ultimately a two-term US president.

Then there is Barack Obama, who had a broken parental family history and had a diverse but disruptive upbringing in Hawaii, Indonesia, and the US mainland. This disruption and stress quite easily might have been detrimental. However, he developed and thrived through this unique background to become one of the outstanding transformational figures of our time and a two-term US president.

All these examples could be analyzed based on parental qualities; however, from the initial perspective of genes (nature), as well as upbringing (nurture), it is not overtly evident in the cases of Clinton, Reagan, or Obama that their background characteristics would have predetermined or hinted at their future genius or greatness.

A more in-depth study of Steve Jobs's upbringing does not give us obvious indications of his future brilliance from nature's perspective. However, it gives us a strong "nurture" hint about the origins of his obsession with design quality. Jobs's adoptive father, Paul Jobs, was an outstanding Coast Guard mechanic who built a workshop in his garage for his son to "pass along his love of mechanics." Jobs greatly admired his adopted father's dedication to high-quality craftsmanship. Once, when building a new cabinet for their home, Paul fine-finished it all over, including the inside and back. When Steve asked why he made the effort to polish the back, as "no one would ever know," his father replied that he would know. This obsession with style, design, and quality was a prevalent passion throughout Jobs's career. For example, he obsessively insisted that the interiors of Apple computers and mobile phones needed to be as elegant and beautiful as the exteriors. Undoubtedly, his father's example and passion for quality greatly influenced Steve's love and passion for high-quality design excellence.

In my case, as I look back over the years, from my perspective, apart from the crucibles I discussed in the preface, I had a generally positive but unexceptional nature and nurture upbringing. As a result, my leadership skills developed gradually and experientially over decades. They were, fortunately, further enhanced by highly diverse work experiences gained in multiple different job roles (sales, marketing, training, consulting, technology), in various industries (travel, finance, dot-coms, media, and consulting), plus through the opportunities to work internationally in the United States, Hong Kong, Singapore, the UK, and Spain, including extensive global responsibilities.

This variety of professional and personal experiences living overseas provided broad exposure to different cultures, work climates, knowledge, and skills. Unquestionably, these experiences expanded my horizons and knowledge, providing me with a broad perspective to draw upon from the different work challenges and diverse groups. These years of unique work experiences in various locations greatly enhanced and expanded my leadership perspectives and capabilities.

Hence, while it may be that leaders may be born in rare cases, it is clear from research, the cases of Steve Jobs, Ronald Reagan, and Barack Obama, and backed up by my own experience that leaders undoubtedly can be made. Therefore, whatever your starting point and position, have faith, stay focused, keep moving forward, and never stop learning. Effective leadership is a critical skill set that can be learned, actively cultivated, and effectively developed over a lifetime. So now, let's continue our leadership development journey.

On Becoming a Leader

Tools and Techniques Exceptional Leaders Use

From my experience and observation of working with scores of leaders and highly creative people, it's clear that not everyone has a brilliant breakthrough idea for every issue. For areas where you have an instinctive knack, apply your native abilities to envision approaches and concepts that apply to those situations. However, if an issue is outside your experience, or you don't feel accomplished at envisioning the future, following are several practical tools that can ensure you can create a vision and set a new direction for virtually any situation. Let's explore techniques and tools you can use to create a future vision for virtually any product, market, or challenge.

Associative Thinking (The Intersection of Concepts)

Associative thinking is a powerful concept that you can learn, practice, and perfect to begin your visioning process. Take any idea, concept, product, or problem and consciously analyze how it is similar, related, and even dissimilar to other things. Next, document, visually picture, or create a mind map of your concept or problem to link your issue graphically to similar or adjacent subjects. This allows you to consider how to correlate and apply your issue to related, orthogonal, or opposing topics. This will stimulate ideas or allow you to form judgments on how your product or idea can be expanded, extended, or resolved through complementary or contrasting concepts, products, or solutions.

A vivid and highly value-creating example of associative thinking is the original creation of the Jet Ski, which was envisioned and conceived from the convergence of a snowmobile, motorcycle, airplane, and kayak! This associative thinking approach inspired me to apply high-performance fighter pilot heads-up display navigation techniques to financial currency traders' user interface displays while designing investment banking trading systems at Reuters.

While this type of visioning and creative product innovation may appear like alchemy to the uninitiated external observer, there is nothing magic to this at all. This technique can be applied with practice to set a vision for a product roadmap, innovate a service, develop a market entry strategy, or transform a company in productive new directions.

System Thinking / Scenario Planning

Our second tool kit for visioning is to step back and look holistically at the company, product suite, service catalog, or problem using holistic system thinking. This may seem obvious, but we often get lost in the trees and can't see the proverbial forest and vice versa. We need to train ourselves to look at the overall picture, not just the issue or problem in isolation. How does it fit into the overall system, organization, or market, including all the influencing and conflicting factors? Anyone can do this; the important thing is to remember to do it! System thinking helps us identify missing, dysfunctional, or even redundant components in a system, be it a product, people, process, or technology.

Once we have identified the opportunity or defect, depending on the complexity or challenge, you can use scenario planning to create alternatives to conceptually or graphically lay out options to resolve or mitigate the issue. Scenario planning is a valuable tool that can be as simple as a list of bullet point alternatives on a workshop flip chart or even a series of detailed options analyses to inform a stakeholder decision.

Build a Taxonomy (Extrapolation, Modification, and Adaptation—Map the Gaps)

A noteworthy approach I used in my innovation labs to develop new products or map future strategies was to create formal product, functional, or technical taxonomies. These taxonomies were often wall-sized hierarchical branching categorizations, sometimes Excel spreadsheets, and occasionally complex mind maps. Regardless of form, these "inventories" of products or technologies were designed to evolve over time through successive generations of technological or functional developments. The fascinating and invaluable approach is mapping the critical path of the products or technologies over time, as well as tracking all related factors such as promising emerging technologies, the latest market developments, new business models, plus financial or legal implications. In developing these charts, challenge participants to be expansive and extrapolate aggressively to be creative in designing comprehensive taxonomies.

I recall one such mind map taxonomy we developed at AOL when I was head of mobiles and broadband in Europe in the early days of mobile internet. In our performance and usability testing, the original WAP (Wireless Application Protocol) mobile internet performed very poorly from a speed and usability perspective. Consequently, we mapped the future mobile network projected performance from 2G, 2.5G GPRS, and 2.75G EDGE through to 3G against the future roadmap for mobile handset and mobile internet technology developments. This permitted us to project forward mobile internet performance to determine a target future convergence point where network speed, device capability, content maturity, and mobile internet developments would align to provide a satisfactory user experience. This multidimensional taxonomy showing the multiple parallel roadmaps was invaluable in informing and developing our mobile internet strategy.

Based on this, I recall presenting a proposal to the AOL board to develop the mobile technology, infrastructure, and services for the new WAP internet protocol. Once I received the approval to proceed, I continued with the second half of my presentation, demonstrating the performance and usability problems on the current devices. As I concluded, I then firmly recommended, to their surprise, that we not launch the products I had just presented due to the anticipated adverse customer reaction. When questioned about the rationale for building something we would not launch, I explained the critical necessity and extended time lines for constructing our mobile internet capabilities. This included device development, network provisioning, content creation, hosting and serving, service modeling, and tax requirements. The board agreed and gave me the go-ahead to develop but not launch the technologies and services until a future point when technology would catch up to service requirements.

The taxonomy roadmap and scenarios informed and prompted our conscious decision to develop but not launch the WAP phone! However, it also highlighted the critical need, high complexity, and long time lines required to create all the organization's intellectual, resource, and physical capabilities. In addition, the roadmap and plan ensured we were prepared and provisioned to launch the products and services the moment the network, devices, and technologies converged. This ultimately gave us a significant market advantage to plan and prepare in advance and launch against a future capability that was unavailable at the time.

In the same manner, when I was a chief technology officer at TUI Group, the global tourism group, we developed a detailed taxonomy mapping a five-year vision and plan for the consolidation of eight operating systems in twenty-four countries, including the evolution of multiple parallel business, legal, process, and technical work streams.

For both examples, the complexity of these projects threatened to overwhelm typical business case analysis and decision-making. The taxonomies aided us significantly in visualizing the future landscape, focusing on the critical path plan, identifying financial and resource requirements, eradicating irrelevant issues, spotting opportunities through product or service gaps, and presenting clear visions for senior management approval.

Horizon Scanning/Radar (Tech Tracking and Trendspotting and Thought Leader Research)

Thanks to my time at PricewaterhouseCoopers Menlo Park Technology Think Tank, I learned and developed invaluable market horizon scanning/technology radar tracking skills. Our center for technology and innovation produced a PwC Technology Forecast for corporate finance and technology investors each year.

These research approaches involved trendspotting and tech tracking using multiple research sources. The key to this research methodology was to rapidly survey and summarize the key trends, issues, and technologies across a vast number of diverse research, news, industry, supplier, and customer sources. Then, as we surveyed and tracked the emerging trends, we rigorously logged them on Excel spreadsheets with the trend, source, implications, suppliers, competitors, costs, and timeframes. This type of taxonomy in database form allowed us to detect and track leading issues, technologies, and standards as they emerged, evolved, crystallized, and eventually adopted.

I would say that horizon scanning, tech tracking, and trendspotting are essential activities that leaders should do continuously as an integral part of their ongoing leadership visioning. Using these tools is vital for your continued future forecasting and planning, keeping you sharp, and maintaining your credibility within your organization. Furthermore, this information and these ideas will assist you immensely as a part of the associative thinking process we discussed earlier. Finally, it is just plain fascinating for your own intellectual stimulation!

Open Innovation (Collaborate across Your Team, Company, Partners, Suppliers, and Customers)

As you embark on setting an ambitious and far-reaching vision, the concept of open innovation is invaluable to broaden your horizons to embrace the world of possibilities. The concept of open innovation is based on the fact that no one and no organization has a monopoly on great ideas or visions. Besides your internal research, external horizon scanning, and market research, expanding your innovation stakeholders to include partners, suppliers, customers, universities, and the like can dramatically enhance the volume and value of your research. These enormously valuable sources of ideas, potential tools, and technologies often come at the cost of no more than a handshake and the building of a collaborative partnership.

As you will appreciate, each organizational ecosystem is a complex matrix of internal staff creating products, partners who provide additional services, suppliers who are experts in their own adjacent services, and customers who are the ultimate barometer of the value of your product or service. Moreover, each of the players has slightly different roles and perspectives on products, services, and customers. Thus, it stands to reason that involving all these players or actors in the innovation process is bound to elaborate and enrich the viewpoints and ideas surrounding your products and services.

Relative to open innovation, recognize that the richness and accuracy of your vision are directly proportionate to the quantity and quality of the inputs into your planning and visioning.

Ideation Generation (Brainstorming, Incubation, and Collaboration)

Ideation, brainstorming, incubation, and idea generation are naturally intrinsic parts of creating a vision. We discuss this topic extensively within the upcoming section on creativity, providing an array of proven ideation-stimulating methods and tools. Remember to conduct idea generation expansively with your team and partners and take advantage of the research and data capture tools I describe.

Finally, recognize brainstorming and idea generation are not once-a-year off-site workshop activities. Instead, idea generation should become an integral part of crafting a creative vision and enriching virtually everything you do as a visionary leader. It can be formal in the form of an off-site idea generation or visioning session, an in-house workshop brainstorming a new strategy, product, or solution, or simply continuous encouragement of staff to think outside the box and be creative and constructive in everything they do.

My only caveat and caution is to ensure you also rigorously prioritize and execute. Don't fall into the trap of continuously generating exciting new ideas but failing to focus on their execution and delivery.

Let's explore through real-life examples how to engender meaning and purpose through a clear vision to lay the groundwork for realizing more fulfilling day-to-day work.

Finding My Personal "True North"

My lifelong ambition and aspiration into my twenties was to be a neurosurgeon. I even had the honor to intern in Neurology under Dr. Thor Sundt at St. Mary's Hospital and the Mayo Clinic in Rochester, Minnesota, from 1970 to 1972. However, a perfect storm of heartrending experiences at the hospital and the simultaneous death of a brother from leukemia in 1971 convinced me I didn't want to spend my life riding the emotional roller coaster of a medical career.

Therefore, with my lifelong dream shattered, I reread Viktor Frankl's *Man's Search for Meaning*,[9] quit university and my job at Mayo's/St. Mary's, sold my car, had a yard sale, and gave up my apartment. Next, I bought an Icelandic Air ticket to Reykjavík, Iceland, to see Bobby Fischer play Boris Spassky for the World Chess Championship, dubbed the "Match of the Century," and then continued on to Munich for the 1972 Olympics. Both events were profoundly moving wake-up calls for an impressionable twenty-year-old, especially the shocking conclusion of the Munich Olympics. The Munich Massacre, as it is remembered, occurred when eight Palestinian terrorists from the group "Black September" attacked the Olympic Village, killing two Israeli Olympic team members and taking nine others hostage. During a failed rescue attempt, five Black September terrorists were killed, but tragically, all nine Israeli hostages perished.[10]

Then, after three months of crisscrossing Europe with student rail passes and a lengthy stint in North Africa, I ran out of money and decided to settle down. I got a couple of part-time jobs teaching English and selling real estate and rented a fisherman's hut for a year on the beach near Malaga, Spain. Then, with no clear idea of what to do with my career and life, I began a deliberate quest to rethink and find a new sense of purpose and direction.

Over the subsequent, eventful years, I did find meaning and purpose, all of which have led to the core messages in this book. However, what I discovered was surprising in that the answers I was searching for revolved more around the journey than the destination. Thus, even though I'm not actively saving lives as a doctor, I have found new meaning and purpose for my life through my work, why and how I do it, and in my interactions with my fellow journeyers.

As Stephen Hawking once said: "Work gives you meaning and purpose, and life is empty without it."[11] Clearly, his unique circumstances make him an especially relevant testament to the value of purposeful work.

Let's talk then about the leadership journey.

Choosing the Right Path

Fast-forward to a particularly good personal example of finding meaning and purpose through work. Fifteen years ago, while at PricewaterhouseCoopers London, I was headhunted and offered a very good role as chief technology officer for a major European online gaming company (a polite way of saying online gambling).

At the same time, as IT strategy director for PwC, I was consulting to the world's largest travel company, developing a common systems strategy during a major merger. This involved harmonizing IT systems from both companies across twenty-four countries. Shortly after our proposed strategy was approved, the client offered me a permanent role to take responsibility for the implementation.

However, the online gaming company offered me 40,000 Euros more per year than the travel company, so I had a dilemma. Should I accept the higher-paying chief technology officer job for the online gambling company, working in an industrial estate in suburban London? Or should I take the lesser pay for an IT strategy director role for the travel company based in Palma Mallorca?

Perhaps if I had been thirty years old with a young family and unemployed, I might have been tempted by the gaming role. However, the online gambling role did not align sufficiently with my values, and in my mid-fifties, I wanted to remain faithful to my principles. Thus, I chose the travel company whose explicitly stated purpose was to provide holiday experiences that brought smiles to their customers on much-needed short vacation breaks or once-in-a-lifetime adventures. It was no contest; I went for the travel company in Mallorca and never looked back except to share the rationale for the decision with you.

The critical message here is that every individual should challenge each opportunity against their principles and vision. The core question is: Who do you want to be, and what do you want to do to ensure your work and career are a close reflection of who you are? The ironic thing about this was that two years later, the gaming company director who had offered me the CTO role became my boss anyhow. He also left that company to come to the same travel company I was at!

In summary, every decision you make and any job you take becomes a stepping stone or launching platform for the next role on that same trajectory. Therefore, be very careful what positions you take, even in the short term, as you must project them forward to envision where they may lead you in the future. If you can't believe in or buy into a company's final product or service, do a quick 180-degree turn as I did and do something else, period. Be authentic and true to yourself, as anything else is "selling out" and may potentially be an unpropitious career and life move for you. Further, unless you are leading an authentic life in the right role and leading your teams with vision and purpose, you are unlikely to be a credible and effective leader. As the saying goes, "the wrong path never leads you in the right direction."

Setting a Vision with a Purpose

All of this led to discovering my new purpose as the chief technology officer of TUI Group Destinations, where we delivered and supported millions of customers on vacations in sixty countries. But more specifically, as mentioned, we helped provide enjoyable holidays, creating smiles for those customers. I earnestly believed in and bought into this vision and could see how my actions and those of my team could impact and enhance the experience, services, and support we provided to customers while on their vacations.

In our responsibilities in IT, this translated into: How could we streamline the user experience, shorten the hotel check-in time, help the customer select a suitable excursion, provide cashless payments, or give visibility to guests as to the status of their transfer pickup? Our actions could literally change a fraught and stressful activity like a homebound departure transfer into an efficient and painless experience. Thus sustaining the customer's holiday glow all the way home instead of finishing a relaxing vacation in a state of high anxiety.

From my position and vantage point, I could see how IT could enrich a guest's experience. I believed in it so passionately that I communicated this mission to every candidate interviewed and employee hired. I regularly reminded our technical staff why they spec'd a functional product change or wrote a line of code. Eventually, these tasks translated into either an anxious or agitated customer or a delighted guest.

I regularly stated to each of them: "The entire machinery of the world's largest travel company, all our websites, travel agencies, airplanes, coaches, and hotels with all the associated tasks, processes, and logistics all comes down to ensuring guests have hassle-free, memorable moments, lying on a beach, exploring a medieval village, cycling or sailing. The purpose of everything we do is to create great experiences for our guests."

Thus, my purpose was to help everyone in the IT team understand how critical their labors are and that they are essential pieces of a puzzle or links in a chain delivering these high-quality guest experiences. This was, in our way, our "butterfly effect,"[12] where a line of code in an application either worked or didn't, and the associated effect and impacts have significant downstream customer experience implications. I repeated this powerful message in every interview or staff onboarding, constantly reinforcing it as a permanently ingrained ethos of our culture.

Occasionally, when someone needed encouragement, to drive home the point of our personal responsibility and impact on each and every customer, I'd often repeat my travel industry–modified version of a story by anthropologist Loren Eiseley. After a major sea storm washed thousands of starfish up onto the beach, a young girl ran along the beach valiantly throwing starfish back into the sea. An adult happened along and grimly informed the girl of the futility of her actions, saying, "There are just too many; you can't really make any difference." Immediately, the young girl boldly picked up another starfish, threw it into the sea, and countered, "It makes a difference to this one!"

I drive this point home by personalizing our millions of customers through visualizing a young family with children playing in the sand at the water's edge for the very first time. Along with the pleasure experienced by customers on their vacations, the staff felt committed to creating these smiles, and I had the self-satisfaction of devoting myself to a mission and purpose that was benevolent and pleasurable. As stated, I'm no longer attempting to save lives as a doctor; however, I'm contributing to many others' enjoyment, even if in a small way, and consequently, I'm living a contented life!

In Summary

This vivid and graphic example is easy to understand and extrapolate into virtually any other context or company. These issues all come down to getting in touch with and honoring human nature for ourselves, our employees, and our customers. All multinationals, most companies, and viable start-ups have mature marketing organizations that clearly articulate their USPs and product/service advantages. Furthermore, our role as leaders on the ground within the organization must be to translate those visions into clear and meaningful staff missions and actions that bridge the gap between the high and lofty boardroom product strategies and the tactical, day-by-day activities performed by the staff.

Surprisingly, the striking disconnect between the corporate vision and the departmental staff performance objectives is often greater than we would imagine and expect it to be. We need to translate it and "land it" into our staff's day-to-day operations and tasks. They must appreciate how their work is directly linked, no matter how far it is from the department or corporate strategy, to the ultimate end product, result, and customer, which as in the case above, was a guest's enjoyable, hassle-free holiday.

Creating and communicating a vision to align and motivate employees is a universal business requirement with only contextual variations. The critical thing is that you consciously and conscientiously identify the emotional outcome and help staff understand how their role contributes to a worthy higher purpose beyond themselves.

Not only does this enhance and enrich the work lives of your staff, but it also translates into significantly improved job satisfaction and self-actualization for you as a leader. Especially when you see considerably enhanced employee engagement, contentment, and morale as a consequence of creating a positive and constructive culture in your teams.

Ideally, every organization should have a clear vision, a noble cause, and a motivating mission beyond the financial metrics to instill and inspire meaning in its objectives and purpose. These are the things that encourage you to want to get out of bed in the morning, make your efforts more meaningful, give you a reason for being, provide direction, and sustain you with energy and courage to overcome any obstacle to achieving your goal.

Companies must have a noble cause, and it's the leader's job to transform that noble cause into such an inspiring vision that it will attract the most talented people in the world to want to join it.
—Steve Jobs, former chairman and CEO, Apple Inc.[13]

"How you do it" versus "What you do and why you do it"

When you want to build a ship, do not begin by gathering wood, cutting boards, and distributing work, but awaken within the heart of man the desire for the vast and endless sea.
                                        —*Antoine de Saint-Exupéry*[14]

We've discussed finding your passion and your true north as essential components of finding a purpose in your career work life to bring value to whatever you do by answering: "Why you are doing it?" This meaningful purpose, aspiration, mission, or vision is the fundamental link between what we do and why we do it. We determine what we are doing at a deeper level by defining why we are doing it.

Any job, role, or task absent some overarching meaningful purpose lacks the essential emotional connection to why we are doing it. Unfortunately, this can result in an all-too-common perception of purposeless, soulless, mindless, tedious, or monotonous work. Therefore, the critical task for any worker, particularly for the leader who guides and mentors staff, is to ensure that each task we do is linked to a positive, purposeful reason we are doing it.

There is an insightful bestselling book[15] and TED Talk titled *Start with Why!*[16] by Simon Sinek that I heartily recommend. Sinek explores basic human nature, again elaborating on the fact that people are motivated by why people do things rather than what we do or how we do it. Identifying and communicating this *why* through the purpose behind issues or actions is much more inspiring and motivating than simply dispassionately defining or describing things.

As Nietzsche[17] once stated and was famously quoted by Viktor Frankl in *Man's Search for Meaning*: "He who has a WHY to live can bear almost any HOW!"[18]

Building on that fundamental foundation, the next critical component in our quest for meaning and purpose in work after *what you do* and *why you do it* is to explore the secret sauce of the leadership alchemy, *how you work*!

Unless you are one of the fortunate few who instinctively knew your passion early on or perhaps somehow rapidly figured out what you wanted to do, you join the millions (or billions?) of the rest of us, who persistently ponder throughout our careers what we want to do and how to apply ourselves gainfully and happily for the decades of labor ahead. Further, even though most of us have dreams and even real aspirations of what we would love to do, circumstances don't always automatically play into our hands. Thus, things (and jobs) don't always work out exactly (or sometimes even remotely) the way we want. Again, as mentioned, this was the dilemma that was preying on many people's minds due to the enforced reflection during the hard reset of the pandemic lockdowns.

Picking up my career journey where we left off, after extensive self-reflection at my serene fisherman's hut in Spain during the turmoil of the Vietnam War (having missed the draft by one number in the first lottery) I crafted my plan. After deciding not to proceed with my medical career, I seized on my next altruistic vision to work for the Red Cross. In my wildest dreams, I imagined becoming the director-general of the Red Cross. Many of us, especially when starting our careers in our early twenties, have such prodigious and often unrealistic fantasies. However, don't be utterly discouraged; sometimes luck and fortune conspire to make magic happen, lightning strikes somewhere, and someone eventually gets that job.

Failing that, however, if I couldn't do exactly what I wanted, I needed a backup plan. That was simply to do something I loved, which was to secure a job in the travel industry. So, with no avenue to the Red Cross, I returned to the United States and fortuitously got a job as a management trainee at American Express Travel. AMEX was my first big break, and I stayed there in successive roles for the next twelve years. Thus, I purposefully began my career in the travel industry, and as we will see, I also happily returned to travel in the later chapters of my career.

To get ahead of myself for a moment, remarkably, I did, however, eventually get a shot at my dream during the intervening years! After conceiving and kicking off the NGO Humanitarian Web Service Reuters AlertNet.org[19] (now Trust.org), which had received a Millennium Innovation Award from the UK government, I received a call from Korn Ferry Executive Recruiters. It was regarding their search for the director-general for the International Red Cross! Surprised but thrilled, I developed a lengthy paper on reinventing the Red Cross for the digital age and submitted my CV/résumé. These events earned me a seat at the table, and I was interviewed in London for the director-general role in 2000. Ultimately, I received a very courteous call from the executive recruiter thanking me and letting me down graciously. While you couldn't say this today, he stated, "With the outgoing Director General being a Norwegian woman, given current international sensitivities, this is not the time to consider a white American male!" Unfortunately, I wasn't selected, but at least I did get my shot at it! I always knew it was a long shot; however, despite my high hopes and disappointment, what happened next was the curious thing.

My discouragement lasted only for about half an hour when I then thought, "How many people actually get a shot at their ultimate dream job?" It was a splendid dream, but I didn't get it, and nothing was ever going to change that. Therefore, I needed to wake up from my fantasy and get on with the rest of my life. No more neurosurgery, no more Red Cross director-general (although I applied again to the Red Cross for their CTO role a decade later); however, I would need to make a living for my family for the next twenty years. So, I stopped fretting in that instant and set about looking for the next best thing.

Thus, although we can't always choose what work we do, we can often find a meaningful purpose in that work and discover a passion for why we do it, but critically, we can always choose how we do it. Considering a Zen or mindful approach to life, it almost doesn't matter what we are doing; what is really important is how we do it. Therefore, if your vision of *what you do* is sound, in that you don't compromise your principles, and the purpose of *why you do it* is aligned with your values, then the final fundamental key to being a successful leader is *how you lead*. Beyond the mechanics of management procedures and processes, effective leadership implies leading with vision, integrity, empathy, and authenticity.

Shortly after returning to Minnesota from my two-year post-university grand tour of Europe and starting at American Express, I happened upon Robert Pirsig's book *Zen and the Art of Motorcycle Maintenance: An Inquiry into Values*.[20] It chronicles his motorcycle journey and related philosophical musing with his son on a trip from Minneapolis to San Francisco. This timely and profound book had a lasting impact on me and my future work. I'd only ever been on a motorcycle once in my life, as a teen, which ended in an afternoon of picking gravel out of my palms and knees. Therefore, Pirsig's motorcycle maintenance was a metaphor for me (as intended) for the proper way to live one's life. The dedication to self-discipline and aspiration to realize quality are key to achieving fulfillment in life.

Pirsig contends that becoming deeply engaged in any task, our work, or our lives in general, is a necessary condition for achieving quality, excellence, and satisfaction. He states that the concept of quality is difficult to grasp, but we know it when we see or experience it. Some things are intrinsically better than others, but he asks what's the "betterness"? For me, it represents both a question of the quality of vision and values and a commitment to quality of action and expression through your words, deeds, and actions. He further explains individuals most frequently and easily find engagement and a quality culture in areas closely aligned with their talents and passions.

Setting a vision with a purpose and creating an emotional link between our task and the meaningful outcome is fundamental to attaining contentment and fulfillment. Being emotionally disconnected from our work or lives causes a lack of engagement, resulting in boredom, apathy, and even cynicism. If it becomes pervasive, we can undergo and endure a sense of persistent drudgery, tedium, or helplessness. This can result in a "rat race" form of plodding, being somnambulant or on autopilot, resulting in a default dull and defeatist state of mind.

The feeling of disconnection from our work dissipates when we believe in the purpose of what we are doing and throw ourselves into it. This results in a sense of achievement and accomplishment.

This principle also applies to any professional interest or personal talent, such as art, sports, music, design, and also, significantly, deep engagement with our families.

Pirsig and others have described this optimal experience of dedication and effortless engagement as "being in the zone" or "flow." All of you will have experienced flow at one moment or another, often during artistic or sports activities. In addition, it is frequently encountered in creative work endeavors such as executing a new design or creating a new product. These optimal experiences are inspiring, enjoyable, and rewarding.

In summary, Pirsig argues that art and science, rationality, and Zen-like "being in the moment" can and should harmoniously coexist within any activity and are vital for self-satisfaction and self-actualization in your work and career. He concludes that integrating, rather than separating, "idealistic romanticism" and "pragmatic rationality" is vital to a high quality of work and a higher quality of life.

Thanks to Pirsig's inspiring and timely book, this philosophy for living a quality life has been embedded in my psyche ever since. While I don't always adhere to it in all ways, the message in his book left me with a subconscious ethos of quality that continually bubbles up to guide my motivations and actions. Perhaps it also, in some way, precipitated my own journey from Minneapolis to San Francisco to start a new life some four years later, thankfully by plane rather than a motorcycle!

This is a way to achieve one's full potential through full engagement in activities and dedication to the virtue of quality. Those who live a life of quality strive for and can realize their full potential in the process. Therefore, leaders should encourage and train the individuals in their teams to fully engage with and strive for the highest quality and eventual mastery of their craft, discipline, or profession.

Further, this account is about how to be an outstanding leader of high quality, a leader your colleagues, and your teams will respect, consult, confide in, trust, support, deliver for, and follow into the heat of battle. All of this relates to how you work. Therefore, what is your day-to-day modus operandi? What are the most effective leadership styles, best practice methods, latest techniques, and specialty tools to help you daily as a leader and throughout your leadership career? Let's explore and address each of these issues.

Leadership is hard to define, and good leadership even harder. But if you can get people to follow you to the ends of the earth, you are a great leader.
—Indra Nooyi, former chairperson and CEO of PepsiCo[21]

Creating a Life through Meaningful Moments

Your work is going to fill a large part of your life, and the only way to be truly satisfied is to do what you believe is great work. And the only way to do great work is to love what you do. If you haven't found it yet, keep looking. Don't settle. As with all matters of the heart, you'll know when you find it.

—Steve Jobs[22]

Thus began my career journey, which eventually spanned four decades, working across three continents, in multiple countries, and through various wholesale career changes. What transpired was a kaleidoscope of experiences and myriad encounters that would never have occurred had I stuck to my original plan to be a surgeon.

Having discussed what we do and elaborated on why we do it, particularly with the vision with a purpose, now with the overlay of quality, let's return to the critical nuances of how we work.

A key lesson I have learned, respecting certain self-imposed boundaries (i.e., no unethical or illegal activities), is the following. Once I've found a role I can believe in and set a vision with a purpose and passion, *what* I am doing on a daily basis is less important than the everyday interactions and activities that transpire between me as a leader and my teams, colleagues, and business partners.

In other words, my purpose, passion, and "personal art" are in my leadership function rather than being a technologist, marketeer, salesperson, operations director, or innovator. Perhaps this perspective derives in part from the time in my role as a technology futurist. What I learned is that over the expanse of time, any emerging technology, new tool, great application, or service will eventually always become old hat, antiquated, obsolete, and replaced with the latest, greatest gadget or next big thing. The special leadership "magical moments" of guiding, training, mentoring, and caring for my colleagues create an ever-expanding and never-ending chain of positive experiences that spread continually through me, my family, themselves, and their colleagues, families, and friends.

Beyond the artifacts of our résumés, CVs, or LinkedIn profiles, our work lives happen in the moment, minute by minute in thousands of small interactions or vignettes. If we are authentic, true to ourselves, honorable and ethical, and work diligently, focus intensely, care deeply, and have a sense of humor, we can create a rich and purposeful work life through stringing together these individual moments.

A recent *Harvard Business Review* article explored the concept of "What Is a Good Job?" Beyond all the complexity and noise surrounding the company, culture, team, and role, it all came down to this simple definition: "A good job is one where you feel seen for being the best version of yourself; you sense that your colleagues have your back; you don't feel discriminated against; you feel your position is secure; and you have confidence that you'll get help navigating constant change in the working world." Further, people need to feel that their work matters and that their contributions help to achieve something worthwhile.[23] This is the environment and atmosphere we should strive for when leading and supporting subordinates and followers.

We may also create something of value, enrich our colleagues, and transform our own lives in the process. This may sound somewhat grandiose or hypothetical; however, these individual actions are mutually self-reinforcing and self-perpetuating and eventually become habitual, automatic, and ultimately a way of life.

This is then a healthy and happy approach to work that has served well for me, my colleagues, teams, and contacts, which is contagious and constructive for all. The beneficial aspect of this is that it can result in your and your colleagues' work life being pleasant, self-actualizing, and productive. Simultaneously, this approach has proven highly efficient and effective for projects, jobs, and employers. Finally, contented and self-actualized workers are more creative and highly productive and, as a result, create greater organizational value.

Corporate Storytelling: Allegory, Metaphor, Analogy

Stories are the secret reservoir of values: change the stories individuals or nations live by and tell themselves, and you change the individuals and nations.

—Ben Okri[24]

As we inspire our people and teams by articulating a vision, corporate storytelling is an inspirational way influential leaders create powerful images and messages in their colleagues' and the teams' minds. The power of stories helps people relate to and emotionally engage with the topics at hand. Compelling stories are meaningful, memorable, and motivating.

Jim Rohn, a respected motivational speaker in management, illustrated the fundamental difference in inspirational storytelling with the following comparison. Cicero and Demosthenes were two great Roman orators. When Cicero spoke, the audience would comment, "What a brilliant speech!" When Demosthenes spoke, the people would say, "Let us march!" A skilled storyteller not only inspires us but arouses us and motivates us to act.[25]

Paul Smith, a renowned executive storyteller, author, and coach, wrote the book *Lead with a Story: A Guide to Crafting Business Narratives That Captivate, Convince, and Inspire.* He elaborates on how to craft the following ten stories influential leaders tell:

1. Where We Came From: A Founding Story—how it all started
2. Why We Can't Stay Here: A Case-for-Change Story
3. Where We're Going: A Vision Story
4. How We're Going to Get There: A Strategy Story
5. What We Believe: A Corporate Values Story
6. Who We Serve: A Customer Story
7. What We Do for Our Customers: A Sales Story
8. How We're Different from Our Competitors: A Marketing Story
9. Why I Lead the Way I Do: A Leadership Philosophy Story
10. Why You Should Want to Work Here: A Recruiting Story[26]

Metaphors and analogies are also powerful corporate storytelling tools for creating and communicating dramatic leadership visions and messages. Of course, some people are more extroverted and have sharper humor and timing than others, but everyone can tell a story, and it is also a skill that can be developed and refined rapidly.

Converting a key message into a story or analogy or comparing a complex problem to a similar situation with familiar or related issues within a different context can help distill or deconstruct a complicated topic down to its bare essentials and core principles. These stories or analogies help listeners comprehend, identify with, and relate to a complex or emotive issue at hand.

Leadership storytelling has the benefit of transporting the listeners out of the present moment, current situation, or dilemma, especially if the issue is problematic, political, or emotionally charged, into a safe, neutral, external narrative. This creates a calm and objective perspective for gaining insight or inspiration and helps crystallize the essence of the situation. In addition, this objective and safe vantage point helps facilitate unadulterated, unambiguous, and unbiased decision-making.

Storytelling approaches could apply an existing, proven approach to a novel problem, identify a new insight or perspective on a topic, or cite a motivational illustration to impart courage or commitment to a course of action that holds promise for resolving a dilemma. In addition, stories can provide new perspectives or inspiration, as with the "philosopher and the stonemasons" or the upcoming analogy of "friends of the road and of the heart" for team building. You can also use them to relate a simple guiding analogy, like: "You can't change the tires of the race car while it's on the track."

Stories and analogies are particularly helpful in imparting specialist information to nonspecialists, such as when explaining complex technical issues to a general manager. For example, when trying to explain why a slick mobile application "proof of concept" cannot just be quickly tidied up and launched, you might comment that this is like trying to construct the roof of a building before you've laid the foundation.

Business or corporate stories can set a vision, reinforce mores, establish a culture, catalyze change, motivate a colleague, solve a problem, or formulate a decision. Naturally, a story's effectiveness depends on the storyteller's credibility, the quality of the visualization, the passion and authenticity of the delivery, and the maturity or emotional receptiveness of the listener. But also the story's relevance to the listener's context, appropriateness of the situation or solution, and finally, the fit of the story and the associated resolution of the problem.

Remember, even if you are not already a natural storyteller, all these skills and techniques can be developed and perfected with practice. Given these provisos and perhaps a bit of patience, the corporate story can be a potent tool to cut through the maze of complexity, home in on the crux of a problem, crystallize the options, and zero in on the right solution. They can be beneficial, improve decision-making effectiveness, help create a can-do culture, foster friendly collegial working relationships, and provide positive and constructive approaches to handling difficulties. They can reduce stress and help make meeting challenges and solving problems enthralling.

In addition to setting a vision, creating passion, or initiating action, there are a few practical tips to keep in mind when crafting a story for your colleagues or staff.

1. First of all, the story must have a salient purpose beyond just entertainment or excitement.
2. Make sure you contextualize your story to the relevant situation or problem you are attempting to address.
3. In contextualizing the story, it must also be customized to be applicable to the particular audience. The context must be relevant and address the specific audience's concerns or needs. This ensures the listener can relate to the story and apply it in the appropriate context.
4. If possible and suitable, you can personalize the story by adding pertinent personal experiences that add to or validate the story's authenticity or credibility.
5. You need the story to be inspiring or motivating to help resolve the problem and galvanize the team to action.
6. Conclude with a summary explanation or application of the story crafted to inspire and empower the listener to adopt it and embrace the learning themselves.

Analogy, idiom, and metaphor alternatives and possibilities are as varied as your imagination. I'll share a few useful ones I've picked up, learned, or adapted that have helped me immensely over the years. I've also added a long list of additional special-purpose analogies and metaphors in the appendix at the end. Many I've modified, and the origins of some of these stories are lost in the sands of time.

- An excellent statement to give perspective is: "To find a safe harbor in a storm." That is to say, there may be current challenges, but the situation is temporary and similar to a ship during a storm; you may need to find a safe harbor to ride out danger or adversity to regroup and resurface when the conditions are better. The challenge of coping with the COVID-19 pandemic was an excellent example of this situation.
- If all the facts are on the table, but people are stalled in indecision to force a timely decision before a situation gets worse or run the risk of missing an opportunity, you can comment that you must avoid "analysis paralysis"!
- To caution against costly or catastrophic procrastination when you need to make a decision or implement a solution, explain: "This ship is about to depart, and if we don't make a decision promptly, we're going to miss the boat!"
- When confronted with someone repeatedly making the same mistakes, caution them of the myth of Sisyphus. The corrupt first king of Corinth, Greece, Sisyphus, angered the gods and was condemned to roll an immense boulder up a steep hill, only for it to roll back down just before reaching the summit, thus forcing Sisyphus to repeat the same task (mistake) repeatedly for all eternity.[27]
- Coupled with the story of Sisyphus above, encourage people to "make new mistakes" instead of repeating the old ones all over again!
- Sometimes, people get entrenched in doing things the way they've always been done or applying old thinking to new problems; you can challenge: "If the only tool you have is a hammer, every problem begins to look like a nail." Follow this

famous Abraham Maslow quote with: "You need to use the right tool for the right task."[28]

- If people are looking for a single, simple solution to a complex, intractable problem, you can warn: "There is no silver bullet"! This comes from the old fable of needing a silver bullet to kill a werewolf. If there is no obvious solution to an issue, you can say: "Sorry, there is no silver bullet for this issue.[29] You may need to accept reality and deal with it by mitigating the situation as much as possible."

- When confronted with a significant obstacle or task, the best thing to do is to try to "chunk the problem" and break it down into manageable pieces. A helpful analogy is "What is the best way to eat an elephant? One bite at a time!"

- If you are trying to take action before you have all the information on a complex issue and don't understand the whole situation yet, you can say: "We are like the proverbial four blind men trying to describe an elephant!"

- When decision-making becomes bogged down with too many actors, you may have to enforce rigorous governance to cut to the heart of the situation or decision: "Sorry, we have too many cooks here," followed by: "We need one chef to pull it all together."

- Pandora's box[30] is an emotive analogy to mention as a potential warning. From Greek mythology, this apparently valuable gift was, in fact, a curse containing all manner of dreadful ills. In today's business terms, it refers to unnecessarily lifting the lid on the source of a great many difficulties, e.g., politics. This may also be coupled with: "If it isn't broke, don't attempt to fix it!"

- Similar to the Pandora's box's warning, there is an old saying, "Let sleeping dogs lie!" This naturally refers to not unnecessarily disturbing a large, ugly, and mean-looking dog lest it rears up and bites you. This is a potentially helpful caution when considering whether to embark on a political battle you might not win.

- "You may be doing it right, but are you doing the right thing?" This is an important challenge when strategically considering focusing on the big picture or the right problem. For example, this is a common issue when chipping away at symptoms of a problem rather than addressing the root cause, iterating more of the same, or doing a quick kludgy fix instead of reengineering a proper new solution.

• To gain perspective and maintain motivation and momentum, remind people that: "We always overestimate what we will achieve in the short term and underestimate what we will achieve in the long run!"[31] I've always found this quote I heard from Bill Gates at the London Natural History Museum in about 2001 particularly powerful, especially when investing in major technological change in order to manage unrealistic short-term expectations versus the significant benefits of a long-term transformation.

• There is an old story I heard from the British Poet David Whyte regarding "friends of the heart and friends of the road." Naturally, we love and value our friends of the heart, but they are often few and far between. But, in life and particularly in business, friends of the road are enormously important. As the metaphorical story goes: "If you find yourself in a mountain pass in Afghanistan in the middle of the night during a fierce storm, with the wind whistling, wolves howling and bandits prowling, you are exceedingly thankful for your 'Friends of the Road' who help keep watch at night, mind your possessions and cover your back." We often spend ten-plus hours a day at work in our business lives, including commutes and sleep. Thus, we spend more awake time with our work colleagues than with family or friends. Hence, working collegially, effectively, and even happily with friends of the road is vital for a healthy and contented work/life balance instead of just expecting to enjoy your life while off work.[32]

Please refer to the Appendix for a long list of executive analogies and stories.

These corporate stories help, first and foremost, to articulate a vision and imbue that vision with purpose. But stories are also used to communicate a challenge, discontinuity, juxtaposition, or new perspective on a problem. This often helps people understand the issues better, put them into context, and develop new approaches to the situations. Analogies, metaphors, and idioms can be highly effective when used appropriately and sparingly. When you create an analogy or tell a story, you share a bit of yourself, build credibility, demonstrate creativity, and help resolve problems in new and original ways.

For most of us, making or creating an analogy or metaphor is relatively easy once you understand what they are, how they work, how to craft them, and how powerful they can be. To create or recall an analogy, think of the essential elements, processes, and context of the problem or issue pending. Then, think of a simplistic everyday situation that is at a high level structurally and stylistically similar. The example need not be contextually similar, as often it is more effective to select an example derived from a familiar day-to-day situation. Then imagine how this straightforward example, comparison, or story connects to or solves the more complex problem. Once you have created a simple, relevant account that helps your listener understand and relate to the real problem, you can help resolve the more complex issue according to the same basic principles crystallized in the resolution of the analogy. With practice, you will find that your ability to create metaphors and analogies easily and rapidly on the fly improves dramatically. You'll be pleasantly surprised at how captivating and enjoyable corporate stories, metaphors, and analogies are for successful business communications.

I'll conclude with a popular story within the technology community relating to quality standards. This story is part fact and a little bit of fable, which is often the case with a good story. But it also makes an important point about considering and respecting history to understand why things are the way they are. I have often shared this story to make the point that one cannot look at things in isolation and that existing systems or products are often a consequence of an extended series of activities and events. This can be helpful in assisting teams to understand and buy into the requirement for change.

The discussion starts with the futuristic International Space Station. The American modules of the space station were designed and constructed with components that were initially delivered to space by the

US space shuttle. Therefore, the space station design was considered and constrained by the size of the cargo hold of the space shuttle. The space shuttle itself was designed to provide maximum storage space, respecting the lift capacity of the two enormous solid-fuel boosters that straddled and launched the shuttle. The space shuttle designers in Utah had to consider the fact that the colossal boosters needed to be transported by rail across the country through Rocky Mountain tunnels to Cape Canaveral in Florida. Consequently, the engineers had to design solid fuel boosters taking into account the US railroad network mountain tunnels and train carriage sizes, which have a standard rail gauge of 4 feet, 8½ inches.

The US rail network gauge of 4 feet, 8½ inches, is an exceedingly unusual size. However, with a bit of research, we find that the European engineers employed to design the US rail network specified the US rail network to conform to the same gauge as the British and European rail systems. This was to permit the sale and reuse of European carriages on the new American rail network.

One might logically assume these unusual dimensions were due to a metric-to-imperial system conversion. However, that is not the case. Examining why the European rail system used that size, we find the railcars were constructed from many of the same materials and the same size and gauge as the pre-railroad tramways. Those tramways, in turn, were traditionally loaded and serviced by horse and cart.

Over centuries, the horse and cart wagon wheel width developed to take advantage of and ride within the existing deep grooves already worn in the roads to avoid wheel breakage. These existing historical wheel ruts harken back to the Romans' roads in the days of the Imperial Roman occupation of Northern Europe.

The deep ruts in the roads were worn over centuries by the passage of millions of Roman war chariots whose wheels were 4 feet 8½ inches apart. The chariot wheels were determined by the width necessary to straddle two horses harnessed side by side and hitched to the chariot.

Therefore, following this original design standard back to the present, the space shuttle's size, and consequently the high-tech International Space Station's design, were constructed the way they were because of constraints initially dictated by the size of two horses' rear ends![33]

You have to know the past to understand the present.

—Carl Sagan[34]

My adaptation of Dr. Sagan's quote: *Understand the past, and you can shape the future.*

Key Takeaways–Creating Leadership Vision with Purpose

- In order to lead people authentically, you must first discover your own "North Star" beacon that defines the essence of who you are as a leader.
- Setting a vision with a purpose and creating an emotional link between our task and a meaningful outcome is vital to staff motivation and job satisfaction.
- The next critical element in our quest for meaning and purpose in work, after what you do and why you do it, is to explore the secret sauce of leadership alchemy, "how you work"!
- Use corporate storytelling, metaphor, and analogy to bring your vision to life and to help communicate complex issues clearly and concisely.
- If we are authentic, honorable, and ethical, work diligently, and care deeply, we can create a rich and purposeful work life out of stringing together these memorable moments into a meaningful life.

CHAPTER 2

The Alchemy of Leadership: The Magic and Mechanics of Leadership

Having laid the firm cornerstone of "vision with a purpose" for the leadership superstructure, let's construct the broader leadership landscape with solid, supporting concept pillars. This will help us build a leadership foundation that underpins, enhances, and strengthens the individual's leadership style and skills.

Leadership Concepts and Culture

Leading with the Heart

> *To handle yourself, use your head; to handle others, use your heart.*
> —*Eleanor Roosevelt*[1]

Leadership is a science as well as an art. In other words, leadership behavior comprises the mind's cognitive capabilities plus the emotional resonance of the heart. In setting a vision, we discussed the self-reflective identification of the deep personal drivers that empower one's vision with purpose. Equally important to a leader's effectiveness is a genuine concern, consideration, and compassion for those colleagues and staff within your responsibility and sphere of influence. As we will see, this emotional sensitivity and altruistic benevolence are the catalysts and sustenance essential to deep relationship bonding through "leading with the heart." Nelson Mandela, an outstanding example of an extraordinary leader, astutely remarked, "A good head and a good heart are always a formidable combination."[2]

When we discuss "leading from the heart," we are not implying some fluffy, touchy-feely, new age team-building exercise. Instead, we are referring to formidable leadership interpersonal skills that exceptional leaders possess in connecting and bonding with staff. These leaders create a steadfast, trustful, and committed relationship through which the leader inspires, motivates, and manages staff.

What is it then, that firmly bonds the leader and individual team members together? What is beyond the organization and programs that result in a leader metaphorically charging up the hill toward a goal in the full knowledge that the team is right there alongside them? It is not solely about the target, goal, or project; instead, it is about the trust, loyal connection, and commitment between the leader and team members. Undoubtedly, there are key associated elements of vision, honesty, integrity, and loyalty; however, at a personal and emotional level, it is when someone touches your heart and ignites a personal bond in a meaningful and intimate way that something unique and special happens. A powerful connection and firm commitment are created that are more rousing than lackluster quantitative objectives, targets, and KPIs. It is a heartwarming, emotional affinity that brings about a positive, benevolent change in the symbiotic and reciprocal relationship within the individuals' beliefs and behaviors.

In leading from the heart, again, it is not so much what we are doing as to why and how we do it. The most successful leaders are the ones who have the ability to create steadfast relationships and to inspire and nurture others through their vision, passion, creativity, and commitment. Critically, underpinning those team-based relationship behaviors are the leaders' fundamental character attributes of altruism, benevolence, integrity, honesty, empathy, and reliability.

When a leader leads in this manner, they radiate an ethical and moral guiding light that permeates all aspects of the leader's behavior. This creates a positive, self-reinforcing culture of mutually supportive relationships between the leader and the staff. In other words, does a leader need to be a saint? No, essentially, to lead with the heart intrinsically means that a leader must strive to be the best person and team leader they can be!

These overriding positive character and behavioral ethos infuse virtually all leaders' actions. We will shortly examine each in detail, but at the outset, let's recognize that these behaviors originate from and are reinforced through "leading from the heart." From that overarching foundation, there are a number of related nuanced leadership models identified by academics and leadership consultants that warrant further mention and investigation.

Authentic Leader

Leading from the heart emerges from being authentic, true to yourself, and carefully guided by your ethical, moral, and philosophical values and beliefs. Being authentic means being conscientiously genuine and unpretentious. It further implies unswerving honesty, including to yourself, and conducting yourself with integrity in all actions, especially in interactions with staff, colleagues, and partners.

Trustful Leader

Trust is fundamental to creating and sustaining any close relationship and is part of the unwritten "social exchange" covenant between the leader and staff and among colleagues. It is built on consistent integrity and truth, which must be initiated and maintained until an enduring trust bond is created between individuals and throughout the team. This reciprocal relationship can develop what the political scientist Robert Putnam calls reciprocal "social capital."[3] This bond is powerful but fragile and can be easily broken, and once broken it is very difficult to rebuild.

Empathetic Leader
Heartfelt leadership further implies feeling and expressing natural empathy and compassion to colleagues and staff as a prerequisite to gaining their trust and building loyalty. The strength of the relationship and the extent of the staff commitment are directly linked to the leader's bona fide level of compassion, encouragement, and nurture of the staff under their responsibility.

Service Leadership
The leader is only one of many essential roles in an organization, and to the extent that a leader exemplifies this behavior implies that they conduct themselves and recognize their primary purpose and responsibility is one of service. This means guiding, caring for, and developing staff altruistically for the genuine benefit of those individuals and the advancement of the team's efforts.

Support Leader
In addition to guiding and developing the staff, leading from the heart entails recognizing your and your team's humanity. This is to appreciate that we all have desires, needs, and concerns, be it a career, finances, family, or health. This leader is a sensitive and concerned mentor who is a pillar of strength and support for team members, providing praise, encouragement, feedback, guidance, comfort, and consolation when necessary.

Loving Leader
We will develop these concepts and behaviors extensively throughout the following discussions. However, to distill these key leadership characteristics and behaviors down to one overarching theme or premise it is

"leading with the heart." Here again, we are referring to a genuine universal love of humanity as it applies to the care and nurture of your team and colleagues. This is perhaps best described by the ancient Greek term "agape," referring to universal and unconditional love.

When leaders are authentic, honest, and genuinely concerned for their staff and colleagues, their ideals and values will resonate through their actions by exhibiting and showing deep, legitimate compassion and commitment to their welfare. Consequently, the staff will appreciate that commitment, instinctively sense your inherent concern and empathy, and realize you have their best interests at heart.

This mutual concern and investment in each other through goodwill, trust, honesty, and respect reinforces the mutually symbiotic relationship. The employees and staff will recognize that the leader values them, appreciates their efforts, and reciprocates through their respect, loyalty, and dedication. Moreover, human nature is such that they will likely transcend the requisite work basics and be motivated to give their very best to achieve or exceed the teams' tasks and objectives.

Of all the concepts and ideas we will discuss, this is an overriding theme that drives the successful leader's actions and substantially benefits the firm, the staff, and the leaders themselves. Leading with the heart can nurture the soul, enrich the team, and help realize your organizational objectives.

Takeaway: Aspire to be the best leader you can be, leading with authenticity, honesty, compassion, and empathy, and your teams will reciprocate with loyalty, dedication, and commitment to your vision and mission. A faithful and devoted team will always be significantly more productive than a group of ambivalent people obediently ticking off tasks on a project list.

The Alchemy of Leadership

Leaders must invoke an alchemy of great vision.
                                          —Henry Kissinger[4]

Building on the essence of leading from the heart, something remarkable, almost miraculous, happens when leaders and their staff and team truly connect, click, and bond. I refer to this as the "alchemy of leadership."

Alchemy is an emotive word for the ancient mystic discipline that is the forerunner of modern chemistry and speculative philosophy, describing the transmutation (change) of something ordinary (i.e., base metal) into something extraordinary (i.e., gold).

This analogy works on various levels to describe the emotional chemistry created between the altruistic servant leader and individuals in their teams and the mutually beneficial transformation that emerges through this synergistic relationship. The advantages of the connection and bond are many for the employees, the leader, and the team. An aligned, cohesive, and harmonious team focused on a passionate vision can achieve remarkable things that might not otherwise be possible or practical. This is what we have oft seen in sports exhibition games: a top regular team defeats an all-star team of the best players selected from all teams across the entire league. The existing team has that unique advantage of subconscious knowledge and almost automatic responses that bind them together, allowing them to move as one, much like the murmurations of a flock of starlings moving virtually instantaneously in concert.

These special relationships can originate from either side, especially with mature, senior specialist teams. However, it is often most effectively initiated from the position of authority or power from the leader to the team members. The resulting affiliation is a unique combination of reciprocal trust, shared mutual concern, collegial friendship, spontaneous symbiotic nurturing, and often even bona fide friendship. That's a mouthful, but it means that you are highly collegial, watching each other's backs, and positively investing in cultivating the relationship. Consequently, both parties grow and gain from the alliance beyond what might have previously existed, providing significant benefits to each and the overall organization.

But how does that happen, and what does it mean? A little additional research will help understand and articulate what had occurred between my teams and me in these positive team relationships. In their book *Strengths-Based Leadership*, Rath and Conchie propose people follow leaders based on four basic needs: trust, compassion, stability, and hope.[5] Axiomatically, if these are the fundamental requirements for building relationships, then absence of trust, lack of empathy, job insecurity, and hopelessness represent a recipe for leadership inadequacy and team malfunction. Likewise, Patrick Lencioni provides a valuable contrasting study of defective team behavior in the *Five Dysfunctions of Teams*. He cites the following barriers to effective teams: absence of trust, conflict avoidance, lack of commitment, avoidance of accountability, and inattention to results.[6] A review of these studies and books provides an excellent juxtaposition of effective and ineffective team behavior.

A basic premise of social exchange theory is that each person acts constructively and reciprocally out of self-interest but also at the same time from a mutually interdependent perspective. As a result, each person has something of value to offer and conceivably receive from their counterparty.

In leader and staff connections, elements of potential value exchange are endless and often self-evident in a mutually supportive and cooperative relationship. The particulars of value to be mutually exchanged or shared can be economical, activity-based, or emotional, and psychological. It could be providing career opportunities, such as rewarding diligence and hard work with a promotion, employee empowerment resulting in the staff member taking more responsibility, or an external training opportunity resulting in improved job contribution and career development.

The critical issue is that someone, typically the leader, must consciously initiate a benevolent action, offer, or opportunity. In turn, the staff will express or demonstrate gratitude for the generous and genuine effort of the leader to provide a constructive prospect or benefit to the employee. This positive symbiotic sharing is core to mutually reinforcing and rewarding both parties' self-interest.

Consequently, the initial charitable action acts as a catalyst for stimulating a favorable reaction on the part of the recipient, which begins the process of reciprocal affirmative self-reinforcing responses. As a result, there is a tendency for it to result in increasing returns, such that the parties are more likely to repeat the action: the more mutual reinforcement, the more liable the positive behavior is to recur continuously.

This all starts getting slightly analytical. But without needing to get deeply into game theory or psychoanalysis, I'm sure we all have experienced this in one way or another and can appreciate the basics above. In fact, overanalysis and intentional exploitation of the leadership and staff relationship rapport run the risk of tainting the integrity of the behavior and, thus, the affiliation's authenticity. From a personal perspective, this positive reciprocity becomes the foundation for a mutually supportive relationship that can grow into a constructive collaboration, invaluable mentorship, and even a steadfast long-term friendship.

I will add a couple of additional logical observations. First, common sense, instinct, and basic psychology imply that the more these positive interactions occur and are reinforced, the stronger and longer the relationship bond between the parties will become.

Second, be aware that a single act of kindness does not create a culture. You might catalyze this alchemy of leadership, but to become firmly established as an organizational modus operandi, corporate culture, departmental ethos, and your own servant leadership style, these altruistic, empathetic, and benevolent behaviors must be authentic, pervasive, and consistent.

Third, in organizations and especially teams, there is a broader social element and network effect to this. If a leader treats someone fairly, naturally, that person is pleased and more likely to promote positive messages about the leadership experience to colleagues. Others will observe these positive behaviors, have a predisposed benevolent attitude toward the leader, and further share their experiences. As favorable behaviors are reinforced in individual relationships, there is a tendency for these constructive behaviors to spill over to the collective. It will then replicate or proliferate across the entire team and organization until the attitudes and behaviors become fully established as cultural norms.

A leader who is aware of and sensitive to staff reinforcement will recognize the team's reciprocal response to their attitudes and actions. This will, in turn, perpetuate positive feedback loops with continued affirmative behavior toward staff. A good leader will recognize, repeat, and reinforce the overall improvement in staff morale, collaboration, and support. In short, "good begets good" (Paul Auster).

Following this somewhat analytical discussion of social exchange theory, let's look at some relevant practical examples of leadership practice. Beyond leadership theory and science, there are significant elements of leadership art, chemistry, and alchemy in compassionate, committed servant leadership.

How do we create, tap into, and leverage our own secret sauce or transformative alchemy of leadership? It can be difficult and take time to develop in some cases, but also, in other ways, it is easy, instinctual, and immediate. It may seem trite, but it is important to say, "Be yourself, your authentic self," and be the person you are when you're with your best friends and family, even in your professional life. If you are a capable, caring, and competent leader, you won't relinquish any management power by being your authentic, altruistic, and benevolent persona. You will, however, be more effective as a leader and create higher staff morale and organizational productivity.

There is no single silver bullet to the alchemy of leadership. Similarly, as Robert Pirsig said about quality, it is hard to define, but you know it when you see it. It is the same for leadership alchemy. It is a synthesis of all your activities, communications, and behaviors.

Be generous with your empathy, encouragement, compliments, feedback, communications, and especially time. If you invest heavily with your time and efforts in your team, your team will benefit enormously and return your efforts multiplied manyfold.

Remember, your leadership style and credibility comprise thousands of small actions, friendly gestures, quick comments, and consistent behaviors that determine who you are and how you are perceived as a leader. The scores of little things create a composite of one's perception of another individual.

The following example is simple and may seem trivial, but as a representative example, it illustrates one of a myriad of similar small but powerful leadership habits. Remember, even slight gestures can be exceedingly meaningful and heartening to employees or colleagues!

Start your day on the right foot cheerfully and positively. I always enter the office with a cheerful "good morning" to everyone I pass. I intentionally go the long way around, passing as many people as possible, greeting everyone at the row of desks, and ensuring I make quick eye contact with everybody. To put it in perspective, it never took more than a minute or two. This simple habit became a minor cultural norm that evidently was anticipated and enjoyed by everyone in the team. Many even found it humorous. Occasionally, if I had an off-site morning meeting and would arrive after lunch, I'd still pass by everyone with a cheerful "good morning," which made them all chuckle. It started each day on a positive note for everyone, especially during challenging and trying times.

Moreover, this habit seemed to break the ice between team members and me and help maintain rapport. Because of this simple gesture on my part, they felt that they had a personal relationship with me and could approach me and talk to me at any time.

So don't just dive into the office with your blinders on each Monday morning, with your head down and the weight of the world on your shoulders. The critical issue here is that even if you are having difficulties, colleagues may interpret your emotional distance as you having a problem with them, even if it has nothing to do with them. You set the work climate and culture from the moment you enter the office. If you are chirpy and lively at the outset, everyone will relax, settle down, be positive, and be able to work uninhibited by anxiety or the specter of heavy-handed management hanging over their head.

In the same vein, I recall once when we had a particularly complex technical system development we had worked on for weeks that was becoming time urgent. It required a challenging weekend launch, and most of the team had to be on duty throughout the weekend. Eventually, after two harrowing days, the release failed, and we had to roll the system back to the prior version at midday on Sunday. It was a big disappointment for everyone and meant a significant delay. When I entered the office at 8:30 on Monday morning, I could see rows of intensely working, serious, and glum-looking technical staff. I fortified myself for a cheerful entry, and the same as every other day, I walked in positively, greeting everyone. I arrived at the IT team where the release had been managed, smiled, and asked with a wry smile: "No one died, did they?" They burst out laughing, breaking the tension. Then, they briefed me on the situation, and we proceeded to resolve the problem calmly and efficiently.

Anxiety and stress are not helpful emotions for getting difficult jobs done effectively, with quality, and hopefully happily.

On a related note, there is a rather odd custom in some business meetings, training, and conference situations when people enter a meeting or training room. They often greet only the people they know and perhaps the stranger next to them. I've always found this peculiar, probably because of my small-town upbringing and time living overseas in places with less reserved cultural habits. I always greet everyone at meetings, walk around the conference table, and introduce myself to everyone. This sets a friendly, collegial tone for the meeting and warms me up to participate and connect with everyone.

It's a small gesture but has constructive outcomes for a cheerful atmosphere, good collaboration, and teamwork. This is especially effective if the meeting involves diverse groups, particularly external partners or suppliers. Remember, it is only an accident of fate that they may have a different logo on their business card than yours.

A smile, encouragement, or recognition for some positive effort is an excellent way to start any discussion with a staff member, regardless of the meeting's objective, and also as a public recognition for a job well done in a meeting or public forum. Ensure this is genuine and gracious to ensure it is not interpreted as contrived gratuitousness. Regular but deliberate and authentic behaviors, as described by Ken Blanchard in the *One-Minute Manager*,[7] require only minimal effort on the part of the leader but are exceedingly motivating for the staff. A slight gesture to you may be a major ego booster and confidence builder for a team member. The important thing is that you consciously remember to do it and do it genuinely, not merely routinely going through the motions.

Finally, a dedicated servant leader must be generous, kind, caring, and selfless when dealing authentically with a team. Don't think of your people as staff, assets, resources, or employees; look beyond that to them as individuals. Invest in them as human beings, not just as employees. I've often found that key staff under my watch had vital knowledge and abilities well beyond my experience in their particular domain. We could never have achieved as much as we did without their enthusiastic alignment and generous contributions.

Moreover, get to know your staff personally and be aware of their families, interests, and hobbies. Get to recognize their talents and aspirations, not just their knowledge and skills. Be sensitive to their fears and anxieties, their problems and concerns, as well as their expectations and challenges. This will help you see the real person behind the role and function to encourage and empathize with them, support them, and bring out the very best in them.

A sound working relationship built on an amicable, symbiotic commitment to each other can strengthen into a unique working relationship that is rewarding and mutually gratifying. As discussed, these are your "friends of the road" with whom you share most of your waking hours. Accordingly, a significant part of your and their professional and personal success, happiness, and well-being depends on high-quality, collaborative, and amiable work relationships.

This, therefore, constitutes critical elements of the alchemy of leadership. We have proposed leading from the heart and discussed the magic of the alchemy of leadership; now, let's embody this heartfelt altruism and alchemy in our perspective and focus on how we shepherd our teams as servant leaders.

Takeaway: People thrive in an environment based on trust, stability, and hope. Create a work culture where people feel safe and valued and feel satisfaction and promise, and you will find your team will rally around you, your vision, and your mission.

Servant Leadership

The servant-leader is servant first. It begins with the natural feeling that one wants to serve first. Then conscious choice brings one to aspire to lead.
                    —*Robert K. Greenleaf "Essentials of Servant Leadership"*[8]

Leading from the heart, comprising and catalyzing the alchemy of leadership, naturally blossoms into an authentic and altruistic leadership style now referred to as servant leadership. Robert Greenleaf, the acknowledged founder of the servant leadership movement, explains:

> The difference manifests itself in the care taken by the servant first to make sure that other people's highest-priority needs are being served. The best test, and the most difficult to administer, is: Do those served grow as persons? Do they, while being served, become healthier, wiser, freer, more autonomous, and more likely themselves to become servants? And what is the effect on the least privileged in society? Will they benefit, or at least not be further deprived?[9]
>
> The emergence of servant-leadership has promise in meeting the deep desire in our society for a world, and in our case, a workplace where people genuinely care for and nurture one another. A place where workers and customers are treated fairly and the leaders can be trusted to serve the needs of their followers rather than just their own.[10]
>
> A primary motivation for leadership should be to serve others and to transform society through service, according to Snyder, Dowd, and Houghton.[11]

Hence, servant leadership is a particular leadership style representing a shift of focus from traditional top-down leadership to one of service to others. The leader/staff roles are recast and almost reversed in servant leadership. The leader guides, nurtures, and supports staff rather than directs and controls staff activities focused primarily on corporate objectives or career advancement. Clearly, this primarily relates to modern knowledge worker environments rather than factory-style conditions such as supply chain warehouses, enormous manufacturing facilities, and massive call centers.

Kathleen Patterson states, "Servant-leadership theory provides a marked contrast to transformational leadership theory. While a transformational leader's focus is to align their professional interests with the issues of the group, organization, or society, the leader's primary focus in servant-leadership theory is serving their followers individually and personally."[12] Solid and consistent effort in staff development results in happy and productive staff, a collaborative relationship, and superior team results and performance.

One could make the case that an astute or shrewd leader would recognize that a large, high-performing, and empowered team will achieve outstanding results. Further, motivating and supporting them to the best of your ability would enhance team morale and, thus, productivity. This is undoubtedly true and not necessarily a bad thing; however, the moment you taint and pollute the intent and diligence of your servant orientation and motivation by the explicit expectation of improved efficiency and productivity or your own personal advancement, you have lost the plot and have missed the point of servant leadership entirely.

The servant role is inspiring but simultaneously demanding, as it evokes a high standard of leadership. In addition, it also entails an element of ego suppression that can be challenging for some. However, if one's servant leadership style is authentic, unconscious, and natural, then it is genuine and unadulterated.

Perhaps the litmus test of genuine servant leadership is: What is the end result? Are the members of the team happy and healthy? Are they developing and self-actualizing? Are they growing and developing? If the answer is yes to each, then it is likely that the leader is an authentic servant leader. They focus first on the well-being, nurturing, and growth of the team and subsequently on the organizational objectives. This does not minimize the goals and objectives; it respects and achieves them. However, the starting point and approach are distinct from a top-down, dispassionate, detached corporate perspective.

Servant leadership, therefore, includes a philosophical and emotional dedication to service rather than just the effective management of activities.

From my perspective, it is an overriding and all-encompassing mindset and behavior rather than simply a theory, science, or systematic method of leadership. This authentic and altruistic attitudinal behavior comes from genuine concern and caring for the people you work with and serve.

Furthermore, servant-leaders are self-aware, true to themselves and their values, and work in a symbiotically nurturing and fulfilling manner for their teams and themselves. The servant-leader gives generously of their time, heart, and effort to get to know team members intimately, understand their needs, and create a genuine two-way communication dialogue. This leader empathizes with them, mentors and supports them, and takes great satisfaction in seeing them healthy, happy, and fulfilled personally and professionally.

Ultimately, servant leadership is a leadership philosophy and pathway of life that, in many ways, again represents the art rather than the science of leadership, overlaying the technical discipline of leadership and imbuing it with heart and benevolence. We don't need to elaborate on the day-to-day how-to specifics of servant leadership, as it represents this book's overall message, philosophy, and ethos rather than a rigid prescriptive model for a set of rules, tactics, methods, or procedures for working.

Over the past forty years, the times when I was truly happy working always involved roles when I was leading teams, both large and small. Looking back, the requisite conditions seemed to be when the team vision was established, there was a healthy organizational culture, and I was intensely engaged with the individuals in the team, guiding, mentoring, training, and supporting them as a servant leader. However, these relationships took on a more profound aspect, where we connected on a human level and touched each other meaningfully, not as leader and staff, but as colleagues, mates, friends, companions, and in some ways through creating a "work family."

One vivid example was running the Reuters Usability Labs in London. It was thrilling, exciting, and rewarding. To a person, the staff members were motivated, inspired, and enthusiastic to be working in the world's foremost usability labs at that time. In addition to being the founder and director, my responsibility was to be the person attempting to inspire, encourage, and support the transformational agenda. However, as this was a team of specialists and experts in cognitive psychology, human factors, ergonomics, customer experience, testing, and interface design, my role was to lead and set direction, but also often to encourage and enable people who had more knowledge and expertise in their specific disciplines than I did.

Once the team was in place, mobilized, and fully operational, my role as their servant leader was to guide, empower, enable, and support them in getting the job done. Sometimes, the most important thing a leader can do is check the compass to ensure they're on track, bandage an emotional wound, give a passionate speech of encouragement, or run interference for them. This could mean running political, contractual, or financial interference or facilitating and supporting with new tools, facilities, or resources. Do whatever needs to be done to ensure the team is freed up to do what they do best. Occasionally, the best thing to do is to get out of the way of their critical path and head out for takeaway croissants and coffees or pizzas and beers!

Among my foremost actions and contributions as a servant leader was my considerable effort to provide development opportunities for my staff, particularly to work and lobby long and hard for their compensation, benefits, and promotions. The conscientiousness and creativity I spent writing extensive rationalizations and justifications for ambitious salary increases and promotions did not go unnoticed or unappreciated by my staff.

This doesn't mean a leader is irrelevant, weak, or has to be a softie—precisely the contrary. It means a heartfelt servant leader genuinely cares for the staff, recognizes their value and needs, and does their best to mentor, nurture, and support them. With a motivated, high-performing team, the servant leader guides and supports them to successful outcomes and shares the rewards accordingly.

Takeaway: If you are generous of spirit, care deeply for people, and find your greatest joy as a leader comes not from tactical successes but from helping people to be happy, grow, and be successful, you may find happiness and fulfillment in corporate life by devoting yourself to the calling of becoming a servant leader.

Emotional Intelligence

Gifted leadership occurs when heart and head—feeling and thought—meet. These are the two winds that allow a leader to soar.
—*Daniel Goleman*[13]

Examining the concept of servant leadership further and digging deeper into the servant leader's character, we can identify various prominent leadership perspectives and classes of behaviors that have become known as emotional intelligence.

Emotional intelligence is a cluster of leadership behavioral characteristics that define leaders as self-aware, self-confident, self-motivated, emotionally stable, socially comfortable, excellent communicators, unpretentious, nonpolitical, benevolent to others, and generous of spirit.

It is now well established and accepted that emotional intelligence is an indispensable coequal component of a leader's effectiveness alongside cognitive intelligence and technical skills. In today's complex work context, especially with senior, highly mature staff, emotional intelligence is equally important as the traditional business requirements of intelligence, education, experience, business/financial skills, and technical knowledge.

Further, emotional intelligence represents a number of personal, social, emotional, and team "soft skills" or "people skills" behaviors that enable a leader to be highly competent in motivating and leading teams and training and mentoring staff.

It initially requires acute self-awareness as a starting criterion to drill down into the nature of emotional intelligence. A leader needs a keen ability to be self-conscious, insightful, reflective, and aware of your own and others' behaviors. Moreover, leaders need to recognize and regulate their conduct and emotions intuitively and instinctively in interactions with the people around them to help guide and manage others. This person, therefore, possesses significant self-discipline and control with an ability to masterfully handle organizational challenges and emotions for themselves and their staff.

In addition, a mature, emotionally intelligent leader must also have a high degree of empathy to sense and appreciate your team's and colleagues' emotional needs and actions. Emotionally intelligent leaders with highly developed self and social awareness have a sharp perception and deep insight into human nature, which assists in developing mature relationships and skillfully managing delicate social interactions.

The emotionally intelligent leader creates a positive team-based culture to inspire and motivate staff, manage expectations and objectives, and interact capably within the team. In addition, this emotionally intelligent and empathetic leader is perceived as trustworthy and highly proficient in communication, collaboration, and teamwork. This is a strong indicator of a successful leader who is respected and admired by staff. These characteristics help establish leadership credibility and trust within the team, resulting in stronger commitment to the leader, loyalty to the team, and a higher alignment with the mission and objectives. Consequently, increased emotional intelligence directly translates into greater leadership effectiveness through higher staff morale and motivation, resulting in improved performance and successful outcomes.

High emotional intelligence also strongly correlates with leadership success across the broader organization. This leader is perceived as a good team leader and is also highly valued as a senior coworker. Therefore, as a colleague, the leader is viewed as a person of good character, trustworthy, reliable, levelheaded, effective in dealing with stress, having clarity of decision-making, being a good communicator, and a respected leadership team player.

In addition to my own examples throughout the book, I believe the best way to internalize the concept of emotional intelligence, based on the descriptions above, is for you to reflect consciously on highly successful and, conversely, ineffective people in your own or former organizations.

Finally, within your own experience and a quick mental survey of political and celebrity culture, you can quickly identify examples of individuals with high and low emotional intelligence. It is also fascinating to note cases of people of high intelligence but, unfortunately, low emotional intelligence. It is a sad critique of current society to see many hugely successful business people who do not possess strong people skills or ethical values. On the other hand, the most successful and respected leaders have a healthy balance of intellectual and emotional intelligence.

Takeaway: It is an established fact that emotional intelligence and people skills are equally important in business today as cognitive intelligence and technical skills. However, with respect to building teams, emotional intelligence is arguably the most important criterion for team leadership.

Mindfulness

Mindfulness enables leaders to be fully present, aware of themselves and their impact on other people, and sensitive to their reactions to stressful situations.
—Bill George, CEO of Medtronics and professor of management[14]

Mindfulness is a prominent personal practice beginning that first gained popularity in the West with the human potential development movement of the 1970s. Further, it has exploded in popularity, along with yoga, since the turn of the millennium.

However, it is much older, rooted in meditation practices and Buddhism in India and the East for hundreds of years. Its popularity and prominence as a meditation practice for centering and relaxation have developed from being a cottage industry to becoming virtually mainstream for individuals and groups. Companies and corporations are adopting these salubrious mindfulness techniques to encourage focus, manage stress, fortify health, and stimulate creativity.

Although not a professed expert, I am aware through numerous personal and professional contacts of the benefits of the principal techniques, which I frequently practice in my own abbreviated and tailored way to center and focus. In layperson's terms, mindfulness is a modern term for the Eastern meditation practices describing: "In the moment" awareness of the present moment and the environment and current activities surrounding you. It involves a continual practice of aspiring to stay "awake" to bring yourself to complete attention and full awareness. Being awake and being present, plus intentionally paying attention and being nonjudgmental without preconceived ideas, allows you to be objective, unbiased, and impartial in assimilating and comprehending your current context, feelings, and nuances about people, situations, or issues.

To achieve this heightened awareness, it is helpful to follow some of the time-honored mindfulness techniques to bring yourself to full attention and maintain that focus of attention. In mindfulness, we are reminded that the present moment is all we can ever experience; the past is history, and the future has not yet happened, so this instant, this moment, is all we ever really have. Mindfulness practitioners encourage us to focus on breathing to capture this moment, help us pay attention, and bring us into the present. Observe nonjudgmentally and benevolently your environment, the people and things around you, and accept them for what they are. Then, attempt to continuously sustain that attention as much as possible throughout your daily work and life. This will help you be fully conscious, put things into perspective, and be more accepting and less anxious.

It is intriguing and valuable for you to contrast this with the contrary mental states of being inattentive, or letting yourself be distracted, daydreaming, or metaphorically "sleepwalking." This corresponds to the related theme of German philosopher Martin Heidegger, who discusses this phenomenon relative to what he refers to as the "awake and asleep" consciousness modes.

These personal development practices have also spilled over into corporate life as professional methodologies to enhance performance. These techniques can assist you in snapping to attention to focus intently on critical issues and stimulate creative thinking. Therefore, let's further explore these leadership mindfulness techniques and how you can employ these tools formally and informally to enhance your efforts and those of your team. There are undoubtedly hundreds of books and workshops you can attend to dive deeply into this topic, and many aficionados recommend the benefits of a continuous commitment in this area. However, even some small, daily practices and activities can have considerable professional and emotional rewards.

Decades prior to my exposure to the mindfulness phenomenon, I recall a technique recommended by a time management instructor who mentioned a mantra he would repeat throughout the day to remind himself to pay attention and focus on his priorities. He stressed the idea of constantly asking yourself, "What is the best use of my time RIGHT NOW?" not in twenty minutes, an hour, or tomorrow, but right now!

Attention, laser focus, clarity of purpose, and creative thinking are critical attributes in business. So, how do we achieve these and avoid distractions, inattention, and daydreaming? Like anything, the first step has already been taken: becoming aware of the issue. Then, adopt some regular modest mindfulness practices that can help you snap back to attention, put you in the moment, and sustain focus. Just as there is an appropriate context for brainstorming, extrapolating, and thinking outside the box, there is the converse critical requirement for focus and concentration. Both require distinct but mindful discipline. Pay attention to and regulate your breathing. This helps maintain focus and also reduces anxiety and stress.

Developing a daily routine is one way to internalize and habitualize these positive lessons into productive new behaviors. Starting with planning your day, we've all started and stopped the daily to-do list, but restart this practice daily. Creating your to-do list will aid enormously in helping you set priorities and regain focus throughout the interruptions and distractions of a busy workplace. This is also extremely important in the new remote working home office environment, with different but equally disruptive distractions. You can repeatedly refer to your checklist throughout your workday to ensure that you are making consistent progress against your daily plan. Through mindfulness techniques, bring yourself into a conscious presence and continuously challenge your priorities with the mantra of what is the best use of your time right now.

Next, try to stay focused and prioritize, working through your important and urgent tasks and discarding the time-wasting urgent but unimportant issues. Also, even if efficiently multitasking, use another mindful technique to do one thing at a time and handle each piece of paper, email, or task just once from start to finish. Finally, keep on task and don't furtively and unproductively shuffle the same documents and tasks repeatedly, wasting a staggering amount of time.

Try to focus fully and completely immerse yourself in your task, even if doing multiple things simultaneously. You will be more present, focused, efficient, and productive. It seems contradictory to say handle each task once when multitasking but focus on the most efficient and effective way to manage all these tasks simultaneously. This is a challenging and fun exercise or mind game to see how efficient you can be with your personal time and motion processes.

Try consciously to "slow down to speed up." Again, it sounds counterintuitive, but instinctively, you know it's right; if you do things carefully, systematically, and with discipline, you will do things right and avoid busywork, errors, and rework. As you will appreciate, each activity, whether a project or a sport, has its own optimal speed or pace to be productive without rushing, tripping up, and overwhelming the task, resulting in errors or slippage.

Each time you finish a task, physically or mentally, check it off, as this will give you incremental self-satisfaction of accomplishment. But, again, don't just tick off urgent but trivial activities; focus on high-value essential activities. And then consciously, breathe, breathe, and breathe! Mindfulness, meditation, and yoga experts will all instruct you that focusing on and managing your breath will help bring you back into the present moment and away from your busyness and "autopilot mode" to regain attention, focus, and direction.

In meetings and conferences, I have found the mindfulness techniques highly effective, particularly in meetings and presentations, to stay focused, be in the moment, stimulate creative thinking, and get with the program.

The best way to deal with a high-pressure meeting or meeting new people is to break the ice immediately. I once heard a wise person say: "Enter talking." In other words, in our context, walk into a meeting or conference, and before you sit down, engage the presenter and participants from the outset. Then don't just sit in the back cynical and skeptical about the event; sit up, "lean in," listen actively, and strike up a rapport.

If I detect myself drifting or daydreaming, I focus my attention rapidly and intensely on the speaker and topic to engage my mind, be present, and focus my attention. This, along with a conscious awareness of breath, helps me wake up, start participating, and get my creative juices flowing. This is particularly effective if the subject or presenter is dry or even dull. A further technique is to ask questions, engage with the presenter to get involved, and even help them tease out the nuances of the issue at hand.

The same goes for a large conference with many participants, where asking a relevant early question will get you into the game as a participant, not an observer. I once raised my hand in a large public presentation and interrupted Tom Peters, the celebrated management guru who wrote *In Search of Excellence*, which resulted in a lively debate and, subsequently, a very fruitful professional relationship with him.

In an online interactive meeting, especially a videoconference, promptly engage with the topic and presentation, ideally in the first five minutes, by asking a question or adding a relevant supporting comment. There is nothing worse than sitting back for forty-five minutes in stone silence, waiting for the right moment to participate while the conversation has progressed, and letting an opportune moment pass by without you. Again, if you break the ice early on, you become a part of the conversation and an active participant rather than a stagnant spectator.

When you are conscious and aware, it's intriguing to look around and observe how many people are tuned out, spaced out, zoned out, not fully conscious, or in the moment. Unfortunately, this is unproductive for them, the presenters, and the group. Without directly embarrassing them, posing thoughtful, pointed questions will often gently bring them back to awareness.

The bottom line is regardless of the dryness of the topic or quality of the presenter, barring departing the meeting or presentation, which is rude, you are there for the duration, be it an hour or a day, and you might as well make the absolute most of it. But it is all about being present, in the moment, on top of your game, and being at your best.

Another significant benefit of being mindful when collaborating with colleagues and teams is the positive impact on creativity. When you are in the moment, fully present, actively listening, and engaged in the dialogue, your subconscious mind begins to associate, extrapolate, and converge ideas, feeding them to your conscious mind. You begin to use those associations and extrapolations to build on ideas, develop products, and see points of convergence and gaps that can be filled. Being mindful is a dynamic cognitive state that focuses you, clears the mind of noise, and frees it up for lateral and out-of-the-box thinking, stimulating your creativity.

Mindfulness has become a prominent leadership discipline in the corporate environment that can benefit you and your teams professionally and personally. Starting small initially with a few minor applied mindfulness habits can positively impact your and your team's performance, pleasure, and productivity.

Takeaway: A regular practice of mindfulness can help you relax, focus, and clear your mind of extraneous distractions, assisting you with clarity of problem solving and being more creative. Even starting small initially, with a few minor applied mindfulness techniques, can positively impact your and your team's performance, pleasure, and productivity.

Motivation

Motivation is a fire from within. If someone else tries to light that fire under you, chances are it will burn very briefly.
                                        —*Stephen R. Covey*[15]

The Stephen Covey quote above raises a fundamental issue relative to leadership motivation. As you appreciate, staff motivation is a critical leadership responsibility to ensure the optimum achievement of organizational objectives while assuring positive worker morale and job satisfaction. The key for leaders is not to try to "light that fire under the staff" but to create a climate and culture conducive to employee engagement and to communicate a meaningful challenge to the staff to excite, encourage, and earn their commitment to the objective. However, as the quote astutely states, simply trying to motivate an employee externally may only have a fleeting effect, if any.

As discussed earlier, this is a function of leadership vision-setting and defining a purpose to secure the employee's psychological buy-in to the objectives and communicate how the individual's efforts contribute to the overall vision. This, in turn, stimulates the employee's initial alignment and further sustains staff motivation and momentum throughout the project or activity, especially when things get tedious or arduous.

This relates to the extrinsic motivational aspects of setting a vision and delivering the outcomes. However, intrinsic personal aspects of motivation also need to be recognized and woven into the equation.

Ideally, the leader can inspire and motivate employees to buy into the team projects and overall organizational objectives personally and intrinsically. For example, as in my case, in the travel industry, my teams and I bought into the concept of providing enjoyable breaks for families in the form of vacations at TUI. When I was at Worldsport Networks, the focus was encouraging physical fitness for youth.

If a task is deemed inherently meaningful or valuable, is seen as beneficial for skill-building or career development to the employee, or gives a sense of autonomy and accomplishment through recognition and reward, staff will be encouraged and motivated to devote themselves to the project and deliver a successful result.

However, suppose the personal motivator and the organizational objectives for an employee are too divergent, incongruent, or conflictive to construct an emotional bridge. In that case, alternatively, you can attempt to recognize their career aspirations or avocational interests instead. If corporate objectives do not align tightly with a person's interests or aspirations, you can still leverage skill and career development as motivational drivers for employees.

Employees are often motivated by a desire to develop new knowledge and skills or through external social or peer pressure, recognition, and career aspirations. Therefore, assigned tasks or work should provide an appropriate challenge and opportunity to stretch the employee. This helps encourage and foster knowledge and skill development, leading to personal job satisfaction and career development. The leader should also give regular feedback, proper help, appropriate resources, and support. Finally, allow sufficient autonomy and decision-making to build competence and confidence and provide commensurate recognition and rewards for achieving the objectives.

The essential thing for leadership and the individual is to align the intrinsic personal motivators and the extrinsic company or team's objectives as closely as possible. Your staff may also have additional personal altruistic passions such as climate change, ecological concerns, or a personal cause such as social equality, women's issues, or child welfare. It's beneficial to make an effort to get to know the employee well enough to surface these deeper emotional drivers and motivators.

Considering employee avocational interests, the leader can be aware of a staff member's interest or hobby, recognize it, and reinforce it as much as possible. This provides a common ground for sharing interests and experiences, which aids in building a bond between the leader and staff member. For example, one employee and I shared a keen interest in chess, which we enjoyed during our lunch hour. This created a common ground for a mutual bond and provided us with intellectual stimulation, often spurring inventive discussions about current projects and organizational issues.

But even if there is no shared interest, with even minimal effort, one can appreciate a staffer's avocational interests and honor them by acknowledging their hobby. A simple example is that I recently heard a Spanish neighbor playing the bagpipes, which I then mentioned to a Scottish employee who I knew also played the bagpipes. This generated an interesting discussion of the Atlantic seafaring connection between the Scottish Celtic bagpipes and the Spanish Galician bagpipe tradition. This was purportedly because of pilgrims returning to Scotland and Ireland from the Camino de Santiago de Compostela in Spain. The opportunities for sharing of interests are endless, and with a bit of imagination, the leader and team bonding benefits are many.

In summary, recognize that employee motivation is more than whitewashing your objectives to make them look more attractive. It requires an extensive and rich two-way dialogue and interaction between the leader and staff. The extent to which you identify, understand, and honor your employee's interests and drivers and align them to your organization's objectives will directly enhance your success in positively motivating and inspiring your staff.

Takeaway: We are all different; consequently, try to get to know your people well enough to understand their primary motivations and hidden drivers. This will help you craft relevant motivational opportunities that can be aligned to your organizational objectives.

Transactional/Transformative

Leaders establish the vision for the future and set the strategy for getting there; they cause change. They motivate and inspire others to go in the right direction, and they, along with everyone else, sacrifice to get there.

—John Kotter[16]

Following discussions of servant leadership and emotional intelligence, it's helpful to pivot our lens to look at two different types of leaders in the organizational context.

The concept of transformative versus transactional leadership was first proposed by James MacGregor Burns in 1978 and later advanced by Bernard Bass in 1985. This is a valuable enhancement of Douglas McGregor's Theory X and Theory Y, which focused principally on task and relationship management behaviors. Burns and Bass introduced rich new principles of inspirational motivation, behavior modeling, collaboration, employee concerns, and intellectual stimulus to the leadership equation.

A traditional transactional leadership style is a more "Tayloristic" (see Frederick Taylor on page 91) approach, primarily based on efficient processes, tight controls, and high-volume production throughput. Transactional leadership skills and styles are highly effective in mass, high productivity-oriented, or care and maintenance organizations. It is most appropriate in factories, large mature public organizations, the military, sales teams, or managing large numbers of minimum-wage staff or contractors. An example could be running large overseas outsourced call centers in India or Southeast Asia.

At the other end of the leadership spectrum is the transformational leader, who is a visionary, motivational leader. The transformational leader leads by setting a compelling vision, inspiring the staff, setting a solid cultural example, building a high degree of trust and collaboration, encouraging creativity, and empowering staff. Transformational leaders are well suited for entrepreneurial or emerging businesses, high-growth businesses, or companies requiring extensive reengineering or reinvention. There are many examples of transformational-style entrepreneurial leaders in California's Silicon Valley companies.

Transactional and transformative leadership behaviors, while dramatically different, are not necessarily mutually exclusive. However, not every leader will be outstanding at both strategic and operational issues. Typically, leaders have a predominant and preferred style that ideally should be matched to an appropriate culture and organization. Nevertheless, an experienced and adaptable leader may occasionally need to employ one or the other style based on the particular organizational context. Traditional leadership domains range from strategic thinking, team building, and operational effectiveness to execution. A skilled leader's key asset is the ability to shift rapidly from one style and behavior to another based on changing circumstances.[17]

Be conscious that a significant misalignment of preferences or predominant style will likely result in a discouraged, dispirited, and perhaps unsuccessful leader. It can also lead to poor staff alignment and morale and even performance and productivity problems.

Leadership, human resources, recruiters, and role candidates should carefully analyze job requirements and role specifications to determine the need for a transactional- or transformational-style leader to ensure an appropriate role and candidate fit. Many leaders will have some measure of both styles to draw upon as needed but consider the long-term positive implications of a good fit for the candidate, their team, and the organization.

I recall roles early in my career where my responsibilities were more routine and care and maintenance oriented, which I found repetitive and disheartening. Undoubtedly, there would have been better candidates fit for those roles than I was at the time. However, I came into my own later in my career when my natural transformational leadership style was better suited and thus more effective in subsequent roles, for example, in the Innovation Labs and as a CIO/CTO. It wasn't until I found my niche in these roles that I hit my stride, began to self-actualize, clicked with my teams, and, as a result, was more successful and much happier.

There are several excellent leadership skill assessment tools for identifying leadership styles, capabilities, and preferences in the Leadership Models and Assessment chapter. I refer you in particular to:

- Insights Discovery: A comprehensive leadership styles assessment tool
- Situational Leadership: An excellent model for a leader who needs to employ both models for staff
- Blake and Mouton's Managerial Grid: Provides a clear and practical overview of leadership style and organizational fit.

Takeaway: If you ever feel out of sync with your organization, rather than automatically thinking it's a problem with you or that the company is fundamentally flawed, do a quick analysis of whether or not you and the organization are an appropriate cultural fit. For example, if you are uncomfortable as a visionary in a stable traditional company, find some role in that organization where you can thrive or move on to another company where you can blossom and shine.

Ethical Leadership

> *Moral authority comes from following universal and timeless princi-*
> *ples like honesty, integrity, and treating people with respect.*
> *—Stephen Covey*[18]

Now that we've explored setting a vision and looked at leadership's phil-osophical and emotional aspects, let's interject an indispensable ethical and moral ethos into the leadership character equation. This has many implications, starting with the moral conduct of individuals and extend-ing to organizational principles, policies, procedures, and critical legal implications. Let's start with the definitions and look at business ethics, its impact, and best practices.

What Is Business Ethics?

Business ethics is a wide-ranging topic that encompasses vital aspects of a company's legal, commercial, customer, and employee activities. It considers the ethical and moral principles, policies, standards, and com-munications that guide how the company conducts its business, serves its customers, and treats its employees.

The explicit purpose of the discipline of business ethics is to adopt consistent legal, procedural, and behavioral activities across the com-pany to ensure all actions are conducted legally, honestly, and fairly. Professional and personal ethical guidelines for determining what is right and wrong for conduct follow similar attitudes and approaches of responsibility, integrity, fairness, and compassion. These ethical norms provide a moral compass to guide management and staff toward making the right principled decisions.

Why Is Business Ethics Important?

All businesses and, therefore, leadership have a legal and professional obli-gation to conduct themselves ethically to best serve their investors, custom-ers, and staff. Operating according to ethical standards helps businesses stay on the right side of the law, deliver high-quality products and services, and maintain productive and proper relationships with their employees.

The benefits of ethical behavior in businesses include:

1. Ethical standards, activities, and behaviors ensure that the company, investors, management, and employees operate legally and professionally.
2. Ethical professionalism is a fundamental criterion for investors considering an investment in companies.
3. Ethical leadership is vital to providing sound direction and effective operation of the company and its staff.
4. Staff respect companies and leadership who follow ethical procedures and exhibit ethical behaviors.
5. Companies' ethical activities and processes elicit respect and motivation in staff and foster collegial and collaborative working.
6. First-rate knowledge workers list business ethics as a critical factor when evaluating company employment.
7. Ethical and professional behavior is directly related to higher levels of top-tier employee retention.[19]

Key Ethical Principles for Leadership

Business ethics is a vast field encompassing many aspects of the company landscape. Thus, there are many different lenses through which to view business ethics. Our mission here is to explore business ethics from a leadership perspective.

Let's focus on five critical areas of professional ethics that, in my experience, represent the most critical leadership characteristics necessary for leading and operating responsibly, morally, and legally.

Honesty and Integrity

Honesty and integrity are foundational ethical attributes and characteristics that define a leader's character and establish professional credibility. A leader with integrity has solid, entrenched ethical values and will stick to their guns even in adversity.

Consequently, honesty and integrity are the leadership foundations for establishing team trust and loyalty. Therefore, these leaders will make morally correct decisions and actions based on fairness and equality,

instilling confidence and trust, and inspiring motivation in their employees, colleagues, partners, suppliers, and customers.

Fairness and Trustworthiness
Building on the ethos of honesty and integrity are the ethical cornerstone
principles of fairness and trustworthiness.

Fairness is an innate ethical leadership characteristic based on justice
and equality. Ethical leaders act fairly and justly in their responsibilities and activities. This pertains to organizational conduct in marketing,
sales, and support practices with customers, suppliers, and partners.

Fairness also applies to the just and equal treatment of individuals
within your organization and team relative to hiring, appraisals, discipline, and compensation.

Trustworthy leaders are open, honest, transparent, truthful, and generous in actions and communications. Customers and staff perceive companies and leaders who keep their commitments and promises as being
trustworthy. This has a positive impact internally on employee trust and
customer confidence in the marketplace.

Concern and Compassion
Following honesty and fairness, an ethical leader should recognize everyone's humanity and develop a strong sense of concern and compassion for
all they interact with through their heightened emotional intelligence.

Leaders should genuinely attempt to sow empathy, benevolence, and
compassion in all their communications and actions in dealing with
staff, colleagues, partners, suppliers, and customers.

Loyalty and Respect
Loyalty is an essential aspect of company team working, which emerges
from other leadership principles of honesty, integrity, fairness, and trust.
Once these preconditions are assured, the requisite conditions of reciprocal social exchange theory are satisfied, and then a relationship of trust
can be established and loyalty created.

The way you treat your staff must demonstrate respect for them as
individuals and their views and opinions, even if they differ from yours.
If you show them appropriate respect, despite differences of opinion, you

will still retain respect, loyalty, and morale. Even criticism can be delivered constructively and compassionately to maintain staff self-respect, commitment, and productivity.

Accountability and Responsibility
Accountability is a principal ethical leadership quality. The ethical leader accepts personal responsibility for their decisions, actions, deficiencies, and defects, as well as their staff, colleagues, and the company, within their accountability. This leader does not shirk from or shift responsibility; instead, they deal with problems head-on and take appropriate action to rectify or mitigate concerns.

Ethical leaders recognize and accept their responsibilities to the company, stakeholders, customers, and employees. They have an additional duty to demonstrate and lead with ethical behavior through their decisions and actions to provide role model examples for the staff regarding appropriate conduct in challenging circumstances.[20]

Ethical Organizational Challenges Today
Organizations today comprising top-notch knowledge workers confront an entirely new class of issues related to ethical standards and work-life balance. One only has to look at recent events where Facebook, Twitter, Amazon, and Google were all challenged by employees to take a public stand on developing social and political issues. Thus, leaders must employ distinctly new thinking, skills, and approaches to grapple with these new and novel socioeconomic and geopolitical challenges, whether at the organizational, team, or individual level. In addition, leadership credibility, commitment, emotional intelligence, and maturity are evaluated and judged daily by the public press, shareholders, company leadership, and continuously by team members and colleagues within their responsibility.

With today's knowledge workers' persistent quest for meaning and purpose in their lives and work, these staff increasingly demand their organizations rise to the social and political responsibilities of being good ethical citizens through their commitment to good causes.

Along with these issues, a powerful vision, perks, and compensation, an organization's alignment to virtuous causes has become a critical motivational factor and requirement to earn an employee's loyalty. This is particularly true among the brightest and the best superstar workers who will never want for a good job and a successful career.

Considering these emerging employee interests and aspirations and the ensuing organizational challenges, traditional KPIs and metrics for employee management have moved beyond conventional hygiene factors such as salary, bonuses, and stock options. Instead, employee attention and emphasis have evolved to motivational factors such as job satisfaction, morale, net promoter scores, community connectedness, and involvement in social causes. Today's leaders must possess high social and emotional intelligence and consider ethical and moral leadership issues relating to employee calls for more profound political, social, and spiritual involvement.

As enlightened and influential leaders, we must rise to the occasion and deal with these issues, engendering greater moral and ethical obligations toward work. Moreover, these new values and work ethics foster a more robust integration of ethical values such as social benevolence, ethical authenticity, collegial reciprocity, social diversity, and political activism. This is resulting in an evolution of ethical standards and a transformation in company cultures.

One can envision and aspire to create a culture where leaders and individuals are encouraged, supported, rewarded, and develop and flourish while achieving greater professional and personal fulfillment. Nurturing these constructive changes will require leaders to be at the top of their game, exhibit the highest ethical and moral behavior, act with integrity and honesty, mentor with concern and compassion, and manage with empathy and fairness.

Takeaway: Companies, decisions, and leadership today are increasingly under the watchful eye of the customers, the press, and staff and are being held accountable to a high standard of ethics. Develop an ongoing discipline of evaluating the impact of any strategy or decision against a business ethics check in the same way you would conduct a compliance, quality, or fiscal review.

Values

Try not to become a man of success but rather try to become a man of value.

—Albert Einstein[21]

Related to ethics but inherently and subtly distinct, the concept of values is a meaningful cultural or philosophical overlay to leadership and a team-based ecosystem. As we have seen, ethics are an extrinsic set of professional standards, policies, or laws. In contrast, values are intrinsic, personal principles that motivate and guide an individual's behaviors, preferences, and priorities.

Looking at the organizational ecosystem as a whole, for each of the actors, leader, and staff to be fully engaged as a positive force for the company, staff, customers, and the community, they must work within a mature corporate ethical framework but also possess a robust cultural code of values. Ideally, your organization's ethical standards will align closely with your values and principles. This is also critical to assess when evaluating potential companies for a career change.

Considering the culture of mores and integrity, leaders and the company should observe high ethical and moral value standards that adhere to human and organizational behavior's highest aspirations. When all actors and parties are aligned to higher values and ideals, it creates an overall sense of trust and confidence in the leader and the organization. This also lifts a significant emotional load off the employees from the perspective of trust and confidence in the leader, the company, and their colleagues. It further fosters goodwill, increases morale, and allows staff to focus on the objectives and tasks at hand instead of wasting energy and experiencing unnecessary anxiety about politics, team collaboration, and job security. Further, these high ethical and moral value standards cascade down through the organization into its products and customers.

Specifically, what do we mean by establishing and abiding by good values across the people and organization? First, it means setting a principled vision and ethical mission infused with solid values. A vivid, recent example was Google's initial mission statement, "Don't be evil," which instilled everyone in the organization with a solid and unequivocal trust- and values-based vision statement promoting corporate values that were affirmative and constructive.

The high-level vision must be translated into goals and objectives and concrete values-based products and services that are positive agents of good in the marketplace and society at large. So, how does this impact leaders in the future, and how does it play out in the real world beyond the theory and textbooks?

Today's knowledge worker needs and demands greater coherence between their work and their lives, not just a better work-life balance. This encouraging trend contributes to a higher degree of personal and professional alignment and integration of ethical, political, and spiritual values. This was particularly evident in the middle of the COVID-19 pandemic, when many workers were locked down, living with family and working virtually. This reinforcement or resurgence of higher personal and professional values is becoming more deeply integrated into the home office overlay in the virtual corporate culture work environment.

So persuasive are these drivers that this emerging trend will likely remain even post-lockdown restrictions with future employee hybrid working. There are multiple reasons for this, but let me cite a few: One notable positive benefit of the remote home working phenomenon is that it is driving a change in behaviors that were frowned upon in the past but blind eyes were turned toward. Work-based behaviors such as verbal abuse, badgering, bullying, inappropriate language, sexual innuendo, and sarcasm were always unacceptable but are now fortunately inconceivable with one's spouse sitting in the same office and young, impressionable children at your feet on the floor. One's moral and ethical credibility is piqued and challenged by one's better half and one's natural desire to model appropriate behavior in front of one's children. This presents a distinct work ethos from that of the traditional office environment. Now that the videoconference environment brings clear focus and attention to emotional behaviors, people will be on their best behavior. Further, the frequent requirement for videoconference recording makes appropriate ethical behavior paramount.

Perhaps this will bring about a mini-renaissance of ethical and moral behavior in today's workplace. Mutual respect, encouragement, tolerance for error, generosity of spirit, and harmony can again infuse the work culture. This would eliminate some of the above aberrant behaviors discussed in the office, on business trips, and at trade shows and conferences. We should work to live rather than live to work; this is the difference between making a living and creating a life.

Another personal example of values-based culture and decisions is when I decided to take a role in the travel industry instead of accepting an online betting and gambling role. That organizational culture, product range, and customer profile did not sufficiently align with my personal and professional values.

Along with a company's product and service value pipeline, all associated business processes and systems should reinforce this culture of positive values. In addition, company policies and procedures should strengthen the values-based vision, products, and processes. Finally, all this must be reflected in the people-based activities, actions, and communications that foster self-respect, collaboration, team spirit, and camaraderie for the entire leadership, staff, contractor, and supplier organizational ecosystem.

Emphasizing a values-based business culture and collaborative teamwork beyond a single-minded focus on financial metrics and market share outcomes contributes to staff enrichment and long-term enterprise success. Once this values-based culture is established and sustained, the organization will function more efficiently, fluidly, and enjoyably. Products and services will have enhanced and consistent quality. Suppliers and partners will be more collaborative. Teams will be more cooperative and focused, and experience improved morale and higher motivation.

It's about finding your values and committing to them. It's about finding your North Star. It's about making choices. Some are easy. Some are hard. And some will make you question everything.
—Tim Cook, CEO Apple[22]

Takeaway: We hear daily about a politician, professor, doctor, or coach who has resigned in the face of ethical, fiscal, or moral misbehavior. In recent years, business ethics, morals, and values standards have moved from being admirable to essential. Further, business today is fast-paced, so one can't be overly cautious, tip-toeing through life. Therefore, if you aspire to be the best leader you can be, through attempting to be honorable and honest, respectful and empathetic, you can develop a perpetual values-based modus operandi that will guide your decisions and actions appropriately.

Quality

Everything is based on a simple rule: Quality is the best business plan, period.

—Steve Jobs[23]

In chapter 1, we briefly began our discussions regarding quality with Robert Pirsig's book *Zen and the Art of Motorcycle Maintenance* in which he proposed the idea of passionately striving for quality and value in all our endeavors.

We cannot overstate quality as a leadership philosophy and management mantra in business today. It should permeate virtually everything we do in an organization, from creating our vision and setting goals, designing and developing products, managing every task and process, and leading and communicating with staff. Quality should be a pervasive glue that infuses and bonds everything in an organization, its leaders, and people with a culture and ethos of excellence. A vivid example of this we are all familiar with is Apple, where everything they do, from the magnificent devices they make, to the fine packaging, and literally the elegant stores where they sell the products, all exude quality and refinement in every way.

Quality systems, as we know them today, originated in postwar Japan when Americans W. Edwards Deming and Joseph Juran were sent to Japan to help with reconstruction and economic recovery. In conjunction with the Japanese government and major Japanese corporations, their quality control mission and methodologies helped catalyze Japan's transformation into a modern global manufacturing powerhouse. There used to be a perception that Japanese products were cheap and of inferior quality. By the 1970s, this dynamic had changed dramatically, particularly within the Japanese automobile and electronics industries.

This rigorous emphasis on high quality, which became characteristic of this new generation of exceptional Japanese products, made it clear that Japan was onto something. By then, America was falling seriously behind in its manufacturing efficiency and quality relative to Japanese products. Deming and Juran then began spearheading these ideas in the United States and consulting with American companies. This started a major thrust in "total quality management" (TQM), which eventually proliferated across most US industries in the 1980s.

At the time, I was a training manager for American Express and was charged with training and implementing American Express Company's quality systems. To get up to speed, I attended a conference with Philip Crosby, one of the current quality gurus, and read his trailblazing books *Quality is Free* and *Quality without Tears*.[24] Along with total quality management techniques, he also stressed "doing things right the first time" and striving for "zero defects." Employing these methods would improve products and systems immensely and result in significant savings that would more than self-fund the cost of the quality initiative itself; in other words, quality is free.

Deming also echoed these ideas in his work, which he stressed in his book *Out of the Crisis*.[25] He emphasized the ideas that systems thinking, continuous improvement (Kaizen), and increasing quality would produce high-quality products, simultaneously reduce rework and waste, improve morale, and increase customer loyalty.

Systems Thinking

Holistic systems thinking is fundamental to how a leader or manager should look at their work and any particular issue or problem. I was first exposed to systems thinking by my somewhat eccentric biology teacher in college, who introduced me to Ludwig von Bertalanffy and Ilya Prigogine's intriguing work on complex systems.[26] This field took off in the 1980s, exploding with popularity through the work of Stuart Kauffman in evolutionary biology and Murray Gell-Mann, John Holland, and others in chaos and complexity theories.

Systems thinking refers to any system or entity comprising multiple interconnected and interrelated elements in an organism or, in our case, an organization. Systems thinking involves looking at the entire system and analyzing it holistically to understand how all the individual pieces inter-operate and contribute (or not) to the overall organization and its objectives. The value of systems thinking is to place any component or issue into the broader context of the overall system within which it resides. This is vital to understand how it integrates with and contributes to the overall structure or process in order to optimize, replace, or potentially remove it. This approach is also central to Hammer and Champy's business reengineering movement in the 1990s, which we will discuss shortly.

Systems thinking is the proverbial ability to "see the forest and the trees" instead of being blindsided by one or the other. I cannot overemphasize the value of having a holistic systems-thinking perspective for understanding and instilling quality into everything we do. I can attribute much of my success and credibility as a leader to this big picture and simultaneous in-depth perspective. There is nothing magical or mysterious about it, but it may take some effort and concentration to develop it into a fine art.

Takeaway: Quality is not a hit-and-miss or point solution process. Instead, quality is an ethos that should infuse everything you do. From your vision statement and corporate culture to your development and continuous improvement processes, quality assurance and control activities, and finally, in how you motivate and manage your employees. Make a continuous habit of progressing quality.

To crystallize this chapter on the alchemy of leadership, encompassing leading from the heart, servant leadership, emotional intelligence, motivation, values, and quality, I'll share a true-to-life example from my experience of the epitome of a leader who personified for me the best of these characteristics. The following example is not business-related but one that many can relate to, as teachers and coaches are often significant role models for many of us.

My football coach in high school was Rod Poppe from Marengo, Illinois, a distant suburb of Chicago. Rod was football captain and team MVP at Valparaiso University in the mid-1950s. After college, he returned to his hometown, Marengo, to coach football. He was head coach there for twenty-three years with an outstanding record of 144 wins, fifty-four losses, and four ties, including a forty-five-game winning streak.[27]

But for those of us whom Mr. Poppe coached, it was not just those successes that we remember, but the model and mentor we had in him as our leader. Mr. Poppe was quiet, calm, serious, dedicated, and above all, concerned and caring for each athlete on his team. During tense games, you could often witness the opposing coach ranting, raving, steaming, and swearing. Yet, despite the high energy of high school football, in my three years there, in practice and games, I never once heard him raise his voice, swear, or lose his temper. In my junior year, in the last quarter of the semifinal game, I recall a Hail Mary pass that was intercepted almost at the goal line. I heard Mr. Poppe gently whisper, "shoot," not the rude and typical alternative.

Right alongside Rod Poppe was Mr. Reeves, a hugely capable and compassionate teacher, assistant football, and head track coach. Even more impressive and inspiring as a sports coach was that Mr. Reeves had one arm, the other lost in a hunting accident as a teen. Yet, it never held him back but also kept his squads of lanky, languid, lackadaisical teens from complaining and inspired them to achieve the best they could with their individual talents and abilities.[28]

As leaders, they personified the leadership characteristics of having a grand vision of success for our team, being honorable in all interactions, being kind and compassionate not only for the stars but for everyone, and encouraging and supportive of all, including the underdog nonstarters.

Likewise, the famed UCLA basketball coach John Wooden never raised his voice, was revered by his players, and was named national coach of the year a record seven times.

These exemplary coaches remind me of the question posed by Robert Greenleaf, the originator of servant leadership, "Do those served grow as persons?" John Wooden, Rod Poppe, and Ed Reeves were the type of people who made you want to do and be your absolute best. In a word, they had character.

Having laid the groundwork, superstructure, and central pillars for leadership, let's examine the core tenets of leadership through the thinking and writing of the foremost leadership gurus and thinkers of the past and present.

Key Takeaways—Leadership Concepts and Culture

- When a leader "Leads with the Heart," they are radiating ethical, empathetic, and benevolent behaviors that reinforce a "trust-based" reciprocal social exchange relationship with staff and co-workers.
- A Servant Leader is a leader who, through their natural authentic and altruistic instincts, has genuine empathy and concern and is dedicated to nurturing and service to their staff.
- To be most effective, today's leaders must have strong Emotional Intelligence and highly developed people skills alongside their cognitive intelligence and technical skills.
- Ethical leadership and principled values together create a leadership ethos and culture that inspire confidence and trust in the leader, the team, the organization, as well as the customer base.
- Quality as a leadership philosophy should permeate everything a leader does, infusing an organization and its people with a culture and ethos of excellence.

CHAPTER 3

Standing on the Shoulders of Giants: Pioneers, Gurus, Visionaries

Sir Isaac Newton,[1] English physicist, astronomer, and mathematician, made famous the quote by French philosopher Bernardo de Chartres[2]: "If I have seen further, it is by standing on the shoulders of giants."[3] This is to say that we do not necessarily have a greater vision or capabilities but that we have been raised up by the foresight and efforts of our forebearers.

Throughout my career, I've had multiple highly diverse roles in marketing and sales, training and development, usability and design, innovation and IT, and consulting. While all these jobs differed significantly from a role and industry perspective, the constant throughout was the people aspect and the aspiration to be a good leader.

Further, as my career developed, business and technology also transformed dramatically. Consequently, I needed to reinvent and retrain myself continually over the years to remain current and relevant in each new position. I achieved that primarily by "learning to learn" and how to do it rapidly through on-the-job training, research journals, management books, conferences, executive education, and internet research, including online learning resources. Interestingly, with practice, over time, it became easier and faster to absorb and adopt new knowledge and content for each new role. In addition, the continued assimilation of further information made it simpler to transfer and extrapolate learning from one position to another. Perhaps this is akin to learning languages, where each successive language becomes easier and faster to master.

One of the key tricks of the trade I learned in knowledge acquisition was identifying and researching the leaders in each field I worked in. Hence, besides the leadership resources and tools discussed, I've incorporated this chapter on the leadership and management leaders I've studied that helped chart and guide my path.

I'll not attempt an exhaustive review of the related topics of strategy, marketing, sales, or organizational change. Instead, I'll include the exceptional leadership resources that were impressionable and formative in my journey. For example, Tom Peters, Charles Handy, Peter Drucker, Daniel Goleman, Rosabeth Moss Kanter, Peter Senge, Alvin Toffler, Clayton Christiansen (*The Innovator's Dilemma*), Hammer and Champy (*Reengineering the Corporation*), and Michael Porter (*Competitive Strategy*), to name a few. As a result of these studies, I've also been fortunate to meet Peter Drucker, Alvin Toffler, Peter Senge, and Gary Hamel, plus both Bill Gates and Tom Peters a couple of times.

Therefore, this chapter comprises a list of the leadership and management gurus and readings that have been formative career cornerstones and mile-markers for me in my ever-evolving leadership career. I trust they can do the same for you. The list is loosely but not rigidly chronological by publication date. Thankfully and gratefully, I've stood on the shoulders of the following leadership giants.

Sun Tzu—*The Art of War*

4

The Art of War by Sun Tzu[5] was written some 2,500 years ago, circa 500 BC, and remains an influential strategy book that has received renewed acclaim in leadership literature in recent decades. I read it after arriving in Hong Kong in the late 1980s and reread it for inspiration during the dot-com years in the late 1990s. Despite being primarily a military strategy book, this book has some timeless leadership messages and examples. Therefore, rather than dwell on the military strategy aspects, I'll summarize the key leadership messages translated into today's business context.

"Sun Tzu states that the Art of War is governed by five fundamental facets using the analogies of 1) Moral Law, 2) Heaven, 3) Earth, 4) The Commander, and 5) Methods,"[6] which the leader must take into consideration when entering into conflict. A leader must carefully consider and analyze these factors to formulate a viable strategy and robust execution plan to dramatically improve the probability of success. His timeless analogies translate effectively into today's key business domains, processes, and principles.

Moral Law is the governing precept of the leader's vision, purpose, and actions. This overriding leadership principle sets the mission, direction, and strategy for any endeavor. Further, it is the guiding tenet that directs the leader and bonds the followers to the cause. In business leadership, this resonates with many of the messages in chapter 1. One must set a convincing goal, communicate the purpose and value, give assurance of success and rewards, and guide and support the team.

Heaven in today's business context can be interpreted as the environment and associated factors in the ecosystem that have to be considered. This considers the industry, the market, your company, and the economic and business climate for our purposes.

Earth can be seen as the business context within which our activities and battles are played, won, and lost. The organization, culture, structure, and actors comprise the specifics of the objectives, projects, politics, and people to be considered relative to the overall business, organizational context, and goals.

The ***Commander*** represents the leader, their character, capabilities, and experience. Do they have integrity, vision, courage, abilities, and experience? Therefore, do they have the leadership characteristics that can instill motivation, confidence, and commitment within the team?

Finally, the ***Methods*** are the objectives, strategies, people, resources, and execution plan that are established and developed to deliver the tasks to ensure the overall success of the venture.[7]

In the subsequent twelve chapters, he delves deeply into the strategy of warfare and tactics of battle. Here are some of the worthy leadership learnings we can derive from his messages.

Avoid warfare. Sun Tzu stresses that, if at all possible, the best strategy is always to win by negotiation, politics, stealth, or psychological means to break the enemy's resistance rather than resort to battle. Warfare is always risky, as there are few guarantees in battle. Ignoring the warfare backdrop of his comments, avoiding conflict at all costs is excellent advice for leaders in today's complex political and organizational context.

Choose your battles. Further to avoiding conflict, choosing your battles is highly relevant advice for business. You must determine when and when not to fight, depending on whether you are weak or strong. Make sure you adjust your plans to ensure that all circumstances and concerns are advantageous to you at any critical juncture.

Focus on the critical aspects or challenges, and don't dissipate your energies or resources on extraneous or ancillary issues. Not to be too Machiavellian, as the best advice is not to fight; you can also use negotiation and influence management to resolve issues. Still, the reality is that sometimes in business, we are confronted with conflict and battles, even if subtle ones, and often with competitors; thus, Sun Tzu's military strategies can provide invaluable lessons. When bogged down in a quagmire of problems in business today, we can consider changing the game to obviate any subordinate concerns.

Timing is everything. If a conflict is unavoidable, consolidate your resources, strengthen your alliances, and choose a time when you are strong and your adversary is weak. Of course, you must have an excellent strategy, but a critical part of the strategy is knowing when to act. You must plan and deliberate carefully. When you recognize the time is right, you must be decisive and take immediate action rather than hesitate and lose the moment or initiative. In my view, this is very Machiavellian and not my style or approach to leadership. However, timing is critical to any market entry success as it relates to competitive challenges in the market. Beyond battles relative to decisive decision-making, remember the Latin phrase "carpe diem" or "seize the day."

Know your enemy. You must also know your adversary or competitor. What are your adversary's strengths and weaknesses? Who are they and their allies? Are there any unknown factors to be assessed before taking action? Pertinent to today's business and technology ecosystem partnering and competitive advantage, Sun Tzu suggests through his quote "the enemy of my enemy is my friend" that opposing or adjacent parties can collaborate against a common opponent.[8]

A winning plan. What is your counterparty's strategy and plan? What is your plan, counterplan, or contingency plan? Develop a unique, unexpected, and original strategy and choose your timing to surprise, destabilize, and disrupt the adversaries' plan and defenses. Also frequently attributed to Sun Tzu but more likely from Helmuth Von Moltke, a Prussian military commander, is an important tip on scenario planning, contingency planning, and adaptability: "No battle plan survives contact with the enemy."[9] Therefore, beyond your primary strategy, ensure you have considered and matured multiple secondary contingency plans.

Flow like water. While in the heat of battle, you should be prepared first and then be adaptable. He uses the metaphor of being flexible to flow like water through the path of least resistance. Adaptability to continuous change is critical. If you are prepared and adaptable, occasionally, an alternative plan can ultimately become more important or valuable than the initial strategy, product, or service.[10]

While most of this comprises military strategy and is somewhat Machiavellian, which is unquestionably not our style as servant leaders, nevertheless, there are many helpful leadership lessons to be learned in this ancient and powerful book. The book is beneficial for using military strategy as an analog for business, particularly competitive strategy, providing many interesting and helpful insights. If you interpret and tone down the aggressive military language in your business context, you can easily translate and adapt these messages into relevant leadership lessons for today.

I am further reminded of another exemplary military strategist, Napoleon. After his defeat at the Battle of Waterloo, he purportedly said, "Even a mediocre strategy well executed will defeat the perfect plan poorly executed!" The leadership lesson is that having an excellent strategy is important; however, effective execution is essential!

Takeaway: Sun Tzu's sweeping treatise on military strategy is a powerful reminder to keep a continuous eye on the industry, competition, and products, as well as your capabilities as you create and develop your strategy. This will ensure you adapt, evolve, and mature your execution plan to the continuously changing dynamics of the hypercompetitive marketplaces we work in today.

Frederick Taylor

11

It is thought-provoking and often helpful to understand the history and evolutionary underpinnings of *how* we got to where we are in business today to understand better and appreciate *why* things are the way they are.

We will shortly discuss Peter Drucker, the father of modern management, and Warren Bennis, the father of leadership studies. But before we do, let's look at Frederick Taylor as the foremost early transitional figure in the study of the management of workers at the outset of the twentieth century.

From the beginning of the industrial age and the emergence of factory work up until Taylor, there was a great chasm between management and workers. Managers set out the work to be accomplished, and workers delivered it, occasionally in a haphazard, disorganized, and sometimes chaotic manner. Further, with limited contact and virtually no feedback between management and workers, there was no systemization or standardization of work or processes. Thus, understandably employee morale and satisfaction were very low.

From today's vantage point of modern leadership and management practices, some of Taylor's innovations and breakthroughs can be seen as somewhat archaic and outdated. In fact, in my early days of management training, we would often somewhat naively scoff at and ridicule antiquated management "command and control" techniques, calling them "Tayloristic." Regardless, he made many significant contributions to the development of scientific management.

Taylor's groundbreaking book *Principles of Scientific Management*[12] revolutionized worker efficiency and factory work productivity over a hundred years ago. While all these ideas have advanced in the last century and a number have been discarded, he pioneered many of the important principles of scientific business analysis, process systemization, and systems standardization.

Taylor's foremost scientific management principles are:

1. Division of work between managers and workers so that managers allocated their time to planning, organizing, and training, and workers were assigned to perform specific optimized and repetitive tasks.
2. Application of the "scientific method" to analyze work processes to determine the most efficient way to perform specific tasks.
3. Analysis can always identify an optimal method and process that is more efficient and superior to all other alternatives.
4. Rigorous scientific analyses of tasks and processes were performed to standardize discrete tasks and systemize efficient "time and motion" workflow processes.
5. Employment of ongoing communications and feedback between management and workers to ensure improvement and implementation of the most efficient time and motion practices.
6. Use of scientific methods to select and allocate workers to suitably relevant jobs based on individual capabilities and provide systematic job training to ensure maximum efficiency.
7. He implemented "a fair day's pay for an honest day's work."
8. Positive reinforcement instead of punishment as the best way to motivate factory workers.[13]

As you will appreciate from this list, Taylor's contribution at the time was foundational in the development of modern management. While these methods dramatically improved factory work efficiency and productivity, they also split workers' jobs into simple and, in many cases, menial tasks, virtually as "cogs" in the overall assembly-line work. This resulted in worker boredom, decreased morale, and an almost complete lack of career development.[14] Unfortunately, Taylor misguidedly believed that workers were fundamentally lazy, solely money-motivated, and had to be rigorously directed and monitored. For these reasons, many of his ideas have either been discarded entirely or enhanced to improve employee work quality and job satisfaction.

However, we can still observe remnants of these Tayloristic "command and control" methodologies, many of which exist today. They are still prevalent in some emerging economies, mass manufacturing, and service industries, such as the electronics industries and mega call centers of India, Southeast Asia, and Latin America.

You may have followed the news of the challenges of managing immense electronics assembly-line manufacturers in China like Foxconn and Pegatron in recent years. Another particularly poignant and challenging employee issue is the intense pressure-cooker environment resulting from extreme process efficiencies at the phenomenally successful Amazon. Part of the enormous difficulties these companies face is how to be hyperefficient, exceptionally profitable, and yet humane at a colossal scale of mass production and service delivery.

Takeaway: Taylor's scientific methods for analyzing and optimizing the most efficient processes are still relevant today for high-efficiency, process-intense environments. However, his groundbreaking work in matching worker capabilities to suitable roles, equitable pay, and positive reinforcement for staff motivation are applicable across all industries.

Peter Drucker

15

Peter Drucker is renowned as the founding father of modern management. A prolific author publishing forty groundbreaking business books, he was also a management consultant and educator whose work contributed extensively to the theoretical and practical foundations of modern management and leadership.

My original introduction to Drucker's work was through an American Express "train the trainer" program, as we were implementing the MBO (management by objectives) methodology across the company. His MBO concept and processes were simple and logical but effective and thus have barely changed to this day.

"The MBO philosophy maintains that a leader/manager must clearly and accurately communicate the organization's overall goals to their employees. They should then discuss individual and team responsibilities to achieve those goals with staff. Next, there should be a conversation and agreement on individual objectives and setting measurable SMART milestones (specific, measurable, achievable, relevant, and timely) as suggested initially by George T. Doran.[16] Finally, there should be regular monitoring, feedback, and an annual review of the objectives and outcomes."[17] These methods are essential and effective for junior or new employees to provide clarity of requirements and expectations. However, be cautious not to constrain senior or talented staff by limiting their initiative or creativity. Far better to set high-level objectives with significant latitude to provide for senior staff empowerment, ingenuity, and adaptability. Many companies today have taken this methodology to the next stage with quarterly objectives, reviews, and bonuses.

This MBO training program piqued my interest in Drucker's work, and the first book of his I read was *The Practice of Management*; another recommendation would be *The Effective Executive*. Today, most of the ideas in Drucker's forty books are embedded within the fabric of current management theory. Drucker's work and contributions to the field of management are vast, and he is known for groundbreaking work in a diverse list of seminal management theories: corporate culture, social responsibility, organizational design simplification, decentralization, and outsourcing.

Drucker emphasized executive effectiveness through strategic thinking, setting a healthy company culture, sound decision-making, focusing on things that really matter, delivering critical contributions, and investing in team development. He stresses the importance of a leader being strategic and proactive rather than reactive, resorting to firefighting, and being subject to the whims and tactical problems of day-to-day operations. A genuine executive should focus on setting direction and getting the few fundamental decisions right instead of wasting time on lower-level operational details, which should be delegated to capable middle management or specialist staff.

Drucker further emphasizes the critical importance of the human resources of any company. He stresses that the organization's most critical resources and assets are the staff. Critically, he espoused inspiring, training, and empowering workers for their self-development, self-satisfaction, and organizational productivity. To develop and empower the team, you need to take a bit of risk in delegation rather than taking it all on yourself, thus stifling staff confidence and development and the team's ability to grow and scale. When employees recognize the leader and organization's commitment to their well-being, they will reciprocate with hard work, committed dedication, and steadfast loyalty.

Drucker was also a pioneer in what eventually became known as outsourcing. He stressed, "Do what you do best and outsource the rest." He advised companies should only engage in customer-facing activities essential to building the company's core products and services. Therefore, he recommends that back-office generic and commodity activities be handed over to external companies specializing in these areas.[18]

While you may find some of the specific examples in his books a bit dated from today's high-velocity work vantage point, the fundamentals are still rock-solid. Moreover, they are the origin and foundation of many management and leadership principles you will be familiar with today. Therefore, I'd recommend his books to anyone who wants a comprehensive overview of these timeless principles.

I had the honor to have a quick lunch with Peter Drucker in about 1996 at a conference in Toronto, for which I was a guest speaker presenting my work on virtual teaming.

Peter, a powerful and provocative speaker, kicked off the first keynote presentation with a visionary talk on the "eras of humanity" starting with hunter-gatherers, agrarian societies, the development of civilization, and then the evolution of business and eventually the emergence of knowledge workers in society.

He wove a motivational thread of basic human needs through these eras, reflecting on how human nature needed to be respected and reflected in any task or endeavor for workers to function healthily and productively in business and their work. Later, the morning session finished with Alvin Toffler offering a not-dissimilar sweep of time futurists' viewpoint on knowledge management.

At the break, I walked to lunch, and coincidentally, Peter Drucker walked up behind me. We chatted briefly, and I introduced myself, to which he stated, "Yes, I know your work" (likely from reading the conference speaker agenda) and invited me to eat with him. Over lunch, I said I'd enjoyed his speech, for which he was gracious. But then there was an awkward moment when I enthused about Alvin Toffler's presentation about the evolution of civilization and the development of knowledge. He huffed and puffed, saying: "Hum, very superficial if you ask me!" No doubt this was a bit of guru competitiveness! Fortunately, he shifted direction to ask about my work, and we had a pleasant twenty minutes, which was a distinct honor.

Takeaway: Maintain your high-level strategic and proactive leadership perspective, concentrating on strategic thinking and direction setting, to focus exclusively on the critical decisions in order to avoid tactical fire-fighting. Develop, inspire, and empower your staff to take over mid-level responsibilities from you.

W. Edwards Deming

19

While living in Asia and running training teams in Japan, I became familiar with Deming's transformative work in helping Japan's reconstruction efforts after World War II. In those days, Japan had a reputation for low-quality products, and "Made in Japan" printed on products implied cheap, inferior, and unreliable.

Deming worked with Japanese companies' leadership, engineers, and factory workers to apply statistical analysis and control to produce high-quality Japanese products while simultaneously increasing productivity and decreasing costs. It seems counterintuitive to have productivity increase and costs drop as quality improves; however, this is because of quality processes that eliminate waste, reduce rework, and deliver improved products that boost market share. Additionally, staff development, empowerment, and morale increase along with pride in workmanship and company loyalty. He emphasizes quality over quantity, as once quality is achieved, you can scale it out to improve production.[20]

This was the beginning of the dramatic reformation of Japanese industry in the second half of the twentieth century. These quality initiatives helped contribute to Japan becoming a dominant force globally in the manufacture and production of very high-quality products, notably that of automobiles and consumer electronics.

This transition was so dramatic that the quality of Japanese products eventually began to exceed that of American products. Ultimately, Deming and his contemporary Juran returned to America to stimulate a similar renaissance in quality improvement within industrial America. Today, Deming's research, writing, and principles have been embedded in best practice quality systems worldwide. I recommend his book *Out of the Crisis*,[21] which elaborates on Deming's fourteen points for the transformation of management.

Dr. Deming's Management Transformation Ideas

1. Create a "constancy of purpose" (dedication or commitment) for improving products and services.
2. Adopt the new philosophy of "responsible leadership."
3. Cease reliance on reactive inspection to realize quality.
4. Don't award contracts solely based on price; minimize total cost by working with a single supplier.
5. Continuously improve all processes for planning, production, operations, and service.
6. Institute regular training on the job.
7. Adopt and institute leadership and supervision to help people and processes to do a better job.
8. Drive out fear to help everyone work more effectively.
9. Break down barriers between departments and functions.
10. Eliminate mottoes and campaigns for the workforce that create stress and adversarial relationships.
11. Focus on leadership and eliminate solely numerical and quantitative quotas for management and staff.
12. Eradicate obstacles that rob people of pride in workmanship and eliminate annual ratings.
13. Employ a robust program of continuing education and self-improvement for all.
14. Get alignment from everyone to advance the transformation.[22]

Courtesy of Deming Institute—https://deming.org/.[23]

As discussed previously, quality is not simply a static metric attribute. Instead, it is an all-encompassing ethos, attitude, and behavior that should imbue everything we say, do, and create in leadership and business with a culture and characteristics of virtue and value.

Takeaway: Regardless of your organizational context, consider Deming's ideas on quality processes to shift the emphasis from reactive quality control testing to statistical analysis, doing things right the first time, and continuous improvement to reduce defects and rework, eliminate waste, and decrease costs.

Warren G. Bennis

24

As Peter Drucker is the founding father of contemporary management studies, Warren Bennis is widely recognized as the founding father of modern leadership studies.

His book *On Becoming a Leader*[25] is a foundational book of leadership literature. His towering presence and powerful impact on business, with thirty books to his credit, extensive interviews, and articles, have been remarkable over the past thirty years. He was particularly well known for his quick wit and memorable quotes. Many of these you may recognize, and Warren was the originator.

"A manager does things right: leaders do the right things."[26]

"Leaders have the ability to transform vision into reality."[27]

"Leaders believe their vision so passionately they can convince others to share their dream."

"The capacity to develop and improve skills distinguishes leaders from followers."[28]

"The most insidious leadership myth is that leaders are born. That's absurd; the opposite is true. Leaders are made instead of born."[29]

"Most leaders are made by accident, circumstances, sheer grit, than have been made by all leadership courses put together."[30]

Dr. Bennis proposed many leadership models and identified six indispensable personal leadership qualities.

Integrity

Personal integrity, values, and trust are essential characteristics of an effective leader who has the trust and confidence of their teams and employees.

Dedication

Dedication is an essential driver for a leader to be effective and productive and to establish commitment and credibility with management and teams.

Magnanimity

Magnanimity is an unusual but vital characteristic where the leader involves people in activities, credits them with success, and accepts failure.

Humility

Humility is the lack of ego and arrogance, which are so prevalent in business today. Humble leaders command respect while sharing credit and accepting responsibility.

Openness

An open leader recognizes and seeks others' ideas and opinions before jumping to conclusions. Consequently, they command respect and loyalty from subordinates.

Creativity

A creative leader builds value by generating their own ideas and solutions while encouraging, supporting, and recognizing those of others.[31]

Bennis further proposed thirteen characteristic comparisons distinguishing leaders from managers. There will be a tendency to breeze through this list; I suggest you pause briefly for each one to internalize them.

Management vs. Leadership

1. The manager is an administrator—the leader is an innovator.
2. The manager is a copy of something—the leader is an original of themself.
3. The manager maintains old things—the leader develops new things.
4. The manager gives attention to systems—the leader concentrates on people.
5. The manager relies on control—the leader instigates trust.
6. The manager readily accepts—the leader carefully investigates.
7. The manager has a narrow view—the leader has a broad perspective.
8. The manager questions how and when—the leader inquires about what and why.
9. Managers have a bottom-line focus—leaders have their view on the horizon.
10. The manager duplicates—the leader initiates.
11. The manager retains the status quo—the leader looks to innovate.
12. The manager is the classic "good citizen"—the leader develops their own unique view.
13. The manager does things correctly—the leader does the correct thing."[32]

Takeaway: Ensure you are functioning as a leader, not a manager. A manager does things right; leaders do the right things. Managers have a bottom-line focus—and leaders have their view on the horizon. The manager relies on control—the leader instigates trust. The manager retains the status quo—the leader looks to innovate.

Douglas McGregor: Theory X and Theory Y

Photo Courtesy of Antioch University[33]

You will probably have heard of the terms a type X or Y manager. In his book *The Human Side of Enterprise*,[34] Douglas McGregor was the originator of Theory X and Theory Y, which are contrasting models of tactical management and humanistic motivation.

This is a relatively straightforward but important theory to keep in the back of your mind when considering staff motivation. It is also a valuable model to monitor your own management style and supervise your manager's styles to ensure the staff, management, and tasks are all appropriately aligned.

Historically, Theory X typically harkens back to "lower-level" factory or assembly-line workers who were assumed by many to be lazy, less capable, lacking ambition, less responsible, less motivated, and working primarily out of necessity and obligation. Further, Theory X proposes that the typical worker has a natural aversion to work and will avoid it if they can. Because of this presumed distaste for work, from the Theory X perspective, people must be coaxed, cajoled, coerced, or controlled to achieve their personal objectives.[35]

Therefore, Theory X-style management, typified by Frederick Taylor, was centralized, highly directive, task-oriented, and hands-on in assigning and monitoring employee work. It was perceived that the employee needed more supervision and encouragement, plus more tangible monetary rewards and occasional threats to apply themselves fully to work and deliver the desired results.

Conversely, with his groundbreaking Theory Y, McGregor rejects Taylor's view that workers are lazy and will avoid work at any cost.

Instead, he embraced the belief that people, even junior people, often enjoy their work, are capable, creative, and self-motivated, and thus more responsible and need less supervision. Also, they will perform better and be more self-satisfied if they participate in setting the direction and decision-making and are given more independence and responsibility.

Effective Theory Y rewards are often not entirely monetary but are also personally self-directed, related to pride of work and potential recognition. Thus, Theory Y management tends to be more participative, less hierarchical, and highly relationship-oriented, designed and employed to inspire and motivate the staff, who are valuable company assets to be nurtured, invested in, and retained.[36, 37]

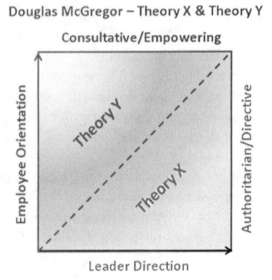

Douglas McGregor – Theory X & Theory Y

Takeaway: Despite almost universal acceptance of the more humane and worker-oriented Theory Y management techniques, we should all be vigilant against oppressive command and control Theory X management styles. Especially in Western supply chain and warehouse companies and the immense electronics manufacturers and call centers of Asia and South America. We must learn to be humane at a colossal scale of mass production and service delivery.

Dr. William Ouchi: Theory Z

38

I recall being intrigued and in agreement with Dr. Ouchi when he announced his Theory Z, or "Japanese Style Management," created as a timely and expedient evolution of McGregor's Theories X and Y.

Building on a Theory Y management-style foundation, Theory Z borrows Japanese "Kanban" management techniques of a strong corporate vision and culture, cooperative teamwork, collaborative decision-making, and consensual problem-solving. The Theory Z emphasis on employee well-being and "jobs for life" resulted in strong company loyalty and job satisfaction. In addition, it combines the best of Japanese consensus-style management blended with American-style leadership and organizational structures.

Contrary to the Tayloristic assumptions that workers are lazy, need continuous guidance, and only work for money, as with Theory Y, Theory Z purports that employees take strong interest in their work and enjoy collaborative teamwork. Moreover, when they receive support from the organization, staff are resolutely loyal.

Theory Z management style and company culture engender improved morale and employee satisfaction, increased commitment, long-term employment, and higher productivity. Also, see Kanban, quality, and continuous improvement within the quality initiatives discussion in the Leadership and Management Tips chapter of book 2.

Takeaway: Theory Z builds on McGregor's Theory Y, employing a stronger company cultural emphasis on cooperative teamwork, collaborative decision-making, and consensual problem-solving, which can result in exceptionally high company loyalty.

John Kotter: Transformational Change

39

Before diving into my primary interest in Kotter, his model for managing transformational change, I want to briefly mention his exposition on management versus leadership. He provides an excellent discourse asserting that leadership and management disciplines are very different but wholly complementary, and both are also indisputably required for almost all organizations.

Management is about directing, managing, and efficiently controlling an organization through governance, processes, and tools to ensure effective operations and delivery of outcomes. Leadership is about creating a vision, creative inspiration, setting goals and targets, motivating and supporting teams, and sustaining the passion and drive to achieve objectives.

Kotter argues it is not a question of being either a manager or leader but rather of when to function in each role and which skill set to employ. For example, an executive may need to use both leadership and management skills at different times, in distinct situations, and with discrete types, levels of maturity, and diversity of staff knowledge and experience.

It is important to emphasize that these two functions are not in conflict or mutually exclusive but are necessary and complementary components of running a business and achieving objectives. Therefore, these roles may optimally coexist in the same individual or be provided through collaborative working by different individuals with complementary skills.

Several times during my career, I've been fortunate enough as a leader to have a highly effective operational manager working with me. You can accomplish great things together if you establish trust and mutual support and empower the manager with complementary leadership and management skills. Working as a cooperative team, you can be effective; your team will recognize and value your abilities and contributions and have an agreeable working relationship.

Kotter is probably best known for his work on Business Transformation. Large-scale transformational change is an issue that is no doubt near and dear (or far and feared?) to us all. Most of us have either done, delivered, or even been an unfortunate casualty of a major corporate transformation. With the incredible pace of social and technical change in the last few decades because of globalization, outsourcing, the internet, digital transformation, and COVID-19, we will likely have seen major transformations come and go every three to five years on average. However, a quick search of the success ratios of business or corporate transformation initiatives reveals that nearly 70 percent of all major transformations fail. Thus, it is fitting for us to focus on exploring best practices in this discipline.

As a line manager for most of my career and as a consultant for two professional services firms, I've seen my share of business and technical transformations, and a few that I would say were truly global transformations. I've been a bit player in many, a participant in perhaps a dozen, and a major player or responsible for a handful. Thus, I've seen some failed transformations and a couple of outstanding ones. Of those entirely under my watch, there was one disappointment early in my career and a major success more recently. I will elaborate on these as case studies later, sharing my personal experiences with these transformations, both the stumbles and the successes as useful learning points.

In between the transformations mentioned above, when I was at PwC as an IT strategy consultant, I ran across Kotter's books *A Sense of Urgency* and *Leading Change* and studied Kotter's 8-step process for leading change. While this step change model initially appears a bit prescriptive and needs to be flexible, the objectives and methodologies of the model resonated with my experience and enhanced my current projects. Thus, I share the basic steps below:

Kotter's 8-Step Process for Leading Change[40]

1. Creating Urgency:

Creating and socializing a genuine sense of urgency is vital to capturing management's attention, mobilizing staff motivation, and creating enthusiasm with everyone for the change. This can be based on a substantial opportunity or a genuine significant risk. You'll need to identify carefully and articulate the opportunities, challenges, threats, and risks to the stakeholders. Then, ensure you understand each stakeholder's public and hidden agendas. Finally, it's imperative you line up at least one supportive senior management sponsor/champion at this stage. You will need this sponsor to lobby for initial support and to run interference throughout the project.

2. Forming Powerful Guiding Coalitions

Having identified the issue and stakeholders, to succeed, you'll need more than the sponsor and champion mentioned above, but also a solid and supportive cross-functional steering committee and a "change coalition." These additional stakeholder "actors" are necessary to provide the political clout and muscle to sell and execute the strategy and campaign, especially in the delicate and risky early stages.

3. Developing a Vision and a Strategy

With a sense of urgency and the stakeholder coalition, you must crystallize the campaign mission and focus on a clear and decisive vision and strategy. This is consistent with the earlier chapter on setting a vision with purpose. Similarly, now you will need to win the stakeholders' hearts and minds to effect any successful transformational change program.

4. Communicating the Vision

With the vision and purpose clearly articulated, communicate and socialize this vision actively, authentically, and passionately across the organization. At this point, objectors and objections will begin to surface, which you will have to quell urgently before any contrarian momentum or political opposition takes root and proliferates.

5. Removing Obstacles

With the above vision, champion, and coalition, recognize that you must have your campaign solidly structured and aligned to ensure you can address objections and obstacles. Even if in your mind your idea or program is a no-brainer, don't be surprised and therefore blindsided when concerns or doubts surface.

Be aware that even if the stakeholders or other actors recognize that the urgency, project, or campaign makes ultimate sense, it may not be financially, organizationally, or politically in each individual's best interest. A humorous but apropos British comment is: "Turkeys voting for Christmas!" Recognize people are disinclined to make or support any choice perceived as disadvantageous to their self-interest.

6. Creating Short-Term Wins

Identify some valuable incremental quick wins while keeping the final objective in sight. Short-term gains will often advance you toward the ultimate goal and, at the same time, give the team confidence and credit for making progress. Importantly, this will also reassure stakeholders and management, win political support, and alleviate pressure from dissenters. Sometimes, people just like or need to see some progress or that you can and do deliver.

7. Consolidating Gains

Along with creating some quick wins, make sure that you consolidate those short-term gains into concrete milestone achievements and actively socialize success stories across the organization to manage stakeholder expectations through continuous improvement and regular progress toward the target deliverable.

8. Anchoring Change in the Corporate Culture

By virtue of the quick wins and consolidated gains, you will continue building support for the initiative with the project team, steering committee, company sponsor, and leadership. Build the wins and milestone accomplishments into success stories to socialize and possibly mount a campaign throughout the company. Over time, ensure that the initiatives' outcomes and growing successes are embedded into the ongoing fabric of the company until they become "business as usual" and thus entrenched into the continuous organizational processes, structure, and culture.[41]

I recall at Reuters Usability Group how long it took to educate and embed product usability into the language and culture of the company. While it was evident to senior management and my team of human factors and ergonomists, it took a long time to convince some deep technologists who thought mere mortals should naturally understand how to operate their elegant technical designs. Eventually, it took video evidence of trader usability trials to drive home the reality of their struggles to learn and operate the systems.

From my experience, Kotter's advice for transformations is spot on and should be reviewed at the outset and during any new large project or program. The two most critical lessons above are the issues related to stakeholder management and alignment and ensuring you have a continuous pipeline of quick wins to maintain political buy-in and momentum throughout the program.

John Kotter's transformation work naturally leads on to Rosabeth Moss Kanter's mastering change. Together they provide a powerful complementary combination of theories, models, and techniques to help effect successful transformational change.

Takeaway: The most critical steps for initiating change are: Developing a compelling vision and strategy. Unless you can create and articulate an inspiring vision and compelling strategy, you will be a non-starter from the outset. Leading on from that, you'll need a strong board-level champion and a powerful stakeholder coalition.

Rosabeth Moss Kanter

42

Dr. Kanter, the distinguished Professor of Business Administration at Harvard Business School, consultant, and author, has been a source of inspiration for me throughout my career ever since I was a training manager at American Express and read *The Change Masters*. Her themes and theories on leadership, strategic visioning, employee empowerment, innovation, and change management have helped chart my course through my various responsibilities as a trainer, innovation director, line manager, and consultant.

Her evocative model of "Kaleidoscope Thinking," presented in *The Change Masters* and developed further in later books, presents a holistic approach to transformational change. This is an excellent framework model for looking at issues, problems, or opportunities in a myriad of ways by adjusting your lenses to view things from multiple perspectives. You can also look at complex challenges as a large matrix of interlocking pieces of a puzzle that must be considered, reassembled, or reengineered correctly.

As mentioned earlier, during my very early career as a trainer, my team was responsible for implementing global credit card policies. While this was years ago, the organizational challenges were the same as today. When the program funding for this program was diverted to another project, we were left in the lurch, with the unfinished requirement but no funding. The challenge was updating and critically maintaining the conventional Rolodex-style printed procedures, with constantly changing credit card and traveler's cheque policies, for hundreds of offices and thousands of staff across forty countries.

As has been said, "desperation is the parent of invention"! At that time, we were also responsible for rolling out and training travel agents on new airline computer reservation systems (CRS). While preparing the training programs, I happened upon the free-form text area within the United Airlines Apollo and the American Airlines Sabre system. As I investigated them further, both systems had a practically unlimited amount of virtually free textual storage space in those days. The idea occurred to me that we could load our entire Financial Services policies and procedures into the open areas of the airline systems.

Consequently, the information would be instantly available worldwide to every office with an airline reservation system. Further, critically, we could update the procedures automatically at will! Remember, these were the days just before the internet! I proceeded to test the systems, pilot the solution, and sold it to my management. We developed the entire system, formatted it, and loaded it into the airline CRS systems, and voilà! We had an electronic financial services system launched and available globally!

Well, actually, no, we did not! Returning then to the Change Masters, this was my first encounter with the realities and challenges of change management within a large global corporation. The solution, pre-internet, was, I thought, brilliant. But I did not anticipate or reckon with a large multinational's matrix politics, territorialism, entrenchment, and resistance to change. I assumed everyone would automatically embrace a new, obviously better solution. Not true! Some people frankly just liked their convenient flip-card procedures. Also, many just didn't "get it" and struggled with the new technology.

Further, the financial service product areas were skeptical and resistant because of the fear of the potential loss of control of the end-to-end procedures. Finally, my management did not have the political clout, power, or influence to drive this innovation through the layers of organizational hurdles to achieve full acceptance of the idea and approach. As a result, the solution was launched and was ultimately only adopted by a few computer-literate users. Unfortunately, despite the immediate global delivery and instant updates, it never realized my vision of transforming the system to take advantage of the ubiquitous and instantaneous benefits we all now take for granted with today's digital solutions. Sadly, it was too far ahead of the curve.

Painfully, as I studied *The Change Masters*, I could see the entire landscape and demise unfolding and unraveling before me, but I couldn't head it off. In retrospect, Dr. Kanter's famous *The Change Masters* model vividly describes the variety of challenges I had at the time and that transformational change programs present to us today. Despite this missed opportunity, fortunately, over the years, I mastered the *Change Masters* tools. Subsequently, I learned to orchestrate the complexity of major change programs—especially securing the vital support of a strong senior sponsor and champion.

Dr. Kanter observes that the first challenge in transformational change is considering and contending with organizational constructs and culture. For example, is your company rigid, siloed, "segmentalist," and change-averse, or entrepreneurial, "integrative," and change-adept? Your organizational paradigms will either stimulate and encourage or hinder and stifle creativity and your ability to effect constructive change. Recognizing these complementary or inhospitable structures will help you leverage the beneficial enablers or overcome obstacles.

Does your organizational structure have rigid hierarchical and siloed job roles, or does it have flexible and cross-functional linkages that encourage communications, the free flow of information, and collaboration? Creating and enabling fluid communications and robust feedback channels across the organization leverages new inputs, different perspectives, and diverse approaches to problem-solving, creative solutioning, and innovation. Logical and sensible, you might deduce; yes, however, getting the buy-in and alignment from different stakeholders with diverse agendas can be challenging.

With a constructive organizational structure and collaborative communications channels, you are now ready to promote and actively progress your change program or project. Critical to any project's success, and one of the challenges I had at American Express, is to get buy-in across the organization, not just within your team, but across the matrix of stakeholders. This includes direct management and related people who influence or are affected by the proposed change, specifically including any product owners. You will need both explicit and implicit agreement and approvals across your stakeholder landscape for your change program to succeed.

As we commented with Kotter, Dr. Kanter discusses the need to establish sponsorship, champions, cheerleaders, and Steer Co's to nurture and support your initiatives initially and stay on course throughout the program. This is particularly important at the project start to promote and get an agreement for a project. Once the project is up and running, it is also critical to manage hurdles and criticism and mitigate attempts by skeptics and objectors to derail the project.

Once the project is approved and mobilized, teamwork and team building may be necessary to get all team members acquainted and aligned. This is essential to avoid conflict, ensure efficient operations, and inspire team motivation. Dr. Kanter cautions, however, about having too many cooks spoiling the broth, as not every decision requires extensive analysis on the part of the entire team. You need to know when to decide, when to consult, and when to delegate. With the team aligned and mobilized, ensure that you, as the leader, maintain focus and efficiency by insulating the team from external distractions, including objections or diversions.

Finally, you must establish a trust culture and articulate a clear, inspiring, and meaningful vision. Ensure you and the team are clear on roles and responsibilities. Positively encourage, motivate, and actively empower the team. The final step in the change process is to promote and publish the change project and the team's successes. Create a constructive story about the change process, including achievements and lessons learned, and enthusiastically recognize individual and team contributions.

The robust kaleidoscope thinking and holistic management of the various dimensions of a change program are crucial to effective change management and vital to creating value for your organization. Initiating sustainable change and stimulating innovation in complex organizations is always challenging and is as much a creative art as a disciplined science. Finally, in the rapidly accelerating markets and turbulent times within which we work, as Dr. Kanter stresses, "Change is the only Constant"! If that is the case, as it most assuredly is, then our critical challenge as leaders is to become what Dr. Kanter refers to as "Change Masters." Fortunately, Dr. Kanter provides a clear road map that helps chart the course for that journey.

Takeaway: To begin a major change program, ensure you have a suitable organizational culture and structure. Your organizational paradigms will either stimulate and encourage or hinder and stifle your efforts. With that constructive foundation, you can build a culture of trust, establish a strong vision, and build sponsors, steering committees, and champions.

James Kouzes and Barry Posner: *The Leadership Challenge*

43, 44

This inspiring book came out toward the end of my time in training at American Express in San Francisco. I began feeling the urge for new challenges and a career change, which would eventually land me at Reuters in Hong Kong. Perhaps it was the timing plus my yearning for change that this book's heartfelt, collaborative, and pragmatic message made such a powerful impression on me. The combination of a relevant conceptual model with a clear call-to-action message resonated strongly with me. I enthusiastically recommend this book, in particular the most recent 2017 update. Here are my key takeaways:[45]

"Model the Way"

For this first behavior, using my language, the authors encourage the leader to "find your center," internalize, and respect your personal value system and operating principles. Once you have validated and internalized these principles, you will have a solid and reliable base of personal integrity and confidence in your vision, values, and modus operandi. From that deep intrinsic self-belief, you will be authentic and true to yourself in your conduct and actions with colleagues and staff. The authors stress exceptional leaders set a positive example by effectively aligning their values and behaviors. As a result, your colleagues and staff will instinctively perceive and trust your actions when you set forth your vision and objectives through these authentic and honest modeling and mentoring behaviors.

"Inspire a Shared Vision"

Kouzes and Posner state leaders are at their best when they envision and champion an inspiring and ennobling vision that speaks to their team's aspirations and ambitions. As discussed in the first chapters, which the authors emphatically echo, a critical leadership challenge is to "crystallize a vision" with a "purpose" that is exciting, valuable, challenging, and achievable. Then, with that vision clearly in your mind's eye, you can communicate that vision with a passion to inspire your colleagues to buy into and collectively share the vision. An exciting shared vision gives work purpose and is therefore effective in motivating staff.

"Challenge the Process"

Challenging the process is about leaders having the vision and courage to do things that have never been done before and take us to places we've never imagined. One of the leader's roles is envisioning and initiating value-creating new change. Further, the leader must challenge the status quo to aspire to great things and then innovate and optimize the successful delivery and execution of the vision.

Therefore, ensure that you and your teams constructively, expansively, and creatively explore the best possible outcomes and solutions for the objectives. Unfortunately, there is often a tendency of inertia or even indolence in the status quo to perpetuate more of the same or simply undertake minor incremental improvements. Therefore, always explore the potential for radical improvement or a broad-based transformation as a prevailing modus operandi wherever possible.

"Enable Others to Act"

The key to effective leadership is effective teamwork. Regardless of charisma and vision, no leader will be successful unless they can create a creative and effective climate of collaborative teamwork. Further, communicating openly and transparently is a precondition to building team trust. That means inspired shared visioning, proactive skills development, delegation, empowered workers, encouragement, support, and shared credit and recognition. With that positive "can-do" culture and climate, staff will engage and flourish, and productivity will be optimized.

"Encourage the Heart"

If things were satisfactory and comfortable with no challenges, then we would simply need a "care and maintenance" manager, not a leader. However, ambitious visions and challenges always involve large and sometimes long journeys that inevitably encounter obstacles and bumps in the road. At times like this, a leader's refined emotional intelligence is required and can make the difference between the failure of a great idea and a successful transformation.

Whether there is a genuine challenge, obstacle, or just a long and tedious path, a leader's courage, caring, and cheerful nature can buoy up the team, lift the spirits and encourage the team to sustain the journey. As a result, with that encouragement and confidence, you open people's hearts and minds to the world of possibilities. With a positive vision of the future, they will be inspired, take more risks, and be more creative.

As you achieve milestones along the way, ensure you recognize and reward individual and team efforts. Follow the "one-minute manager" philosophy as a highly effective way to maintain motivation and momentum throughout the venture.[46] This practice of immediate and incremental personal recognition and reward is far more effective than a time-shifted objectives appraisal discussion long after the fact.

These five action-oriented models for leadership behavior are clear, concise, and remarkably effective in managing a vision through to reality through effective collaboration with teams. If you were to have only a handful of leadership books on your bookshelf, *The Leadership Challenge* should definitely be one.[47]

Takeaway: Fundamental to leading teams is to "find your center," internalizing and respecting your value system and operating principles. Once you validate and internalize these principles, you will have a solid base of integrity and confidence in your vision, values, and modus operandi. From that deep self-belief, you will be authentic and true in your conduct and actions with staff.

Charles Handy

48

My introduction to Charles Handy was through one of my British managers shortly after I arrived at Reuters in Hong Kong. Handy quickly became one of my all-time favorite management thinkers and authors; I have read *The Gods of Management, The Age of Unreason, Inside Organizations,* and *The Empty Raincoat.* As a sociologist, philosopher, business, and management guru, his experience, personal style, and philosophy resonate powerfully, especially as he thinks deeply and writes clearly and eloquently. I didn't read *Gods of Management* first, but as the earliest, let's start with that as it frames organizational structures uniquely and memorably.

Handy's early academic studies in Greek and Roman history and language helped inspire his book *Gods of Management* on organizational structures and design by comparing them through analogy to the Greek gods.

He named his first organizational structure Zeus, after the omnipotent king of gods in Greek mythology. This organization is dominated by a powerful, charismatic leader, frequently the founder and chief executive. Good examples of this would be Apple's early years with Steve Jobs, Microsoft with Bill Gates, and Facebook with Mark Zuckerberg, especially before those companies became enormous mature multinationals. Elon Musk at Tesla and SpaceX is also an excellent current example.

The next type of structure is Apollo, the most important and complex god. Apollo companies represent multinational organizations managed by solid governance and structure, mature processes, and robust systems. Examples are IBM, Siemens, GE, and Toyota.

The Athena organizational culture is named after the goddess of wisdom. It represents a specialist knowledge worker culture focused on project-based work, such as consultancies and creative agencies. Good examples are Accenture, PwC, McCann, and WPP.

Finally is the Dionysian, after Dionysus, the god of wine and patron of the arts. The Dionysian corporate culture represents flexibly structured and adaptable organizations like start-ups, artist studios, or academic institutions where creative types can thrive and work independently or in small teams. The list is endless, but good examples I'm familiar with are IDEO, ThoughtWorks, and Cambridge Consultants.[49]

In his later published works and as a consultant, Handy created a more traditional organizational model with four classes of corporate culture: power, role, task, and person. He develops this in detail; however, in my view, this is a mature mainstream evolution of the gods of management model. Here, the power culture is a Zeus culture, the role culture is an Apollo-style culture, the task culture is an Athenian culture, and the person culture is a Dionysian culture.

Based on these structures, Handy then explores the benefits, liabilities, and unique challenges of each. One of the problems Handy postulates is that sometimes the "tool is not fit to the task" in organizational terms. For example, an organization may outgrow the founding leader's or current leadership's capabilities. In addition, over time, the business may grow to the extent that its structure, methods, and systems may not be sufficiently robust or mature to manage a more extensive, diverse, or multinational structure. Furthermore, an older, more mature organizational design may be too heavy, inflexible, and slow to cope with the pace of change in a new, more dynamic industry. In these cases, there is the risk that disruptive processes or technologies may rapidly render obsolete companies not adaptable enough to reinvent themselves. Finally, a new dynamic, loosely structured start-up or agency model may lack central systems or project and process disciplines to develop and maintain systems at a sufficient scale to sustain themselves or to compete in the long term.

As a senior adviser to Accenture, I watched with fascination Accenture's evolution in recent years as a vivid example of the opportunities and challenges of managing a diverse portfolio of organizational styles. Accenture is a behemoth of a company with 720,000 employees in fifty countries. Over the past decade, they embarked on a wholesale digital transformation, which included integrating scores of specialty tech, design, and media companies. By all accounts, they managed to successfully merge these specialty companies into Accenture. They achieved this by leveraging their scale to incorporate, harness, and respect these entrepreneurial companies' creative culture, spirit, and cutting-edge expertise. The potential for failure was very high; however, they balanced the best of Accenture's marketing, technical capabilities, and systems with the specialty companies' fresh perspectives, innovative business models, and emerging tools. This is a rare example of a successful business model transformation of a vast multinational company.

Therefore, people and organizations must recognize that one size does not fit all contexts. Sometimes, we must employ many or all of our capabilities and tools to cope with dynamic change and complexity without, as mentioned earlier, "simply relying solely on a hammer."[50]

A core Handy theme, particularly in *the Age of Unreason* and *The Empty Raincoat,* is his "village" or community-oriented "federalist model" for organizations. Here, the activity, creativity, and drive occur in the community, the regions, or at the edge instead of primarily at the center of the organization or bureaucracy. The center has a rightful role in resource allocation, standards, and security, among other headquarters functions. But it is a guiding and supportive structure, not the be-all and end-all of the organizational spirit, innovation, or customer engagement. He repeatedly stresses that organizations are not inanimate objects but dynamic systems that must respect the people's and customers' individual needs and motivations throughout the organization. His view is that sociological change and societal evolution have not been adequately reflected in the associated development of corporate company cultures, structures, or systems.

He posited that organizations need to evolve to be more adaptable, decentralized, and flexible. His Irish representation of this is the shamrock, with the unifying stem holding the organization's parts together. The first leaf represents the core organization with the full-time central staff. These are senior management and essential domain experts who intimately know the markets and company products. The second leaf is the resident or related contractors who are closely linked contractually to the company, including former or retired employees. Finally, the third leaf represents professional service or technology consultancies with requisite specialty skills providing essential and invaluable unique skills on an ad hoc or part-time basis.

This decentralized, federated organizational shamrock structure functions much as a community village. The organizational model interacts with the market and the community regularly and effectively to conceive, develop, launch, and interactively support products and services in the marketplace. Along with this flexible organizational model, he presented ideas for career and personal development, including what he termed a "portfolio life" where workers would have multifaceted freelance portfolios of clients, providing a portfolio of tasks, projects, and jobs for different clients.[51] These ideas are relatively commonplace in the "gig economy" of the 2020s, especially during the COVID-19 virtual working phenomenon; nevertheless, this was highly prescient in the 1980s and 1990s!

As a sociologist, business guru, and philosopher, Handy has a big heart. His works are still relevant today and are definitely worth reading at some point during your career. They are especially valuable for professional reflection and direction-setting during transitional times of job change, career shifts, or setting long-term lifetime goals.

Takeaway: There are numerous types of corporate cultures based on industry, location, and organization size. Further, companies go through various transformations as they grow and mature. Likewise, each leader has unique strengths and weaknesses that evolve over time. The critical thing is to ensure that your management's style is strategically and operationally well aligned to the culture and working style of the organization where you labor.

Stephen R. Covey

52

Covey was a prominent American author, educator, speaker, and management consultant who was most famous for his enormously successful book *The 7 Habits of Highly Effective People* and for *Principle-Centered Leadership*. He further pioneered and popularized numerous highly practical methods and tools for management development and operational efficiency, as well as being a leading advocate of spiritual and ethical values in business.

Here is a brief summary of the *7 Habits of Highly Effective People*:

Habit 1: Be Proactive

Effective people are proactive rather than reactive. This is obvious; however, the key is consciously and constantly practicing proactivity until it becomes an enduring, consistent habit. This means anticipating future circumstances and taking the responsibility to act in advance to ensure you control situations instead of simply reacting to the issues or problems once they occur.

Perhaps this is a simplistic but still appropriate analogy for life, but as a teen, I always remembered my driving instructor telling us to keep an eye off into the distance to observe and be ready to react to any incidents and future events coming our way.

Further, I recall when at AOL in the early days of mobiles, I proposed to my teams that we should be proactive in participating in the mobile industry development forums, as it would be easier to help develop the standards than to have to conform and adapt to them after the fact!

Habit 2: Start with the End Result in Mind

Habit 2 is about consciously envisioning a clear end result and outcome in everything we do by starting with the destination in mind and working toward it. That way, you can plan in advance to ensure you set the proper road map, actions, and steps that lead toward that objective. While many things can occur in the course of a large project delivery, maintaining focus on the outcome will help to stay on track with the project's critical path and avoid detrimental deviations.

This advice echoes the advice of the great Cuban chess master José Raúl Capablanca, who recommended keeping the end game in sight before and throughout any match.

There is a saying that if you don't know where you are going, you will be unlikely to end up where you want to be.

Habit 3: First Things First

Developed initially by Covey and Dwight D. Eisenhower, the thirty-fourth US president, this is one of my favorites and most frequently used habits. It relates to setting priorities and time management. This habit focuses on breaking each task down into its importance and urgency and identifying the appropriate action for each: *Important and Urgent, Important and Not Urgent, Not Important and Urgent*, and *Not Important and Not Urgent*. Given this habit's importance, I've reserved a dedicated discussion for this in the Leadership and Management Tips chapter of book 2. As an advance tip, focus exclusively on the important and urgent; don't get distracted and diverted by urgent but unimportant things. If something is not important, who cares if it is urgent? This is a challenging but hugely valuable habit to remember and practice.

Habit 4: Think Win-Win

This is another important theme for me over the years, not only in negotiations but, most importantly, for a collaborative approach to vendor management and working with all manner of externals.

This is about working honestly, collaboratively, and productively with others in a benevolent yet practical manner. However, it also turns out to be the most effective way to work with others to achieve optimal results. It is about developing value-creating trust relationships, particularly long-term relationships, with mutual respect and commitment to a successful partnership. The operative metrics are **Win-Win**: Where both parties benefit and win. **Win-Lose**: This is where you act selfishly and aggressively to win at the expense of your counterparty. **Lose-Win**: This is when you cede position or strength for minor or personal wins. **Lose-Lose**: This is where both parties stubbornly hold their ground, neither party gains an advantage, and both parties ultimately lose out against a more productive approach.

Game Theory and Social Exchange Theory concepts inform and support the Win/Win approach, which says that in any relationship, any Win-Lose or Lose-Win position ultimately deteriorates into a Lose-Lose. If a situation is unequal or one-sided, there will be resentment, and eventually, some sort of retaliation will probably result. For those interested, this Win-Win status can be likened to a game theory situation known as the Nash Equilibrium. This is where all participants simultaneously optimize their positions in a negotiation or decision-making interaction, arriving at a steady state or equilibrium where no participant has a viable or better option to improve their position.[53] While a Win-Win negotiation has an element of benevolent intention, a Nash Equilibrium is a highly analytical and pragmatic stable state position.

Habit 5: Strive to Understand, Aspire to Be Understood

Habit 5 is about effective communication through creating a trust relationship where both parties make an effort to listen, fully understand, and appreciate the issues. This avoids jumping to conclusions and offering suggestions that may not fully appreciate the nuance of the other's concerns. Covey states we should deeply understand the other person and their concerns by practicing empathic (active) listening. This effort to understand each other's context and position deeply significantly increases the likelihood of enhancing the relationship's quality and successfully resolving any issues.

Throughout my life, I've always enjoyed the idiom "walk a mile in another's moccasins," which is about making a sufficient effort to understand another before judging. This quote is often attributed to Native Americans but comes from a poem by Mary Lathrap.[54]

Habit 6: Synergize!

With Habit 6, Covey discusses this well-known but not always maximized maxim: synergistically working with others, perhaps even with a different point of view, to leverage diverse perspectives in solving problems or creating new opportunities. Synergy means the proverbial "two heads are better than one" for collaboration, ideation, sharing, and teamwork. Exploring and valuing differences, diversity, and creativity yields more appreciable results than one can achieve individually.

Habit 7: Sharpen the Saw: Growth

Covey encourages and emphasizes human potential development in all areas of our lives, spiritually, mentally, socially, and physically. To achieve our best, personally and professionally, we need to exercise discipline and devote time and effort to continuously improving ourselves in these dimensions throughout our lives. This positive personal habit should be encouraged and developed throughout your teams and organizations to unlock all our talents, maximize potential, and live happier, more fulfilled lives.[55]

Takeaway: The success of the 7 Habits has been so pervasive that one begins to take these ideas for granted. However, knowing something is a far cry from making it habitual. Don't be confused by and reactive to an urgent but less important task. These are the pervasive time wasters that should be rigorously discarded. Focus exclusively on essential tasks, both urgent and then nonurgent.

Recognize in any negotiation or relationship, a win/lose or lose/win situation always deteriorates into a lose/lose endgame. Always strive for a win/win in any negotiation or partnership.

Peter M. Senge

56

I had just been appointed Training Director for Reuters Asia in Singapore when *The Fifth Discipline: The Art and Practice of the Learning Organization*[57] was published. I took it to heart as it was directly related to my core role, but it was also written from a technologist's perspective, so culturally as well as linguistically, it was "speaking my language." I also had the fortune to meet Senge at a conference in London in the mid-1990s.

According to Peter Senge, "Learning organizations are organizations where people continually expand their capacity to create the results they truly desire, where new and expansive patterns of thinking are nurtured, where collective aspiration is set free, and where people are continually learning to see the whole together."[58]

As a training director and, subsequently, a line manager, I adopted and promoted this idea of a "learning organization" through various organizational iterations. In my view, and my own words, a learning organization is a complex adaptive system that continuously learns, develops, and grows in constructive ways toward achieving its stated purpose and objectives, evolving beneficially for the organization and its staff.

Peter examines "mental models" that assist in becoming a learning organization through individual, team-based, and organizational development. Dr. Senge was also an ardent follower of physicist and philosopher David Bohm in advancing an overarching and integrating idea of "systems thinking."

In terms of a company or an organization, system thinking refers to an entity comprising multiple interrelated and interconnected components. Systems thinking involves looking at the entire organization and analyzing it from a holistic perspective to understand how the individual pieces interoperate and contribute to the overall organization and its objectives. This is particularly valuable in linking and understanding seemingly unrelated issues, such as stakeholder agendas and politics necessary to progress projects or transformations successfully. In practical terms, I've found it's crucial to understand how individual, perhaps seemingly insignificant or trivial things, can significantly impact the whole system. This is clearly important when considering small bits of computer code that can disrupt or bring down the entire system. Also, consider how a single isolated event can dramatically affect an overall customer experience, for example, a delayed airport transfer, in my case, working within the travel industry. More dramatically, recently, IT contractors accidentally deleted a tiny bit of the overall FAA air traffic management code, bringing all US airline operations to a grinding halt.

Senge also encourages creating and communicating a shared vision for the organization to align people to the vision and its objective's purpose and processes. Along with the vision, the people and organization must develop and align shared mental models of principles, ideas, and assumptions that will influence and guide staff actions. This is important in that managers can never plan or anticipate every staff action required to keep a business operational. Mental models establish the framework and principles that staff can be guided by to interpret and apply to their activities and tasks.

Moreover, there must be internal organizational and staff commitment to personal mastery, which is a process of maximizing learning and development for personal and professional development. In addition to personal mastery, there must be collective team-based working and knowledge linked to the shared vision and model in order to become a learning organization. This enables everyone to achieve more by working together toward the organizational objectives. This can be a powerful motivator to gain staff alignment when leading transformational changes involving challenging emerging and disruptive technologies.

In Senge's view, empowered and collaborative teams are the fundamental learning and working communities in a company. If the company, the leader, and the staff are aligned around a mutual commitment to personal mastery and professional development, the individuals and the company as a learning organization all benefit.

By ardently following these learning organization disciplines outlined by Senge, an organization can grow and progress rapidly and become more cohesive and adaptable to manage change, compete effectively, become more productive, increase employee job satisfaction, and thus, overall staff morale.[59]

Takeaway: Without getting lost in the complexity, ensure your strategic organization view encompasses a holistic "systems thinking" perspective. Make sure you recognize how the components and parts of the organization are interconnected and interrelated to understand how they interoperate. A leader, like an orchestra conductor, may be the only person who appreciates how all the pieces of the organization work together like an orchestra to produce a symphony.

Alvin and Heidi Toffler

60

Among my foremost professional inspirations were Alvin and Heidi Toffler, whom I had the good fortune to see at two conferences, once in London and the other in Toronto, along with Peter Drucker. To a certain extent, Alvin, a futurist, "pulled back the curtain" for me by helping me take a "long view" of things from the distant past into the far future. His viewpoints on the stages of evolution of humanity from the earliest ages to the accelerating changes in society, business, and technology in the present and far future gave me new and unique perspectives on what's occurred, what's happening now, what might happen next, and most importantly, why.

Alvin and my father, a science fiction enthusiast and inventor, helped me think beyond the moment and to extrapolate things of today forward into the future to envision how they could evolve. This process is invaluable for any leader for product innovation and to visualize how products and markets will develop in the future. To a certain extent, this approach relates to both the systems theory discussed with Peter Senge and the story I told earlier about the historical evolution of the International Space Station. At a high level, if one thinks holistically about an issue or perhaps a product, almost as in two dimensions, that of its functional usage and its technology, you can add a third dimension, that of time, both historically and forward into the future. You can then begin to extrapolate to foresee how trends and technologies will evolve, morph, and leap in step changes through continuous and disruptive changes over time. I'll remind you of the example I cited earlier while at AOL. Following these same methodologies, we mapped multiple interrelated mobile internet technologies through a series of anticipated evolutions over a number of years to forecast and plan our future product developments.

This further reminds me of Thomas Kuhn's theories on "paradigm shifts." He argues that scientific and technological advances do not happen in a continuous linear or straight-line evolution; instead, they occur in fits and starts, step changes, and periodic revolutions.[61] Thus, as you project forward, make sure you do not predict simple linear trends over a consistent trajectory.

Given the groundbreaking nature of the works at the time, I naturally read Alvin and Heidi's trilogy: *Future Shock*, then *The Third Wave*, and finally *Powershift*. While the time and context have changed, the visioning lessons and methods are still relevant today.

In *Future Shock*, Alvin vividly illustrates the challenges and concerns of the accelerating pace of change in modern postindustrial society and today's digital age. With the exponential rate of societal change, the evolution of business and technology products, and emerging technologies, associated workers' and users' skills are rapidly and consistently obsoleted. Inexorably, this constant and rapid change outpaces people and society's ability to adapt to and cope with these shifts. This causes significant confusion and stress for people, resulting in a feeling of estrangement and disassociation from modern society, and in particular from the youth, new activities, and emerging work opportunities.

The term "information overload" popularized by Toffler is one key symptom of this situation. He further coins the term "future shock" to classify the human reaction to this overwhelming and disorienting pace of change. A person has to look no further than one's own family to observe some older people's difficulties in coping with computers, the internet, smartphones, and digital applications. Virtually every "modern convenience" from the bedroom clock, the bathroom scale, kitchen appliances, and the living room digital theater TV and media player present significant learning and operational challenges for many senior citizens today.[62]

The second book of the trilogy, *The Third Wave*, charts the evolution of civilization from the earliest age of humanity with the hunter-gatherers through each significant social anthropological change depicted as "waves." The first wave, the agrarian revolution, replaced the hunter-gatherers, which was supplanted by the second wave, the Industrial Revolution. The third wave is the postindustrial revolution. Arguably, we are in the fourth wave, the digital age.[63]

The trilogy concludes with *Power Shift,* which describes the information age and knowledge society, which has resulted in a new shift of power. In the past, power relied on strength and occasionally violence to gain authority and control; this later progressed into being accumulated through the acquisition of wealth. Today, in the digital information age, power transfers to those who have and control information and knowledge, which then translates into influence, wealth, and power.[64]

This trilogy provides us with a vast amount of food for thought about product evolution, user experience, design simplicity, and the potential impacts of technology and transformational change on our employees and customers.

This may seem esoteric and hypothetical; however, let's look at this in the context of some burning issues for big tech today. There are many current social, ethical, security, and financial concerns that were never envisioned by the founders of companies such as Google, Facebook, and Amazon. For example, the abuse of Facebook by bad actors relating to politics and elections, the impact of Amazon on small shops and warehouse workers, and privacy issues pertaining to Google search, Google Maps, and Apple location-aware AirTags. No one has a crystal ball; however, despite many well-intended and perhaps initially altruistic company objectives, possibilities for misuse and abuse abound. Clearly, the current explosion of AI technologies has vast technical, social, and economic implications, as well as profound potential risks. To the extent we can envision and mitigate these issues while rigorously adhering to our ethical and value systems, we, the company, and society will benefit.

The thinking and approach modeled by Alvin and Heidi Toffler is a fine example of how leaders should observe and consider the influence and impact of social, business, and technological change on ourselves, our teams, and our customers.

Takeaway: Your organization does not exist in isolation but rather within a larger ecosystem of customers, industries, and society. Attempt to cast your mind forward in time to appreciate the future ramifications of your company's products and services. Failure to have a long view has thrust many big tech companies into situations they never envisioned. For example, the transformation to AI has many short-term benefits with uncertain future ramifications. Make sure you are not navigating with blinders on.

Gary Hamel and C. K. Prahalad

65, 66

Gary Hamel and C. K. Prahalad are not "Leadership Gurus" per se but rather business strategy gurus. Nevertheless, a good leader wears many hats, and effective strategy is one of the most critical skills any successful leader must possess. Gary and C. K. were keynote speakers, along with Peter Drucker and Alvin Toffler, at a conference in Toronto I was fortunate enough to be invited to attend and speak at.

At the conference, they presented the key messages from their book *Competing for the Future*,[67] which had come out the year before. I wholeheartedly recommend their books *Competing for the Future* and *Leading the Revolution*. Presumably, there are many excellent additional titles by both authors.

Gary is known for his radical strategy tactics and was responsible for groundbreaking new concepts of core competencies, strategic intent, and new aspects of industry revolution, all of which are now embedded in today's business vernacular. These concepts and principles were quite revolutionary when they first appeared. Today, they are foundational to current business strategy.

Hamel and Prahalad proposed that the pace and trajectory of business change today are not linear in trajectory and have an exponential rate of change. (Again, a concept initially put forward by Thomas Kuhn.) Hamel insists organizations must continually reinvent themselves and avoid "company blindness," which is an inability to see things differently based on your company's biased lenses. Like Clayton Christensen, he states that if you take your company and its orthodoxies for granted, it will be virtually impossible to see beyond your current way of doing things. Recall Einstein's comment that no problem can be solved by the kind of thinking that created it.[68] There is also another humorous business saying appropriate to "company blindness." That is: "We love our own babies." This is to say that our affection and loyalty to our company, its products, and our projects create this blindness, which induces resistance to change.

Secondarily, a company must understand its core competencies, not only to look at what you do but what else you could potentially do with your existing knowledge, skills, and capabilities. This applies equally to the current organizational capabilities, such as products, systems, infrastructure, and the organization's people and talent.

A third approach identifies discontinuities that exist in your environment and industry that could be replaced, reengineered, or reinvented to be transformed to be much more advantageous. Again, there is a strong correlation here to Clayton Christensen's ideas on disruptive technologies.

Hamel contends that a "revolutionary" is someone who challenges the status quo and is willing to change it. And that innovation is more often created by heretics than prophets![69] A quick reflection on Steve Jobs's and Elon Musk's careers and modi operandi effectively proves this point.

Takeaway: In business today, continuous change is the only constant, and even if things are going well, we must avoid complacency and having a narrow, internally focused perspective. This leads to company blindness and the tendency to self-reinforce our own decisions or solutions. While it is difficult to see beyond our current way of doing things, recognize that, as Einstein said, "No problem can be solved by the kind of thinking that created it." Constantly interject new ideas and thinking into evolving your strategies.

Michael Porter

70

Michael Porter is not specifically a *leadership* guru; however, he is an almost essential read for leaders because of his landmark ideas on competitive strategy and tools like the eponymous Porter's Five Forces. I've read *Competitive Strategy*,[71] skim-read *Competitive Advantage of Nations*, and ardently used Porter's Five Forces over the past thirty years in virtually every role I've had. First, it's useful as a marketing and product tool; further, I've employed it as a project or stakeholder alignment and assessment tool.

Porter's *Competitive Advantage* discusses how to gain leverage in the market by 1) Establishing a "cost advantage" where you attempt to provide the same or similar products or services to customers but at a lower cost. 2) Create a "differentiation advantage," or make your products or services stand out to the customer by design, innovation, or quality. Finally, 3) Adopt a "segmentation strategy" where you narrow your market by geography, demographics, or behavioral segments to provide a unique and targeted product or service to a narrowly defined market segment.[72] This concise strategy differentiation is vital to keep in mind to ensure you are not trying to be all things to all people.

Porter's Five Forces is from his book *Competitive Strategy* and can be used to analyze industries, company strategy, and even internal organizational structures and topics. I've adapted the concept many times and found it invaluable to do a snapshot, 360-degree assessment of virtually any opportunity, issue, or risk.

Porter identified Five Forces that play a part in shaping markets and can be used to measure market attractiveness, the competition, their potential competitive capabilities, and your comparative internal company competencies. They are:

1. **Competitive Rivalry.** Considers the number and strength of the competition. How many are there? Who are they? Where are they, and what is the relative quality of their products compared to yours?
2. **Supplier Power.** How many different suppliers do you have? How dependent are you on them? Is their product or service unique, and how easy would it be to switch to another supplier? Could they disintermediate you and become a competitor?
3. **Buyer Power.** How many buyers do you have, and how easy would it be for them to switch to a competitor? Are your buyers powerful enough to dictate disadvantageous terms to you?
4. **Threat of Substitution.** Is it possible or probable that your customers could find a different way of operating that could obviate the need for or eliminate your product?
5. **Threat of New Entry.** How easy would it be for new players to enter your market or industry?[73,74]

"How Competitive Forces Shape Strategy"[75] by Michael E. Porter, March 1979. Copyright © 1979 by the Harvard Business School Publishing Corporation; all rights reserved.[76]

Takeaway: Avoid trying to accomplish everything for everybody with your product or service strategy. Attempt to gain competitive advantage by 1) establishing a cost advantage, 2) creating a differentiation advantage, e.g., innovation, design, or quality, or 3) adopting a segmentation strategy by demographics, customer behavior, or geography. Use Porter's Five Forces to analyze the market situation by competition, suppliers, buyers, and threats.

Michael Hammer and James Champy

77, 78

Sometimes, as they say, timing is everything. But let's also leave some margin for a bit of serendipity as well! I arrived in London in January 1993 to begin my task of redesigning Reuters Investment Bank Trading Systems. Shortly thereafter, Hammer and Champy published *Reengineering the Corporation*.[79] Given my enormous yet still imprecise new challenge, it wasn't long before I picked up *Reengineering* at my local Waterstones bookstore in Hampstead, London. At the time, I found it perceptive, penetrating, and spot-on relative to our current predicament with the poor usability and kludgy operation of the product range I was now responsible for improving.

I'll elaborate on this detailed case study later. But, in brief, when I reported to the Reuters CEO Peter Job for my new role in January 1993, he told me in simple and no uncertain terms: "Greg, your job is to fix our products." Without any playbook, I had to invent one, and Hammer and Champy provided me with an invaluable part of the approach and solution, positive reassurance, and all-important motivation.

They recommended thinking entirely freshly, outside the box, and with a "clean sheet of paper" rather than just considering incremental or marginal improvements. They espoused revolution and reinvention rather than incremental continuous improvement. That was music to my ears and resonated with the reading I had done by Edward de Bono on lateral thinking and thinking outside the box.

Hammer and Champy suggested eliminating (obliterating) work that doesn't add value and carefully examining each step of every process you are reviewing to eliminate redundant and unnecessary steps. This made great sense to me, particularly as the first thing I was doing was analyzing customer interactions, support calls, and operational failures at our customer helpdesks.

With the trading systems of the day, it was instantly apparent that the customer journeys and user experiences were simply automated replicas of the old verbal and manual trading processes. Worse, many of the processes were irrelevant and time-consuming in an automated foreign exchange trading context, where seconds delays could mean significant missed opportunities and losses in the millions for investment bank traders.

Hammer and Champy further prescribed reengineering to radically redesign the company and associated business and technical processes to achieve a dramatic leap in performance. In my case, it was directly relevant to maximizing the operating efficiencies for high-flying investment bank currency traders.

The book is definitely worth reading, and the still-relevant core principles are:

1. Organize all activities around outcomes, not tasks.
2. Identify and analyze all suboptimal processes and prioritize them for redesign or replacement.
3. Analyze and optimize real-world business processes.
4. Look objectively at all decentralized global processes to centralize and standardize them.
5. Link up, integrate, and de-duplicate all parallel workflow processes instead of just merging the results.
6. Put milestones, decision points, and controls into the workflow processes instead of just validation check-point reviews at the end.
7. Capture and process information only once and always at the source.[80]

As mentioned, this book arrived at the right time for me and the industry. At that point, many multinationals, such as ours, had expanded rapidly with globalization. To manage that growth, the associated systems and processes had proliferated and scaled rapidly, often out of urgent need, but in turn, had suffered from uncontrolled and bloated designs. The industry, in general, was ripe and desperate for rationalization and simplification. *Reengineering the Corporation* provided that playbook.

Technical footnote: The principles of reengineering apply equally today, with the explosive expansion of digital "minimum viable product" systems occasionally being launched prematurely and half-baked. The market and fierce competition demand speed; however, these systems sometimes need hard resets and reengineering to remove accumulated "technical debt" in order to achieve bulletproof, industrial-strength stability. This is a critical issue concerning security, data protection, system reliability, and brand reputation.

Takeaway: To streamline your organization or processes, adopt a fresh perspective about how to radically redesign the company, its processes, and technology to remove and replace duplicative, parallel, and suboptimal systems. Focus your reengineering designs on outcomes rather than machinate with existing processes or endless tasks. For your data model and information strategy, ensure you evolve toward a "single version of the truth."

Joseph Badaracco

81

Shortly after I joined PwC in London, a work colleague, Jason, mentioned a thought-provoking book, *Leading Quietly*, by Joseph Badaracco.[82] I found it inspiring and encouraging from a few perspectives; first, it supported the old American Express axiom I mentioned previously: "If it is against the law, if it is against policy, if it is against your conscience, DON'T DO IT!" Badaracco provides a similar principle from West Point Military Academy—"Cadets don't cheat, lie, or steal or tolerate anyone who does." This also resonated with the culture at PwC, as this was immediately after the Arthur Andersen/Enron fiasco. It also aligned with and reinforced my own "quiet leadership style." Further, again as a technologist, he spoke the same language I did.

A key theme and premise of the book is that contrary to some of the heroic leadership stories by some management consultants, many of the most significant and invaluable leaders are not charismatic leaders like Elon Musk, Bill Gates, and Steve Jobs. Instead, they are quiet, diligent, decent, and responsible behind-the-scenes leaders who get work done and make the world run. These "quiet leaders" are the businesses' unsung heroes. These leaders modestly, tenaciously, and with restraint solve problems, deliver solutions, and lead teams ethically and consistently to deliver the organization's objectives, products, and promises.

He cites various examples and case studies of quiet leaders and provides eight practical guidelines for managing ethically and effectively. He starts with the practical advice that sometimes life and problems are complicated. Leaders should not kid themselves that they have all the answers or even fully understand the situation. This reminds me of physicist Richard Feynman's unintentionally humorous but apropos quote: "If you think you understand quantum mechanics, you don't understand quantum mechanics!"

Badaracco states you must be realistic and practical and view the world through a kaleidoscopic lens to recognize how complex and multifaceted issues can be. Further, you must realize that solutions may be as complex as the problems themselves. While you must act responsibly and ethically, you must also balance self-interest and altruism to improvise and persevere simultaneously. Don't rush into half-baked solutions; buy as much time as you need, consult with colleagues, and drill down into the problem's political and technical aspects to understand and test the intricacies of the problem and any potential solutions.

Before you jump to solutioning, understand those technical complexity and political ramifications, and within your principled professional boundaries, understand the political risks and know what battles to fight and when (Sun Tzu!). Then, apply your ethical and moral principles, accepting that complexity is never an excuse for wrongdoing. Finally, continue to consult, nudge improvisations, and test until you identify the best possible solution or compromise to achieve the most effective yet responsible solution.

He cautions any guideline can also be a "double-edged sword," but if you keep a clear head and a firm sense of the correct course of action, you will know when to compromise and when to stand your ground. Quiet leaders recognize some situations require courageous and decisive action, and even a few demand no small measure of heroism. Just know the risks, limits, and consequences. Go forth with your eyes wide open! Observing this sound advice, you are unlikely to go too far astray.[83]

Takeaway: Every organization is different and has unique needs. Further, there are many types of effective leaders. Some leaders are larger-than-life characters like Steve Jobs, Oprah Winfrey, Bill Gates, Sheryl Sandberg, or Elon Musk. However, most of the most successful leaders are diligent and responsible, behind-the-scenes "quiet leaders" who are the unsung heroes for getting the job done.

David Whyte

84

David Whyte is a unique and worthy inclusion in my list of leadership gurus. He has been a source of inspiration to me ever since I read *The Heart Aroused: Poetry and the Preservation of the Soul in Corporate America*[85] and later *Crossing the Unknown Sea*. I was fortunate enough to attend a conference he spoke at in London in 2000.

David is a powerful and prophetic poet, naturalist, and philosopher. His primary professional business purpose is to reconnect disenfranchised and discouraged knowledge workers back to their hearts and souls, reinvigorating their work lives to become more fulfilling and achieve a healthier work/life balance. I read *The Heart Aroused* with my friend Ernie's recommendation when leaving Reuters after ten years and starting my consultancy in London. At that time, I was searching for a fresh, new path with a more meaningful direction in my life.

The Heart Aroused uses "executive story" allegories and metaphors to provide insights and road maps for redirecting your work to be more meaningful and rewarding. One intriguing image in his storytelling is the recounting of *Beowulf*,[86] the ancient British poem, where he addresses how we must persevere to overcome obstacles through courage, faith, and creativity. I won't attempt the poetic prose of Whyte, but the tale is of how Norse King Hrothgar recruits the hero Beowulf to rescue the village from the horrible monster Grendel. Beowulf defeats and kills Grendel, to the great relief of the townsfolk.

However, during the victory celebration, there is a dreadful cry, and the even more terrible Grendel's mother comes to seek revenge on the town and Beowulf. Beowulf and Grendel's mother fight and, struggling, fall deep down into the lake into Grendel's mother's lair. There, Beowulf's sword and shield melt away and are powerless against Grendel's mother's assault. As Grendel's mother attacks, Beowulf, without weapons or protection, is at mortal risk and eventually is injured. Desperate, Beowulf spies a sword on the wall of the monster's lair, which he seizes and slays Grendel's mother.

The more profound message here is that sometimes in life, the knowledge, skills, and abilities that guided us on our journeys, helped us succeed, and defended us until now may no longer be appropriate or adequate for the new challenges ahead. This is a trial that many of us have had when starting a new role that either entails considerable new skills or a significant jump in responsibility. We must take heart, have courage, reinvent ourselves, and forge ahead to find and learn appropriate new skills and solutions.[87]

I remind you of David's powerful story and message about the friends of the heart and friends of the road. Of course, we love and value our friends of the heart, but they are few and far between. However, friends of the road are enormously important in life and particularly in business. As the tale goes: "If you find yourself in the mountains of Afghanistan in the middle of the night, during a fierce storm, with the wind whistling, wolfs howling, and bandits prowling, you can be extremely thankful for the friends of the road, who can help keep watch at night, mind your possessions and guard your back."[88]

We often spend ten hours a day or more at work, and with commutes and sleep, we frequently spend more waking time with our work colleagues than with our family or friends. Consequently, working collegially, effectively, and even enjoyably with our friends of the road is incredibly important for a healthy and happy work/life balance. This is more satisfying and rewarding than only expecting to live and enjoy your life while off work on evenings and weekends.

While I love and value my family and friends, my work colleagues at Accenture, TUI, PwC, Reuters, and AMEX also enriched my career and my life enormously. Throughout our many shared missions, labors, and journeys, my life and career would have been dreadfully diminished without these fabulous friends of the road. Unfortunately, this traditional work-based support system is one of the clear casualties of the new COVID-19-induced remote working and work-from-home phenomenon.

Whyte quotes Dante and uses Pablo Neruda, T. S. Eliot, and his own poems to find and provide solace in the trials and tribulations of our work lives. He provides insights, motivation, and guidance to help us find our "real path" and to rekindle our spirit.

> *In the middle of the road of my life, I awoke in a dark wood where the true way was wholly lost*
> —Dante, *La Divina Commedia.*

Whyte tells the story of a senior executive at one of his conferences. She lamented: "I turned my head for a moment, and it became my life." She regretted a decision twenty years previously, when under pressure, she accepted an unattractive short-term assignment. This role evolved; one thing led to another, and it morphed to the extent it eventually consumed her career and even derailed her personal life. Sadly, this situation is far too common. Through various circumstances, people feel trapped in a role where their job or career is unhappily, decidedly misaligned with who they are and their personal goals and aspirations.[89] This is precisely the dilemma that many have confronted during the enforced self-reflection caused by the COVID-19 pandemic lockdowns and subsequent remote working experiences. In such a case, one must reset their compass and relocate their north star to redirect their career to better align with dreams and desires.

I also recommend Whyte's *Crossing the Unknown Sea*,[90] a modern business take on Joseph Campbell's profound and powerful "hero's journey" mythology from *The Hero with a Thousand Faces*,[91] which in turn was derived from *The Odyssey* by Homer. It is also thought-provoking for those of us who, through overseas assignments, have spent years or decades apart from family and friends back home. It vividly calls out to us to reconnect with our life's real purpose, heal our past, and craft careers that nourish, not harm, our personal lives, colleagues, friends, and family.

Takeaway: We all have separate business and personal lives. However, to the extent that we can align our roles and work life with our personal values, we will be more productive, happier, and healthier overall. We may spend forty to sixty of our weekly waking hours with colleagues at work. Thus, developing strong, mutually supportive relationships with our work "friends of the road" is vital to our overall quality of life.

Jim Collins

92

My introduction to Jim Collins came at a three-day internal strategy workshop while at Interactive Investor in London during my dot-com years. The consultant hired to facilitate our session provocatively introduced us to Jim's concept of a BHAG (big hairy audacious goal) from his book *Built to Last*.[93] This idea of creating a momentous "stretch goal" intrigued me and has often inspired me to strive to reach well beyond the typical corporate annual target objectives.

To create a true BHAG when setting professional or personal goals, imagine a dramatic but almost impossible long-term ambition. What is your personal or organizational Everest? Consider a moon-shot-level goal that will surprise, inspire, and galvanize your team around a passionate objective. A challenge and target of this magnitude will overshadow the minutia of daily routines, exciting and exhilarating everyone's efforts. As Jim stresses in his following book, *Good to Great*, if you complacently accept good, you will never achieve great. This brings to mind a great David Schwartz quote from *The Magic of Thinking Big*: "Most people fail in life not because they aim too high and miss. But because they aim too low and hit!"[94]

Perhaps it was because of my lack of traditional risk adversity, but having taken some bold chances and risks in my life and career taught me that sometimes, not always, but occasionally, big, ambitious, seemingly impossible things manifest. But if you don't step up to the plate and go to bat, nothing happens!

There are a number of essential concepts derived from the extensive research that went into *Built to Last*. First and fundamental to the success of companies that not only survive but thrive is that they are founded and sustained by core ideologies. These are based on principled values and a key sense of purpose transcending short-term objectives, such as revenue generation and market share. Further, these overriding values and the sense of purpose develop into what Collins describes as almost a cultlike corporate culture that reinforces those values and the corporate mission. A good example is: "Google's mission is to organize the world's information and make it universally accessible and useful."

An additional nuance to the successful companies identified in *Built to Last* was that these companies benefited from and actively encouraged staff and management development from within the organization. Home-growing internal talent has the combined benefits of enhanced staff motivation, preserving the corporate culture and values, providing an essential continuity of organizational knowledge, and ensuring effective management succession planning.

Collins stresses the clear benefits of simultaneously and inclusively preserving the corporate core values and stimulating progress and innovation. He states that long-term successful visionary companies embrace both ends of the spectrum of continuity and change, stability and evolution, and predictability and transformation, creating both a stable, successful company and one that is progressive and innovative.[95] A current serious BHAG would be SpaceX's mission, summarized by the statement: "Making Humanity Multiplanetary"; it doesn't get much grander or bolder than that, yet Elon Musk & Co. are already taking concrete steps to fulfill that dream.

Collins's next book, *Good to Great: Why Some Companies Make the Leap . . . And Others Don't*[96] in 2001, was also a timely book for me, after I had been caught up in the 2000 dot-com collapse and subsequent recession. I'd jumped from AOL to Worldsport Networks in March 2000, two weeks before the stock market crash, and I found myself managing Worldsport's inevitable decline into oblivion when funding dried up. After another short stint with a new media private equity firm in Singapore, I became increasingly skeptical of the current prospects in start-ups. There were many factors, but one was my self-reflection when reading *Good to Great* about where to place my career bets for the future. Ultimately, I chose the safe course and jumped from the tumultuous dot-com world to a stable role in a highly successful technology con-sulting role at PricewaterhouseCoopers Menlo Park Technology Think Tank. It was the right decision at that point in time.

Some of the key learnings from *Good to Great* are:

What Collins calls level 5 leadership is all about "servant leader-ship," exceptional leaders who are not only highly ambitious and driven but also humble and modest. These successful leaders are authentically focused on the team and the task rather than on their career and personal agenda. These leaders set the right tone and culture for employee empow-erment and motivation and are thus rewarded with solid team support, collaboration, and outstanding results.

His second critical lesson is, "Get the right people on the bus!" In other words, above all else, start with *who* instead of *what* and ensure you have the right team and in the right jobs. The idea is simple but pow-erful. In the complex and dynamic marketplace we work in, you never know what challenges lie ahead. If you have the right team, you will be as prepared as possible to confront those challenges and adapt to change. Further, you will already have aligned, self-directed teams who will assist rather than impede any required change of strategy or direction. Finally, the right people will do the right things for the right reasons.

To reinforce Collins's point on the right team, the highly success-ful creation of our new IT organization during the TUI three-company carve-out was achieved because we decided to recruit the senior team and most of the staff exclusively internally from within the parent companies. This experienced, aligned, and acclimated team hit the ground running instantly and knew exactly what was needed.

Collins's next essential message is of needing to "confront the brutal facts!" Don't live in denial, delude yourself that things will automatically resolve themselves, or be naively optimistic. Certainly, we need to be pos-itive and enthusiastic. However, don't be blindsided by false hopes and unrealistic expectations. As we will discuss and model in detailed case studies later, it is always decidedly better to recognize any risks or chal-lenges and deal with them decisively and as soon as possible. This relates equally to products and systems as well as people. It is a fact of life that problems invariably get worse over time and occasionally can become unresolvable if left to fester and exacerbate.

He further makes the strong case that companies that move from good to great are frequently based on successful companies that define and fervently focus on what they are best at, what they are passionate about, and how to drive economic benefit.

Perhaps it goes without saying, but it is essential for organizations to be focused and highly disciplined. Disciplined action is one of the cultural cornerstones that helps ensure the transition to greatness. He uses the flywheel analogy, where dedicated, small, consistent actions eventually turn the flywheel faster until it glides virtually in perpetual motion. This is particularly true of new transformational ideas such as the usability mission we kick-started at Reuters, where a small idea eventually grew to achieve critical mass and began a user-friendly systems transformation.

Collins's books benefit from his robust observational insights, an extensive team of rigorous researchers, and data-based recommendations. Recent and equally influential are Collins's newer books: *Great by Choice* & *BE 2.0 (Beyond Entrepreneurship 2.0)*.

Takeaway: "The greatest leaders we've studied, cared as much about values as victory, as much about purpose as profit, as much about being useful as being successful. Their drive and standards are ultimately internal, rising from somewhere deep inside."

—Jim Collins, *Great by Choice*[97]

Daniel Goleman

98

Dan Goleman's 1995 book *Emotional Intelligence*[99] was a trailblazer for this emerging field and was a big eye-opener for the management community. Goleman didn't say it first but perhaps said it best in this book, catching the essence of the moment and helping to create and perpetuate this new emotional intelligence meme.

In my experience, this was a watershed moment when businesses finally virtually closed the book on what McGregor called Theory X, command and control-style management. By this time, many business psychologists, researchers, and consultants had begun to recognize that there was a whole class of personal, social, emotional, nonintellectual "soft" skills required alongside traditional management skills and methods.

Thereafter, it was recognized almost overnight that in modern corporations, high intelligence, adequate technical skills, and appropriate experience were no longer sufficient in and of themselves to inspire, motivate, and lead high-potential knowledge workers. In today's work environment, without highly evolved emotional intelligence, managers may be incapable, inadequate, and insecure and thus be prone to anxiety, frustration, and emotional outbursts, and experience ineffective interactions and communications with staff. Further, a manager with low emotional intelligence will have difficulties hiring and retaining high-quality staff, building cohesive teams, and motivating employees.

Today, we know and accept that an effective leader/manager must possess high emotional intelligence. It coexists alongside traditional aspects of quick-witted intellect, sharp technical skills, and extensive experience to be accepted and effective as a leader of intelligent, self-motivated, career-oriented, and self-actualizing staff.

If you reflect on your work experience, it won't take long to identify previous managers or colleagues with very high and low emotional intelligence. Of course, no one is perfect, but each of us can dedicate ourselves continually to improving our skills and abilities, especially our emotional intelligence. The key is to be consciously aware of your capabilities and temperament and develop mature emotional intelligence along with the rest of your professional expertise.

Goleman and other analysts have extensively documented and established the fact that emotional intelligence is now one of the critical leadership secret sauces essential to developing and leading high-performing teams, particularly in the digital age.

Takeaway: To become a successful senior leader who is valued and supported by colleagues and staff in business today, your highly developed people skills and emotional intelligence are equally important as intellect, technical skills, and experience.

David O. Ulrich

100

Dr. Ulrich is a university professor, management consultant, and author. He has written over thirty books on human resources, organizational development, and leadership and is regarded by many as the father of modern human resources.

His book *The Leadership Code: Five Rules to Lead By*[101] is highly useful for aspiring leaders. He and his team systematically researched the existing body of leadership literature and compiled a synthesis of the leading frameworks, tools, processes, and leadership studies. From that research, they have distilled the research into a straightforward but thought-provoking model of five fundamental rules to lead by, *The Leadership Code*. Following is a summary of those five rules; however, I recommend this book as this summary introduces the key topics, and *The Leadership Code* provides extensive research to support these five rules and effective habits.

Rule 1: Shape the Future
Leaders are responsible for setting the direction of their company, team, and career. They are strategists who conceive the vision, plot the path, and organize the resources and activities to execute the strategy and plan.

Rule 2: Make Things Happen
With the vision, strategy, and plan in place, the leader is both the strategist and the person making it happen. They translate the

strategy into a plan and put the plan into operation. Then, they take responsibility for leading the teams and executing and delivering on the strategic objectives.

Rule 3: Engage Today's Talent

No executive can deliver the business plan single-handedly; they must rely on the coordinated efforts of many people. A key leadership responsibility is the identification of what skills are required, the selection and recruitment of top-caliber people, and the creation of a cohesive, motivated, and high-performing team.

Rule 4: Build the Next Generation

Along with identifying and building a great team, a good leader continues to mentor, train, and develop their team for future business skill requirements and the team members' benefit. One must upskill and reskill talent over time to bring in new cutting-edge skills to ensure the organization stays competitive and transforms with new technologies and business models.

Rule 5: Invest in Yourself

Fundamentally, to be and remain the best leader you can be, you must continuously develop your knowledge, skills, and talent. This can be achieved by avid reading, taking executive education classes, attending continuing education courses, and through life experience. A well-rounded leader is intellectually and emotionally mature, both professionally and personally. Only then will you have the ability you need to be successful now and in the future. Therefore, continuously challenge yourself to avoid becoming complacent and continually grow and develop new skills. This habit will help your business career and be an excellent role model for your colleagues and teams.

This last habit is fundamental to long-term successful career development, particularly to stay sharp and relevant as one enters middle age and the later stages of one's career. This ensures your expertise, experience, and career advance throughout your working life rather than declining toward the end of your career. Your final working years should be the pinnacle of your career instead of being a slippery slope toward redundancy or early retirement.

Sheryl Sandberg, former COO of Facebook, firmly reinforces the same view of investing in yourself through lifelong learning with her quote: "The ability to learn is the most important quality a leader can have."[102]

The Leadership Code provides extensive research, helpful insights, and countless practical tips for emerging high-caliber leaders.[103]

Takeaway: To be the best leader you can be and remain relevant in a changing world, continuously develop and advance your knowledge and skills. Make a permanent habit of researching and studying the latest trends and technologies, even if they are beyond the scope of your current role. These emerging ideas and tools may be vital in the future or even represent a new career opportunity.

Tom Peters

104

Tom Peters is one of my personal favorites and most influential leadership gurus. I have followed him for decades since his groundbreaking book *In Search of Excellence*,[105] which almost single-handedly kick-started the business book genre phenomenon.

Over the years, I've received tremendous benefit from his forceful messages, authoritative and insightful analysis, and forward-thinking, radical approach to reinventing or reimagining business.

Along with *In Search of Excellence*, I've read his first six books listed below, all of which are still worth a review:

1982—*In Search of Excellence* (with Robert Waterman)
1985—*A Passion for Excellence* (with Nancy Austin)
1987—*Thriving on Chaos*
1992—*Liberation Management*
1994—*Crazy Times Call for Crazy Organizations*
1994—*The Pursuit of WOW!*

While his career and writing have evolved over the past forty years, as has business, I've always enjoyed his passionate, iconoclastic, and captivating messages. Some critics might say that he is the king of the soundbites, but I've always found those soundbites to be powerful messaging that resonates with me as they generally touch a raw nerve that needs to be tweaked or jolted. Within those soundbites and vignettes are potent leadership messages and stories.

First is his consistent message, a bias for action; in other words, get on with it! Many problems occur from inaction or delayed action that either miss an opportunity entirely or compromise the solution due to changing conditions as a result of the delayed response. Analysis paralysis is one of his pet peeves.

The second would be to stay close to the customer. So many problems, missed opportunities, failures of execution, and delivery all stem back to a poor understanding of the customer and their needs in the first place. While the world and his work have changed over the years, these eight principles are still rich and timeless. Summarized in my words:

1. **A bias for action**: take action, avoid analysis paralysis, and get on with it.
2. **Stay close to the customer**: talk to, learn from, and develop solutions for your customers.
3. **Autonomy and entrepreneurialism**: encourage independence and innovation.
4. **Productivity through people**: inspire, encourage, and support people and teams.
5. **Hands-on**: stay involved with your products and teams to stay current and demonstrate commitment.
6. **Stick to the knitting**: respect your core businesses, leverage core competencies, and don't stray too far.
7. **Simple structure, lean teams**: eliminate bureaucracy, strip out redundant layers.
8. **Concurrent loose-tight models**: foster local freedom within a centrally agreed framework.[106]

Peters has always been dramatic, provocative, and pushing the envelope. You love him or hate him, but undoubtedly, he changed the field of leadership and management consulting from being a backroom, doughty, academic research discipline to becoming a high-profile, high-profit, media-friendly, mainstream discipline.

While running the Reuters Group Usability and Design Labs as a Virtual Team, I met Peters various times over the years and collaborated with him on various articles in his *In Search of Excellence* publication, the *Financial Times,* and *Sunday Times.*

Following is a case study elaborating on my experiences and collaborations with Tom Peters and his team.

Takeaway: Be decisive and take action, even if it means delegating a decision or action to another. Being the "go-to person" who gets things done, in one way or another, will become a vital part of your professional persona. Your ability to lead, inspire, and work with and through people in teams is the key to highly leveraged productivity.

Reuters Virtual Team

A breakthrough opportunity happened to me while attending a Tom Peters conference at the Brewery Conference Centre in London. At one point, Peters began an impassioned speech about thinking differently, breaking down the rules of monolithic organizations, and espousing anarchic approaches to destroying bureaucracy. "Think outside the box, break the rules, blur the boundaries. . . . You need to throw out your policy manual and trash the current procedures; it's a whole new anarchic world we are entering," he bellowed.

Having arrived that morning from New York in a jet-lagged but fortuitous lapse of decorum, I intervened and interrupted his presentation. I interjected and countered: "No, I disagree; that doesn't work! You still need guidelines, just new guidelines. We've been running a virtual team of about one hundred consultants from six companies for over a year. We jettisoned all our individual corporate policies but had to create new common harmonized ones by which all virtual team members would be guided." With such a diverse group of people and suppliers, everyone needed to know how to operate. We parlayed back and forth until he stopped and, with exuberance, exclaimed to the crowd: "Excellent, that's right, that's the way you need to do it," and invited me to lunch in front of some five hundred attendees.

We chatted over lunch, and he suggested we write up the Reuters Virtual Team Case Study for his newsletter, *On Achieving Excellence*. So, I went home that night, drafted a summary of how we were working, and presented it to him the next morning at breakfast. He was intrigued and enthusiastic about our approach, and we agreed to collaborate on the article. We met a few times and published several features along with his editor, Des Dearlove:

- Tom Peters's Newsletter *On Achieving Excellence*
- *Financial Times* article "Cherry Picking Top Talent"
- *Sunday Times* article "Making Sure the News Gets Through"

See Appendix II for copies of these articles.

Tom generously credited me through these publications as the person who conceived and pioneered virtual working, at least in Europe. This attention subsequently expanded from an interest in virtual teaming to our work in our Usability Group and Design Labs. These two topics kept me busy on the conference circuit alongside my full-time role for a number of years.

These activities continued off and on for a time and aided somewhat in my being appointed as a Technology Futurist and IT Strategy Director at PwC's Menlo Park Europe Technology Think Tank. This period was perhaps my initial "fifteen minutes of fame."[107]

Having now architected the leadership landscape and examined the foundational theories and thinking of the preeminent leadership gurus from the past and present, let's explore the elements and attributes of leadership character and its fundamental characteristics.

Key Takeaways—Standing on the Shoulders of Giants

- John Kotter is known for Business Transformation in *A Sense of Urgency* with his 8-Step Process for Leading Change. He stresses leadership and management are essential and complementary roles.
- Rosabeth Moss Kanter is a staunch advocate of "investing in staff, staff training, and creative HR practices." In her book *The Change Masters*, she outlines 11 key ideas for initiating and fostering change.
- James Kouzes & Barry Posner's book *Leadership Challenge* outlines a conceptual model for leadership, including: "Model the Way, Inspire a Vision, Challenge Processes, Enable Others, and Encourage Heart."
- Stephen Covey was most famous for his book *The 7 Habits of Highly Effective People*: 1: Be Proactive 2: Start with the end result 3: First things first 4: Win-Win 5: Seek to understand 6: Synergize! 7: Growth.
- Dan Goleman's book *Emotional Intelligence* advocated a whole new class of personal, social, emotional, and non-intellectual "soft skills" required to lead post-industrial age knowledge workers.

CHAPTER 4

Constructs of Character:
Foundations and Pillars of Success

Leadership Character

Thus far, our focus and task have been to examine the overall leadership landscape, its vision and purpose, leadership styles and overarching leadership concept pillars and principles, including leading with the heart, emotional intelligence, motivation, quality, ethics, and values. Further, we have studied the predominant thinking and theories of foremost leadership and management thinkers.

These broad, sweeping themes have set the stage and fundamental parameters for the following field of inquiry into the character and nature of successful leaders and their effective leadership traits and characteristics.

What are the attributes, traits, and behaviors that comprise a high-caliber leader? We will shortly explore such specific qualities as integrity, trust, empathy, optimism, perseverance, and many more. However, to distill all these leadership traits down into one defining concept and statement, it is that exceptional leaders have "character."

Character means different things to different people; however, in my view, it is an amalgam or synthesis of many of the following twenty crucial leadership characteristics.

Some leaders are highly visionary, some more diplomatic, and others inspirational. However, to be optimally effective, leaders must possess a critical mass of these positive attributes, values, and moral characteristics to be considered to have sufficient strength of character to lead, inspire, persevere, and succeed.

Character, therefore, is a distinguishing high-level description of leadership. Without it, one is unlikely to have the charisma, grit, and courage to gain the trust of, motivate, and guide teams of individuals to be successful and satisfied over the long run.

The incredible story of the Antarctic shipwreck of the HMS *Endurance* and the two-year (1914–1916) survival journey of Sir Ernest Shackleton and his crew is a phenomenal tale and a masterclass of leadership, character, and teamwork.

I was struck by Shackleton's entry in his ship's log "South": "I confess that I felt the burden of responsibility sit heavily on my shoulders; but, on the other hand, I was stimulated and cheered by the attitude of the men. Loneliness is the penalty of leadership, but the man who has to make the decisions is assisted greatly if he feels that there is no uncertainty in the minds of those who follow him and that his orders will be carried out confidently and in expectation of success."[1]

Shackleton's comment about the burden of responsibility clearly arises from his responsibility as captain but also from his recognition that his enthusiasm and obsession for the journey had initially clouded his judgment, leading to the fundamentally flawed decision to proceed by disregarding expert warnings of historic poor weather.

Beyond this critical lesson in prudent, informed decision-making, his subsequent rising to the extreme challenge of surviving two years in the Antarctic after the loss of his ship and eventually saving his entire crew highlights multiple critical leadership characteristics that contributed to his and their success.

First, he possessed an *indefatigable will* to survive, which translated into *unshakeable optimism*, instilling *critical confidence* in his crew.

Coupled with this will, courage, and optimism, he met the challenge, took vital, *timely decisions*, clearly *communicated the vision and purpose* to survive, and *set essential objectives and tasks* at critical junctures.

Further, given the constantly changing dynamics of the harsh Antarctic environment, including weather and temperature, he courageously and continuously *adapted and executed* his strategies.

Finally, *he inspired, encouraged, and motivated his team* to maintain hope, survive, and persevere despite the crew's awareness of the seemingly insurmountable challenges throughout.

These critical leadership characteristics and actions won the crew's *fierce loyalty*, realizing their *unquestioned commitment* to his directives and instructions.

Accounts of Shackleton's phenomenal leadership and endurance epic make for an inspiring and informative study of this exceptional leader.

Character is about having sufficient positive leadership traits and behaviors, coupled with a personal ethos and empathy for the team's welfare, to earn genuine reciprocal leadership trust and staff loyalty.

Let's examine in detail the twenty key characteristics that underpin leadership character.

Leadership Characteristics

In my research on leadership, I've studied leadership characteristics as defined by leaders, academics, trainers, and staff. I had hoped to develop a consensus list of the top ten attributes of what constitutes a good leader.

As it turns out, it is much more complicated than that. Perhaps that is why there are some fifteen thousand books on the topic. After my initial exploration, consolidation, and elimination of those characteristics I deemed primarily management skills rather than leadership skills—remember management is about directing, operating, and controlling an organization while leadership is about creating a vision, setting goals, and inspiring and motivating teams—I came up with the following consolidated list of eighty-eight characteristics:

Accountability	Action	Adaptable	Altruism
Ambition	Assertive	Authenticity	Belief
Bold	Caring	Change Agent	Character
Charisma	Coach	Commitment	Compassion
Confidence	Communicator	Conviction	Cooperation
Courage	Creativity	Credibility	Curious
Decision Maker	Decisiveness	Dedicated	Delegation
Dependability	Determination	Diplomacy	Discernment
Drive	Emotional Intel	Empathy	Empowerment
Encouraging	Energy	Enthusiastic	Ethical
Facilitator	Fairness	Focus	Foresight
Heart	Honesty	Hopeful	Humility
Humor	Influence	Initiative	Inspirational
Integrity	Intuitive	Judgment	Knowledge
Listening	Loyalty	Mindfulness	Morals
Motivation	Nurturing	Open-minded	Optimism
	Passion	Patience	

Consolidated list of 88 characteristics.

This comprises a fascinating but not very helpful list to provide memorable guidance for aspiring leaders. Clearly, there is some overlap and redundancy in similar concepts, which provided an opportunity for rationalization. Thus, I worked carefully through the list to identify and crystallize the most important and essential characteristics that resonated with me from my years on the ground, on the front lines, and experience as a leader and manager.

The following short list of twenty characteristics, in my research and experience, represents the most crucial and indispensable characteristics and behaviors of exceptional leaders. No one is perfect nor possesses all the following attributes in equal quantity or quality; however, this is an excellent aspirational list for talented leaders.

Leadership Skill Categories

Integrity	Purpose	Judgment	Courage
Empathy	Passion	Diplomacy	Confidence
Visionary	Enthusiasm	Decisiveness	Commitment
Authenticity	Inspirational	Perseverance	Communicative
Trust	Optimism	Reliability	Creativity

This prominent and authoritative compilation provides a concise and definitive synopsis of leadership characteristics comprising "leadership character."

It will be further beneficial to leaders to classify the twenty characteristics into four related categories to create an effective and memorable
mental model of leadership.

I've structured these four category groups to represent distinctly different but equally important types of characteristics and behaviors. These
include *innate personality* characteristics; some are *emotional drivers*, others are *intellectual capabilities*, and the remainder represent acquired or
learned behaviors.

INNATE	EMOTIONAL	INTELLECTUAL	LEARNED
Integrity	Purpose	Judgment	Courage
Empathy	Passion	Diplomacy	Confidence
Visionary	Enthusiasm	Decisiveness	Commitment
Authenticity	Inspirational	Perseverance	Communicative
Trust	Optimism	Reliability	Creativity

We can plot these four categories onto a matrix to dissect them to
provide clarity and enhance understanding. Thus, we create a vector for
the *Cognitive* criterion on the vertical X-axis and the *Behavioral* criterion
on the horizontal Y-axis. Then, we can also model the *Developmental*
criterion as a 45-degree diagonal trajectory. This gives us the following
four-quadrant matrix.[2]

Hudson – Garrison
Leadership Characteristics Matrix

Cognitive — *Development* — **Behavioural**

Three Vectors – Cognitive, Behavioural, Development

Leadership Characteristics Matrix—Three Vectors.

We can then map our four Leadership Skill Categories into the appropriate quadrants based on the cognitive, behavioral, and developmental criteria in the matrix as follows:[3]

Hudson – Garrison
Leadership Characteristics Matrix

Leadership Characteristics Matrix—Four Quadrants

If we now analyze these four leadership skill categories further, we see that each of these criteria represents four distinct important leadership *drivers*:

The *Innate* Character traits are *Essential* Leadership elements.
Emotional Character traits are important Leadership *Empowerers*.
The *Intellectual* Character traits are powerful Leadership *Enablers*.
The *Learned* Character traits become Leadership *Enhancers*.[4]

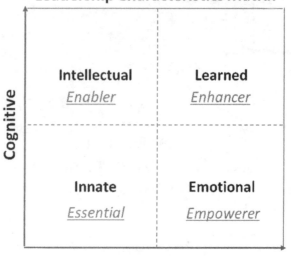

Leadership Characteristics Matrix—Four E's

Bringing the leadership criteria together and mapping all the leadership skill characteristics into this matrix provides a powerful holistic leadership model.

This matrix model helps us understand the quintessential leadership characteristics and behaviors and provides a memorable leadership model to understand and develop a more complete, well-rounded, and effective leadership profile and capability.[5]

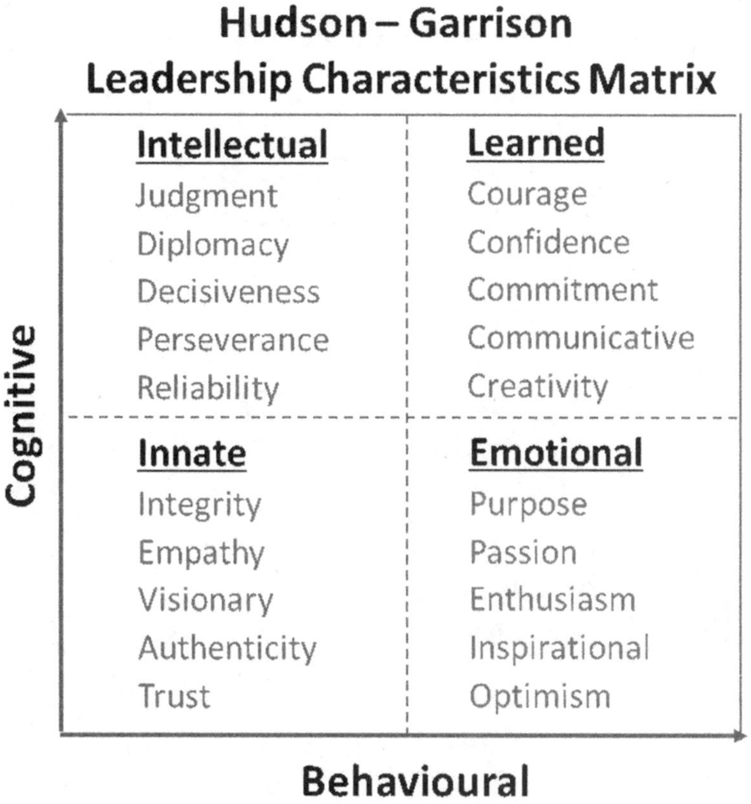
Hudson – Garrison
Leadership Characteristics Matrix
Intellectual
Judgment
Diplomacy
Decisiveness
Perseverance
Reliability
Learned
Courage
Confidence
Commitment
Communicative
Creativity
Innate
Integrity
Empathy
Visionary
Authenticity
Trust
Emotional
Purpose
Passion
Enthusiasm
Inspirational
Optimism
Cognitive
Behavioural

Leadership Characteristics Matrix—Full populated matrix

The First Five: Innate Leadership Traits

Integrity, empathy, vision, authenticity, and trust represent fundamental and indispensable "innate" personal leadership characteristics stemming from deep-seated imprinting and learning derived from family history, familial culture–based ethics, and values. Of course, they will vary by individual depending on upbringing; nevertheless, these attributes represent highly developed human behaviors and ethos that resonate with the human heart, spirit, and conscience. Further, as we all have these in different measure, our opportunity and challenge is to develop these further to strengthen the skills that we already possess.[6]

Hudson – Garrison
Leadership Characteristics Matrix

Leadership Characteristics Matrix—Innate Characteristics

Integrity

The supreme quality for leadership is unquestionably integrity. Without it, no real success is possible.
—Dwight D. Eisenhower, thirty-fourth US president[7]

First and foremost on my list of critical leadership characteristics is integrity. In my view, it is the preeminent and pervasive character value that an exceptional leader must possess. Leading with integrity means striving to be guided by the highest possible level of ethical, honorable, and moral behavior in everything you do, every interaction you have, and each decision you make.

Colleagues and staff expect and even demand an authentic leader who advocates and demonstrates intrinsic and consistent principles of integrity. Further, integrity is the fundamental basis of the leadership/staff trust equation. The leader's integrity and ethical behavior set the tone and culture for the organization and, in turn, influence employee/staff attitudes, behaviors, and commitment.

Life and business are constantly full of challenges and sometimes necessary compromises. One is often confronted with decisions that can potentially challenge and clash with one's sense of fairness and ethics. Nevertheless, if you are true to yourself, truthful with others, and virtuous in demonstrating behaviors that promote integrity, trust, and benevolence, you are unlikely to go very wrong in your decisions and dealings with others. If you are guided by the principles of integrity that are consistent with your ethics and values, it is probable that the outcome or the end result will generally be the best possible solution in the long run.

As mentioned, in my very first job at American Express, during my management training orientation, I was particularly struck and impressed when told of the company motto: "If it is against the law, against company policy, or against your conscience, DON'T DO IT!" Ever since, that simple and straightforward ethical statement has stuck with me as a rock-solid cornerstone of professional integrity. I have repeated this mantra countless times since to my colleagues and subordinates.

I'll share a personal incident regarding professional integrity as a contrarian learning experience. It's not an earthshaking example, but it is a poignant illustration of a minor decision that had significant career implications and is, therefore, a valuable exemplar of leadership integrity. Years ago, at a multinational, I submitted a business case for a global initiative to train all worldwide staff on new financial procedures. This major program was agreed upon by my SVP boss. Upon approval, I began the project mobilization, but the launch got stalled, and I spent weeks trying unsuccessfully to get authorization to kick off the program. Then, unexpectedly, I read an executive leadership monthly report regarding this project's timely and successful completion. Outraged, as this program was critical for all overseas offices, I wrote a rebuttal to various management, stating that this was incorrect. Further, we had not even started the project. When called to New York in a confrontation with my superior, she admitted she had diverted the funds to cover a separate pet project that was going off the rails.

This was perhaps her prerogative; however, no one had been advised, agreed to the change, or put in place contingency plans. Further, the pet project's failure and the non-delivery of the training program were covered up. She had publicly falsified the truth and, critically, left the overseas offices and customers floundering with out-of-date policies and procedures. Finally, in frustration and resignation, she stated somewhat reflectively, "Greg, I fully expected to be long gone before this came to light!" Because of this breach of protocol, she lost considerable credibility in a company that was rigorously managed with high integrity, and she was eventually reassigned to another role. It was a needless and senseless decision and mistake that could have been easily avoided had she simply acted with honesty and integrity.

In business and life, one always assumes that any comment, action, or decision you take can and will always echo or bounce back, either to reinforce you positively or haunt you negatively. As we've seen above, even a minor infraction can have significant consequences.

We often have challenges in the complex business arena where multiple conflicting variables complicate decisions. In these cases, try to deconstruct the decisions into discrete ethical, economic, legal, political, market, staff, and customer dimensions. Then, sit back with a holistic perspective, consider all aspects, and take the long view of the situation, considering the inherent integrity and outcomes of the available options.

Be honest with yourself, listen to your conscience, and overtly state the likely obvious, correct, principled alternative. Then, weigh the other factors against this "integrity barometer" to make a conscious, informed decision recognizing all parameters and the potential consequences. Even if eventually proven wrong, those actions made with integrity will be understandable and justifiable in the context of a decision or action made with the appropriate ethical and moral intent.

Therefore, we can position integrity as a foundational cornerstone of character, underpinning and imbuing our strategies, plans, decisions, and actions with honesty, ethics, and morality. Moreover, this creates a culture of trust and confidence in the leader on behalf of colleagues, partners, customers, and employees.

Only a moment of personal reflection will likely resonate with you as you recall times in your life, career, or even public life or politics when integrity has been exhibited or violated. This will reinforce your appreciation of the criticality of leadership integrity for staff trust, loyalty, and motivation, leading to personal self-esteem, self-confidence, and a clear conscience.

With our character "cornerstone" of integrity fixed securely in place, let's construct the other building blocks of innate leadership characteristics.

Takeaway: As leaders, we frequently must stand up for our beliefs. Listen to your conscience and heart, coupled with your learned behaviors based on ethics and principles, and you'll be unlikely to go wrong with any decision or action. Your personal integrity establishes your credibility and models appropriate behaviors for your staff.

Empathy

Real empathy is sometimes not insisting that it will be okay but acknowledging that it is not.
—Sheryl Sandberg, former chief operating officer of Facebook[8]

Empathy is my second selection for critical personal leadership characteristics, as it is crucial to leadership as an essential prerequisite for the leader's bonding with their team. Axiomatically, without bonding, there is no leading.

Certainly, a manager can issue a directive to an employee and expect them to comply with and carry out the request. However, as you all appreciate, there is a big difference between obediently following a directive and being inspired and motivated to achieve a task. When a leader has genuine empathy for coworkers, those colleagues feel a justifiable sense of loyalty toward the leader, whom they know will have, whenever possible, their best interests at heart. With this empathetic leadership, the staff member and leader have a symbiotic, self-reinforcing, and mutually beneficial relationship. It then logically follows that the probability of a productive and profitable team and organization increases dramatically with a collaborative and tightly aligned reciprocal leader and staff relationship.

I have recounted on numerous occasions that with the strength of the relationships with some of my teams, I've sensed that if I metaphorically were to grab a banner and charge up a hill, I wouldn't need to look back; I would know without a doubt that my team would be charging right along beside me. Why? Because I knew that they knew I was as committed to them as they were to me. There were many reasons for this bond, but perhaps principally, it was due to mutually shared empathy and reciprocal concern and commitment.

Empathy can take many forms and at varying degrees, from attentive listening, sensing colleagues' concerns, training or guiding employees to perform to the best of their ability, mentoring them to develop further in their career, or earnestly sympathizing or empathizing with a personal or professional difficulty.

Critically, empathy must be genuine and spontaneous, or it could be interpreted as insincere and might be discredited and discounted.

However, authentic empathy is not only relationship building as a fundamental leadership skill, but it also makes good business sense. An astute leader knows an individual can only accomplish so much alone and that any substantial program requires many people's efforts. Moreover, the extra time it takes to manage, mentor properly, and empathize with staff will be repaid many times over and multiplied by the actions of a highly motivated team all pulling together in the same direction.

Frequently in the past, I've made a genuine special effort and a personal investment with various employees, sometimes well beyond what might be expected in a typical leadership mentoring role. Subsequently, although it was not my overt objective, I have seen a highly supportive reciprocal response on their part in their "going the second mile" to assist me and contribute to our overall team effort.

While there have been many examples like this over the years, one, in particular, comes to mind. While this is not an earthshaking issue, it was highly significant to the person involved. Remember, leadership and empathy are often about the seemingly small things we do daily that ultimately can make a meaningful difference in an individual's life.

While engaged in a major yearlong development project, one high-performing team member's behavior suddenly changed from cheerful and upbeat to somber and withdrawn. This was a notable and dramatic change in behavior that persisted for some days. Rather than pointing out the change in performance, I took her aside and asked if everything was okay and if I could help in any way. She then emotionally shared a personal incident that clearly explained the behavior change. She was relieved to have a trusted personal confidant and leader to share the issue with, which apparently helped to lighten the load.

Further, it at least took the job pressure off her, which, as a typically highly dedicated person, was adding to her anxiety. I suggested she take a week off, and she countered with a week at home but still fulfilling the same tasks. The week of rest and recuperation helped; she delivered her work during her absence and returned to the office refreshed and rejuvenated. The small gesture of empathy helped her personally and professionally to revive her spirit and help her get back on track in delivering exceptional performance on the project.

These sensitive and sympathetic interactions must be authentic, honest, and spontaneous, as you can't fake or force empathy. If you allow your humanity to shine through in your professional behavior, especially with genuine caring and compassion, you will strengthen the relationship bond with your team. These types of supportive connections and relationships are the personal and mutually rewarding moments we work and live for.

Takeaway: We often hear someone say that person is empathetic. However, we all have empathy; it is just how and where we express it. For example, most people are empathetic with their families and children. Allow your natural love and empathy for people to shine through in your relationships and actions with colleagues and staff, and they will reciprocate, respect, and support you.

Visionary

If you are working on something exciting that you really care about, you don't have to be pushed. The vision pulls you.
— *Steve Jobs, former chairman and CEO, Apple Inc.*[9]

The leader's responsibility is to create and communicate a powerful vision for the team and the organization. Toward that end, we discussed setting a vision with a purpose extensively in chapter 1. Shifting our perspective, let's explore the concept of visionary as an intrinsic personal characteristic of the leader that illuminates their perception with foresight and imagination.

An evocative historical image comes from Michelangelo, who described sculpting as seeing an angel in a rock and setting it free. Likewise, a more recent example was Steve Jobs, who once said, "I have this really incredible product inside me, and I have to get it out."[10]

Visionary leaders look above and beyond the minutiae of today, sometimes wrestling a vague idea into existence. These visionaries have a clear view and emerging image of the future and, critically, can inspire and guide the organization toward that future. Thus, leaders need to lead, and leading implies setting direction through the leader's ability to envision, foresee, or predict through their imagination, horizon scanning, research, or insights.

This unique combination of vision and leadership is indispensable to ensuring that the creative idea blossoms out of the visionary's mind and flourishes within a team to materialize into a new product or service in the marketplace. This imaginative ability and visualization skill distinguishes transformational leaders from transactional ones. Instead of just mechanically going through routine motions, these leaders make a meaningful impact in their roles and teams. Further, leaders are responsible for envisioning the future, guiding the organization toward that goal, and executing the strategy.

Furthermore, it is a distinct organizational advantage when the leader is also a visionary. It inspires the team with confidence in the leader and the goal, thereby establishing credibility and allegiance with the staff. When the visionary leader has "envisioned" or created the goal themselves, then it is natural and persuasive for that leader to be able to crystallize, articulate, and communicate that vision. This gives them the objective's context and helps them intuitively guide the team toward that goal instead of having to understand, adapt, and align the organization to another's vision and target.

Whether you are a natural-born visionary or practice visioning methods exceptional leaders use to crystallize a vision, you can be equally credible and effective in charting the future direction for your team and organization. While integrity was my top choice for leadership character relative to leading teams, one can legitimately argue that leadership vision is one of the most critical characteristics for the organization itself.

Given the criticality of leadership vision, I will reinforce this point repeatedly. As a natural or aspiring visionary, you can use the visioning techniques discussed in chapter 1—associative thinking, systems thinking, scenario planning, horizon scanning, open innovation, and idea generation—to systematically originate ideas and create a vision for your organization.

A final word of encouragement. While Steve Jobs at Apple was unquestionably a creative genius visionary, his successor, Tim Cook, has also undoubtedly mastered the essential skills of creative innovation. So, whether you use your heart and gut instinct like Steve Jobs, or your head and disciplined techniques like Tim Cook, you can still be equally effective as a visionary leader. But, of course, it's also nice to have a good measure of both, as with the likes of Bill Gates and Elon Musk!

Good business leaders create a vision, articulate the vision, passionately own the vision, and relentlessly drive it to competition.
      —*Jack Welch*, former CEO of General Electric[11]

Takeaway: Executive vision is a differentiator between a forward-thinking leader and a tactical manager. The good news is that whether you are a natural visionary or not, you can apply the visioning techniques of associative thinking, systems thinking, scenario planning, horizon scanning, open innovation, and idea generation to envisage a promising future for your organization.

Authenticity

> *True leadership stems from individuality that is honestly and some-times imperfectly expressed. . . . Leaders should strive for authenticity over perfection.*
> *—Sheryl Sandberg, former chief operating officer of Facebook*[12]

Authenticity and the related topic of emotional intelligence, as discussed in chapter 2, are foundational leadership capabilities relating to integrity, honesty, and behavior. Principally, an authentic leader must be self-aware, believe in themselves, possess great integrity, have strong alignment between their values and actions, and conduct themselves honestly and honorably.

Regardless of your level of professional experience, intelligence, or skills relating to the knowledge and capabilities of your role, a leader must inspire, nurture, and motivate teams of people through their social skills and behavior. These authentic leadership behavioral skills are enhanced and refined by the leader's emotional maturity level, expressed through a genuine and forthright relationship with the team.

These emotional and social skills either positively enable and enhance your performance and perception as a leader or detract from and undermine it. This directly determines your acceptance as a leader for your team and as a trusted colleague in the broader organization.

Daniel Goleman posits the following behavior skills as the essential criteria for a mature, effective leader: motivation, self-awareness, self-regulation, empathy, and social skills. The first three relate to personal attributes that a leader must possess personally, and the second two are social behaviors relating to effective team interaction.[13]

Leaders with high emotional intelligence effectively manage staff and organizational challenges with self-confidence, integrity, and courage and foster team trust through open, honest, and empathetic actions and communications.

By incorporating emotional intelligence into the construct of authentic leadership, we have a comprehensive model of an effective leader's emotional and behavioral profile. Therefore, inclusively and ideally, we can state that an authentic leader is:

- Self-aware to the extent that they know their own mind and value systems and can communicate a clear vision to inspire and motivate the team.
- The authentic leader has personal integrity, is honest and forthright, and has a clear moral guiding compass.
- They are positive, compassionate, empathetic, and intuitive and lead with the heart, not just their head.
- The leader has the personal self-belief and confidence to trust in themselves to lead with integrity, passion, commitment, and generosity of spirit.
- They are collaborative, consistent, and communicative by embracing others' contributions and ideas and empowering people through sharing opportunities, responsibilities, and successes.
- They have highly developed communications and social skills to lead, mentor, and guide people toward success and empathize with and encourage staff during difficulties.

Authenticity is the human side of leadership, where we are guided by our compassionate hearts and astute conscience. This is where we are true to ourselves and reflect that in how we mentor and manage our teams. Of course, no one is perfect, and life and work sometimes force compromises. However, to the extent that you are true to yourself and your values in leadership, you will find yourself at peace with yourself, in alignment with your team, and effective in your organization.

In my early career, when the times and work practices were different, I occasionally found my role responsibilities to be out of sync with my values, which caused considerable personal stress and professional anxiety.

It took some years to appreciate and accept that my value system was correct, sound, and credible. I then realized that I functioned far more successfully when I was true to myself and my team, rather than compromising my core values or team's long-term well-being for short-term or short-sighted corporate objectives.

Consequently, as I became comfortable with and refined my personal leadership style, I became more discerning and demanding to seek out roles better aligned with my innate leadership style. This permitted me to create and enjoy a fuller and richer career through a more authentic relationship with my staff and colleagues.

One significant lesson is that it's easy to be open, honest, cheerful, and magnanimous when you are on a roll and the wind is at your back. The challenge comes when you're in the center of a metaphoric storm; the sky is falling, and people or things turn against you. But that is when authenticity and honesty are most important, as those are the things and times that build character. Especially in situations when you, as the leader, need to carry your entire team and sometimes the whole company on your back. You will find that those challenges often cause or allow you to rise to the occasion to do and achieve things you might never have expected.

I will elaborate on the following story as a short case study later. Still, as it is one of my defining moments of leadership and perhaps authenticity, I introduce it briefly here. Once in the middle of a dot-com death spiral in 2000 at Worldsport Networks, after struggling to survive for months, I had to lay off 50 percent of my 256-member staff one Friday afternoon. With a catch in my throat and tears in my eyes, I explained in detail why this had occurred, what we tried to do to avoid it, how we would proceed, who would stay and who would go, and finally, that we would not rest until everyone was successfully outplaced. I told them that after my speech, the redundancies would take place. Finally, I thanked them sincerely for their efforts, trust, and support. Then, when I concluded, the entire room leaped to their feet in a standing ovation! For a moment, my honesty and humanity had shone through, our team's bond held firm even in adversity, and my painful but authentic communique was accepted despite the difficult situation. I believe the climate and chemistry of that moment, with our mutual trust and emotional connection, helped sustain us throughout the ensuing months of disruption and turmoil.

Takeaway: Authenticity begins with being honest with yourself. Unless you can be objective and honest with yourself, you won't be able to be straightforward and genuine with your colleagues. Authenticity is the most transparent leadership criterion; your honesty, integrity, and commitment shine through innately, engendering trust and confidence.

Trust

The ability to establish, grow, extend, and restore trust is the key professional and personal competency of our time."
—*Stephen Covey, educator, consultant, author*[14]

When I previously described the metaphorical image of me grabbing a banner and charging up a hill in complete confidence that my team would be right alongside me, I described a trust-based relationship. First, I knew intrinsically, with certainty and assurance, that the team was aligned and committed to whatever course of action I deemed necessary as their leader.

Why did I have that assurance, and critically, why was it so? I believe the fundamental reasons the team was aligned and committed was that they trusted that if I was to initiate an action, then obviously the action was necessary, we were capable of undertaking the effort and risk, and that I undoubtedly would have their well-being in the forefront of my mind. This was all due to a high degree of mutual trust the team and I developed over time. Let's explore why and how this bond of trust is created and sustained.

Trust is a steadfast connection between the leader and the team; without it, there is no authentic leadership and no team alignment. Of the twenty critical leadership characteristics, trust is at the heart of the reciprocal relationship between the leader and the team. It has its foundation in the integrity, sincerity, authenticity, and mutual allegiance of the leader and the team members. Moreover, it is resolutely reinforced by creating an ethical and communal culture that underpins the team's confidence and commitment.

Hence, mutual trust is a critical core requirement for creating cohesive, confident, and collaborative teams. As previously discussed, the social exchange theory concept reinforces this mutual trust.[15] To reiterate, it means there is a mutually recognized pact (even if subconsciously) and reciprocal exchange of value between parties, be it monetary, resources, or emotional or political support. In the leader/team context, the leader often provides some form of compensation or opportunity, and the team members reciprocate with effort and loyalty. I refer you to chapter 2 and the alchemy of leadership discussion for a detailed refresher on social exchange theory.

In addition to the two-way trust reciprocity, there is another essential trust-based criterion. That confidence in each other. This comprises an element of bilateral assessment of first the leader's competence and then the team's capability. Obviously, having an emotionally trusting relationship with an incompetent person is not helpful. However, without sufficient confidence and respect for each other, generating the personal and professional assurance necessary to fully commit, accept risks, and dedicate oneself to shared tasks will be challenging. As in the banner example, we would both know that the mission was crucial and achievable because of the mutual respect, understanding, and confidence we had in each other. Additionally, there must be a benevolent, mutual self-interest and caring commitment to each other that overlays the reasonableness of the task with honesty, integrity, and good intention.[16]

To sustain this trust and allegiance, the confidence in the mutual capabilities and the relationship's benevolence must be continuously validated by the communications, behaviors, and dedication of the team's interactions. This reinforces the symbiotic team-based culture that is sustained by the mutual, two-way, trust-based relationship. Over time, the trust-confidence bond can be so strong that it can weather difficulties and even conflict. There is a pervasive sense of leadership/team trust that can overcome even significant challenges to the collective's best interest.

For a real-life team-trust example, I recall some annual salary discussions in my IT Team at TUI, where I operated with a high degree of transparency regarding how I would assign salaries and bonuses. As you will appreciate, salaries and bonuses are a highly emotive issue. My operative principle for this exercise was that there would never be enough money to delight everyone. Nevertheless, the process I would conduct would be open and fair, based on effort, contribution, historical trends that were important to be recognized, and, to a certain degree, need.

One year after a merger consolidation, I explained to the staff that for former historical reasons, in our newly created team, several individuals had previously been suppressed at salaries well below their peers and at a level not commensurate with their contribution. After a careful explanation, the team generously accepted the fact that the majority of that year's annual increases would have to be apportioned to those individuals to bring them up to a comparable level. The following year, the negatively affected staff members were adjusted appropriately to compensate for the prior year's deficit.

Money is always a sensitive issue. However, this challenging multi-year adjustment to everyone's salaries was only possible because of collaborative communications, a strong trust relationship, and a sense of collective commitment within the team that had been established over many years.

Takeaway: Trust is the cornerstone of a symbiotic relationship between a leader and the team, built on honesty, integrity, and confidence. It can take some time to develop fully but can be damaged instantly. Once established, it is a critical component of a cohesive, collaborative, and productive team.

The Second Five: Emotional Leadership Traits

Purpose, passion, enthusiasm, inspiration, and optimism are "emotional" behaviors that build on both innate personal as well as behavioral characteristics. These behaviors dramatically enhance and empower leadership vision, effectiveness, and team commitment. These characteristics are the leadership behaviors that inspire individuals and motivate staff into action.[17]

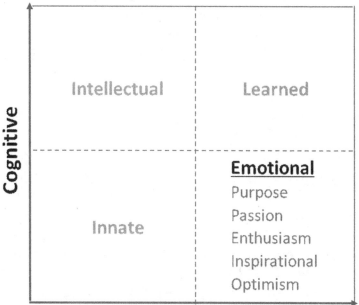

Hudson – Garrison
Leadership Characteristics Matrix

Leadership Characteristics Matrix—Emotional Characteristics

Purpose

When you are surrounded by people who share a passionate commitment around a common purpose, anything is possible.
—*Howard Schultz, former chairman and CEO, Starbucks*[18]

Leadership scholar Warren Bennis once wrote, "The No. 1 requirement for a leader is a strongly defined sense of Purpose."[19] Further, we've extensively discussed the requirement for a leader to create a "vision with a purpose" to build an emotional bridge from departmental objectives to meaningful motivators for staff.

Having defined that requirement and activity, let's dig deeper into the leader's intrinsic nature and character to understand how a leader can authentically and convincingly create and communicate messages. Employees in business are often inherently cautious and skeptical of management and are acutely sensitive to authenticity or bullsh*t. Touted up, glossed over, whitewashed objectives and empty promises are instinctively and immediately detected and discredited.

Therefore, for starters, let's return to the first principles of honesty, integrity, and authenticity. Then, taking that ethos as an overlay, how does a leader find the meaning and wellspring of inspiration to craft a vision and purpose?

A leader must begin by identifying and internalizing their personal and professional purpose or raison d'être as a prerequisite to setting a team's vision and objectives. We must first discover and align our personal vision and purpose by examining and recognizing our values, motivations, aspirations, and passions. From this cornerstone, we can orient our internal compass toward what Bill George refers to as our personal navigational north star, as discussed in chapter 1. This inner exploration or self-reflection helps us establish and solidify the essence of who we are as a leader and lays a solid anchor point for any professional goal, vision, or purpose we set or aspire to.

You can create a meaningful and credible vision for your teams from the foundation of your personal value system, built on intrinsic beliefs and conviction. Then, aligning the organizational objectives to that, as a leader you can instill that vision with a "higher purpose" that resonates with your and the team's values and interests. The leader's challenge is then making the vision come alive. From your cornerstone of purpose and passion, plus a little creative imagination, you can craft a powerful purpose to bridge the personal emotional gap between the departmental vision and the final product or outcome.

This, for me, is a superb way for each of us as leaders to enrich our lives, help make our team's daily efforts more meaningful, and enhance the quality and value of our deliverables. Further, setting a vision with purpose is not only about what we do. Rather, more critically, it is about why and how we do it. This, in turn, inspires the team, creating the enthusiasm and motivation to dedicate themselves to achieving that vision. Further, along with an emotional bridge, defining and communicating a purpose also builds employee engagement and motivation by aligning their beliefs with the organizational vision and objectives.

In my introduction, I shared my story of articulating the vision for the IT teams at TUI. I explained that each of our daily tasks were links in a chain of processes and events that, when connected, created travel activities whose purpose was to create smiles on the faces of young families for memories of a lifetime. Whether your purpose is to build quality automobiles, develop engaging websites, produce healthy food products, or create a vaccine, creating the vision with a meaningful purpose is far more effective than declaring staff need to improve productivity by 15 percent!

This alignment of employees' values, beliefs, goals, and emotions engages staff with the stated objectives through a compelling vision and meaningful purpose. This provides a powerful motivator that excites us, energizes us, encourages us, and sustains us. However, it begins with the leader affirming their value system, finding their purpose, and following their moral compass. Then, and perhaps only then, will the staff vision and team objectives you create and communicate be recognized as authentic, convincing, and value-creating and be fully embraced by the team.

Takeaway: Whatever your industry, products, or services, use your creativity to envision a higher purpose for your team's efforts. Then, craft a compelling management story to give the purpose deeper meaning. Everyone wants their time and effort to have value, to be appreciated, and to be a part of something greater than themselves.

Passion

Without passion, you don't have energy. Without energy, you have nothing.
　　　—Warren Buffett, American investor and philanthropist[20]

The leader's contagious passion is the alchemy that transforms vision and purpose into an infectious mission that transforms the vision into reality by inspiring, meaningful action.

As we said in the initial story of the stonemasons, people yearn to become a part of something significant that is perhaps greater or beyond themselves. Additionally, they are also naturally drawn to a charismatic leader with a meaningful mission. This gives the task, their job, and their lives purpose and some consequence.

The passionate mission is the spark and flame that creates the energy, excitement, and enthusiasm that fuels the staff's motivation, commitment, and impetus, igniting their ambition to take up and dedicate themselves to a cause.

Once the mission is catalyzed, the leader's continued enthusiasm and courage will sustain the team's energy and momentum throughout the campaign, project, or program. In addition, this passion will permeate the team's corporate culture with continuing optimism, conviction, commitment, and perseverance throughout the activity, thereby dramatically enhancing the probability of success.

Having established a powerful vision, purposeful mission, and creative culture, you are well on the way to creating an atmosphere and environment that is exciting, vibrant, creative, and productive; a setting where people will thrive, achieve high performance, and self-actualize; and a place where people will want to work that will be a boiling cauldron of creativity and be a magnet for attracting and retaining the best talent. Talent, of course, is the key to any successful project, program, or company.

Considering what examples of passion from my career were most significant and evocative was an intriguing exercise for me, as there were many times when I felt excitement, enthusiasm, and passion. These examples often occurred when I was consumed with a new idea or invention and became passionate about creating and inventing something new.

Interestingly, the other times I identified my passion were not about exciting new innovations. On the contrary, they were somewhat mundane but large-scale complex business transformations that required the efforts of large groups of people, all working and pulling together. In these cases, it was not the task that was the focus of the passion but the process of mobilizing and working with groups of people toward a common objective. This team leadership challenge was, in its way, immensely exciting.

Looking at these entirely opposite products, projects, and issues, I examined why they elicited passion for me and the teams. In retrospect, I think it came down to having a mission. Further, it was the intrigue and intellectual challenge of creating something new. Finally, there was a considerable and challenging goal that needed large teams and significant effort to accomplish successfully.

I'll cite a passionate personal example, exploring briefly why it generated so much emotion. It was the creation of AlertNet.org (now Trust. org) while at Reuters. This was an idea that sprung out of my frustration at the inefficiencies of the global humanitarian relief effort during the 1994 Rwanda genocide. The idea was to create a combined news agency and relief organization website and system. It would provide rapid response, logistics, and support to NGOs using the existing Reuters News Agency's high-technology satellite communications networks, trading systems, and database tools. The passionate objective here was an urgent desire to strengthen the weak links in the global relief response capabilities during profound humanitarian and geopolitical crises.

In this case, as with most innovations and transformations, we had a critical mission with immense challenges, which required several significant innovations plus an urgent initiative to overcome those obstacles and hurdles. Our mission, passion, and mutual commitment inspired, motivated, and sustained us until, ultimately, we were successful, thanks to the concerted effort of all involved.

In summary, dare to dream, and as a leader, express your dreams passionately, and you may find that your passion gives the wings to those dreams to take flight through your colleagues' embrace and uptake of the mission.

Takeaway: Your role as a leader is to inspire and motivate your teams. Once you've formed a clear vision and compelling purpose you ascribe to, tap your passion for the vision and purpose to generate meaning and excitement for your team. If you exude passion for the mission, the team will instinctively recognize it and buy into it.

Enthusiasm

> *I consider my ability to arouse enthusiasm among men (people) the greatest asset I possess. The way to develop the best that is in a man (person) is by appreciation and encouragement.*
> —*Charles M. Schwab, American business executive*[21]

As we just saw in the discussion about leadership passion, an emotional behavior vital for an effective leader is boundless enthusiasm derived from a powerful and effective combination of commitment, drive, and passion.

Enthusiasm and passion are directly connected and display a significant yet subtle difference. Passion has an essential emotional component, whereas the enthusiastic leader has a conscious, positive, and optimistic outlook with a firm belief in oneself, the vision they espouse, and the team's ability to achieve success. This self-fulfilling prophetic enthusiasm is essential to articulating an exciting vision and inspiring team energy and dedication to achieve success.

The leader's self-confidence, passion, and enthusiasm for the vision and mission are infectious. This is the crucial catalyst for igniting the team's excitement and motivation for the task or project. If you are excited and energetic, the team becomes enthusiastic, and everyone catches the buzz of excitement, which is contagious and thus mutually self-reinforcing and self-perpetuating.

The leader's optimistic attitude and dynamic behavior are vital for setting an overall can-do positive organizational culture. Besides setting the initial vision, generating initiative, and getting projects kicked off effectively, enthusiasm is perhaps even more important for maintaining team confidence when confronted with challenges, setbacks, or even failure. Ensuring a positive, enthusiastic attitude, especially in difficult times, is crucial to avoid team discouragement, burnout, or meltdown.

In the three-company merger carve-out project previously mentioned, we had three suppliers working together to deliver the new business setup. It was essential to set the vision, but critically, to get alignment among the external partners. To that end, I painted a persuasive picture of success for the program and everyone's part in it. Next, I stated that we would operate as one team and that "it was only by an accident of fate that a third of the teams each had TUI, Telefonica, or Accenture logos on their cards. We were individually all capable and motivated IT professionals." Our home base organizational alignment became temporarily secondary to the new operational team we had joined. We set a strong one team collaborative culture, which everyone bought into, and consequently, it worked exceptionally effectively.

However, during the project, we had an existential threat to the delivery at one juncture, for over a month, with a major systems setup failure. After exhausting all currently proposed solutions, I called all the team and company engagement leads together for a crisis meeting. The tension was thick as smoke with the project leads, their management, and the commercial heads all in the room.

I told them, for better or for worse, we were one team and that we, no one else, would have to resolve this situation as partners. Further, we were all going to pitch in and share the responsibility and pain, as that was the only way to turn a likely failure into a sure success. Either we all would celebrate a major success for the rest of our careers in this critical project, or we would all be painfully spending the next three years in court with our lawyers dissecting this failure and what part we all had in it. I continued with zeal as the lead, "However, I choose success with no alternative. I trust you, and I believe in you, and we are all going to solve the problem and deliver the solution and celebrate success." Mercedes Oblanca, Accenture's director, chimed in, stating that as the prime contractor, they were committed to the cross-company team and would invest in the solution to make it work, regardless of the risk and cost. All the project and commercial leads then added their agreement of mutual responsibility, joint commitment, and total dedication to resolving the situation.

A solution was found; we delivered on time, on budget, and with zero defects. What defined the success? Belief in the individuals and teams, respect and empathy for each partner's challenges, the courage of our convictions, continuous communications, and boundless enthusiasm and confidence in the potential for success.

Takeaway: Leadership enthusiasm is a powerful and effective combination of optimism, commitment, passion, and drive. Further, enthusiasm is contagious, and to the extent that you can generate and arouse this excitement, your teams will be energized, motivated, more productive, and generally enjoy it more.

Inspiration

Management is about persuading people to do things they do not want to do, while leadership is about inspiring people to do things they never thought they could.
    —*Steve Jobs, former chairman and CEO, Apple Inc.*[22]

Inspiration is a complex but critical characteristic comprising a delicate combination of personal emotional leadership traits plus an element of visionary and creative leadership. A leader's heart might be in the right place to mentor and guide staff. Still, unless they likewise have the creative and visionary trait as well, it will be difficult to be credible when inspiring creative knowledge workers.

It is particularly challenging if you have done your work well as a leader and hired exceptionally talented staff. The benefit is that your expert team can also be a positive, constructive challenge for you, inspiring and propelling you to greater heights. This two-way process of mutual inspiration and creative challenge can be motivating and value-creating for you and your team.

Therefore, an inspiring leader must lead by example through both their creative and intellectual talents. This is all well and good for a leader who is also a domain specialist in the area they are managing, such as an innovation director managing an innovation team. However, it can be somewhat more difficult for a generalist leader. In the case where a leader is perhaps not the domain specialist, they can still inspire the team in related and supporting areas and business outcomes that the delivery of the projects will achieve. For example, you don't have to be an artificial intelligence automation expert to appreciate the benefits of automating low-level, repetitive tasks in a call center. In other words, you don't have to be the subject matter expert, but you can focus on the outcomes to positively inspire the team to deliver value to and through the activity.

Moreover, as the leader, it's not necessary to be better at everything than your specialist staff. You are not in competition with your star players. Instead, you need to see the big picture and understand how all specialist areas fit together synergistically or potentially how they create a new product or service. This is why you are the leader, not the specialist.

To capture the team's imagination, inspire them, and win their support, you must conceive and articulate a captivating vision of the future beyond the status quo or business as usual. Everyone wants their efforts to amount to something and to be a part of a grand venture that is larger than themselves. Elon Musk's vision for SpaceX is a grandiose but excellent current example of dramatic, inspirational leadership. Elon often waxes lyrical about how earthlings must reach for the stars and become a space-faring civilization living among the stars.

Perhaps these comments from a lesser leader might elicit skepticism or even ridicule. However, when he and SpaceX's team back this up with the roar of a massive rocket blasting off for the International Space Station and a continuous stream of new innovations, including thousands of Starlink satellites, one begins to see a thread from the vision through to a future reality. This is what a leader needs to achieve: set and communicate a grand, captivating vision, but one based on the reality that it could actually be achieved.

You will no doubt have inspirational examples within your own context. The leader's function is to lead and synthesize solutions out of customers' needs, challenges in the market, new technologies, and the team's labor. In that context, you bring added value to the team and your company by envisioning and conjuring up new products, ideas, and solutions. It is through those situations you inspire your team, colleagues, and leadership.

Your mission is to create inspiration at the outset and then inspire your teams to action. A sufficiently inspired team will overcome any obstacles, transcend the moment, and realize seemingly impossible things.

Takeaway: Inspiration is a complex alchemy of vision, mission, intellect, and enthusiasm. Once you identify a compelling objective, create an exciting executive vignette or story that people can relate to, generating their enthusiasm to buy into the mission.

Optimism

One of the most important qualities of a good leader is optimism, a
pragmatic enthusiasm for what can be achieved.
    —*Bob Iger, chairman and former CEO of Walt Disney Co.*[23]

Optimism, while related to enthusiasm, inspiration, and passion, is notably different in that the others are more external emotional behaviors. In contrast, optimism is an emotional attitudinal behavior with a "state of mind" or dispositional underpinning.

Optimism is the proverbial "cup is half full" attitude. However, it is not an unrealistic or misguided perspective but a positive attitude toward any situation, person, or problem. This constructive or optimistic attitude is critically important for leaders because it translates into a productive can-do attitude and approach to problem-solving and decision-making to overcome challenges.

Further, it also lifts the team members' spirit out of the doldrums when they may be anxious, discouraged, and defeatist into a fresh, new, constructive perspective. By adopting a more positive attitude, team members can think and act creatively and optimally because of reduced fear and a mental shift from an anxious, threatened, or defensive posture to a more right-brain-inspired thinking mode.

I believe optimism is one of my most powerful tools as a leader. While it can be learned and conditioned over time, it must be authentic, not forced or faked. Your staff are intuitive and insightful and will immediately detect hyperbole, unrealistic, false, or put-on behavior. The wellspring of optimism derives from experience and a big-picture perspective. Perhaps age and experiences have seasoned me to the point that I can generally view a problem from a distance to recognize that most problems are not earthshaking issues, usually are not existential threats, and will likely have a solution.

I've found that even when embroiled in some of the worst corporate challenges, from a long-view standpoint, one can often see the absurdity of the situations. However, if you call it like it is and provide a big-picture perspective on the problem, generally, staff will appreciate it and realize the current catastrophe will eventually be just an ironic memory. I call this cheerful, confident optimism.

Often, in the middle of an intractable and protracted problem, I would arrive at the office happily (genuinely), greeting everyone cheerfully and just being normal. As a result, staff who may have lamented the difficulties the evening before and lost sleep over the issue are startled out of their stupor and contagiously cheered up. They will realize I'm in charge, optimistic, and not worried, or at least can see a way out of our current morass. This is highly reassuring and encouraging.

Finally, if in a difficult situation when everything is melting down and the teams are about to fall apart, I've often looked around and said: "Listen, everyone, no children are dying here, we'll figure this out, and in six months we'll all be laughing about it!" It's amazing how putting a problem in perspective and in its place, especially relative to huge and severe issues in the context of the sweep of time, can help you regain the high ground and shift to a more constructive approach. Of course, things occasionally go amiss; fortunately, optimism is a highly beneficial behavior to manage difficulties to the best resolution and result.

Eventually, people will recognize through your example that an optimistic attitude has a favorable influence on people and issues from which new ideas and fresh solutions are more likely to result. This is in contrast to a pessimistic attitude, where being anxious and in the doldrums adds to the challenge of finding or implementing an optimal solution. Thus, indefatigable optimism is a powerful and potent leadership attitudinal behavior for overcoming difficulties, righting floundering projects, gaining team support, and generally creating a pleasant and positive can-do culture within your teams.

Thomas Edison provides one of the best examples of boundless optimism in making the very best out of a catastrophic situation. When his factory was destroyed by fire along with his life's work, he quipped that the disaster had burned up all his mistakes, and thank goodness, as he could start anew![24]

Takeaway: Optimism is a potent leadership attribute and attitude as it inspires hope and confidence in your team. Used judiciously as a positive "the cup is half full" perspective rather than one of false hope, it can establish an upbeat can-do attitude within the team. If optimism is your natural personal perspective, develop and strengthen it; if not, it is a behavior that can and should be encouraged and developed.

The Third FIVE: Intellectual Leadership Traits

Judgment, diplomacy, decisiveness, perseverance, and reliability are intellectual behaviors derived from leadership maturity of experience, sound judgment, personal commitment, the leader's mastery of team interactions, and discipline in work activities.[25]

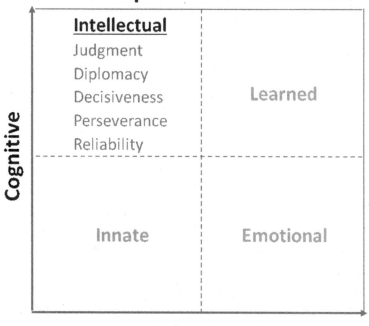

Leadership Characteristics Matrix—Intellectual Characteristics

Judgment

Management is doing things right; leadership is doing the right things.
—Peter Drucker, management consultant and author[26]

Our first "intellectual" characteristic is judgment. Here, of course, we are discussing having "sound judgment" rather than being judgmental. Regardless of all the exemplary behaviors we have discussed thus far, whether it be integrity, vision, passion, or any of the others in surplus, all of it will be for naught without reliable judgment.

When all is said and done, you are the leader, not just for your charisma, cleverness, and courage, but for the successful deliverables, the end result, and the bottom line. Therefore, a critical factor in choosing the right objectives, selecting and managing the team, dealing with leadership, planning the project, making the right decisions, solving problems, and delivering the correct result comes down to solid and dependable judgment.

So then, what is judgment, and how do we develop and deploy it? Hopefully, from the outset, you will have benefited from a good family upbringing where your parents and grandparents provided constructive models for judgment in all contexts. Further, your education and work experience are formative for developing trustworthy judgment by observing effective decision-making and management behavior, perhaps by mentoring or trial and error during on-the-job training and experience. Finally, through all this, you will have honed your common sense and judgment toward making decisions and forming opinions wisely and effectively in planning, politics, projects, prioritizing, and people.

Good judgment behavior implies:

- Clearly understanding the issue at hand, the objectives, and the priorities.
- Doing your research, collecting relevant information, and looking at all sides of an issue or problem.
- Communicating and consulting with the appropriate knowledgeable and experienced people and resources to get the facts and research to inform your decisions.

- Identifying the correct perspective to adopt, weighing all aspects and options.
- Considering the options based on all the actors' assumptions, viewpoints, opinions, facts, expectations, and outcomes.
- Reflecting on all aspects of the situation to understand the implications and outcomes of all alternatives for all interested parties.
- If a solution is not apparent or has conflicting points of view, assessing the alternatives against your core value systems, ethical principles, laws, and moral codes.
- Finally, objectively evaluating the situations based on the analysis above to arrive at a fair and sound judgment.

Three follow-on provisos:

1. Choose your battles. In the pragmatic world of corporate politics, you don't have to win every battle, just the essential ones. Keep the big picture in mind!
2. A critical factor to effective judgment is to "know thyself" and recognize your capabilities and liabilities. In a later chapter, we discuss Daniel Kahneman's book, *Thinking, Fast and Slow,* in greater detail.
   a. He discusses the critical concept of knowing when and how to make rapid, sound decisions based on sufficient prior applicable knowledge and experience.
   b. Conversely, in complex and unfamiliar situations, hold back to make a careful analysis before exercising a reasoned and robust judgment and decision.
3. Finally, in evaluating reliable judgments throughout your organization, you need to consider yourself, your leadership, and your team in deciding how, when, and who should make the decisions.
   a. Sometimes, with your experience, you are in the best position to make the decision.
   b. Alternatively, it may be politically or from an experience perspective, wiser for your boss or senior leadership to decide.

    c. It may be best to delegate to one of your key specialist staff if they have the most experience relative to the issue at hand.

    d. As mentioned above, never let your ego or position come in the way of identifying the best person or group to inform or make the appropriate decisions.

Remember that these twenty leadership criteria create a rich composite of your leadership abilities; however, your sound judgment is the ultimate measure of your success. The following prayer, when seen as a leadership maxim, is an exceedingly wise statement and perspective to always keep in the back of your mind when judiciously deciding if and how to proceed with decisions.

> *God grant me the serenity to accept the things I cannot change, the courage to change the things I can change, and the wisdom to know the difference.*
>
> —*"The Serenity Prayer," Reinhold Niebuhr*[27]

Takeaway: First of all, the critical thing about judgment is to determine who should make the decision and when. Be objective and confident enough to ensure the correct person is tasked with the decision. If the issue or decision is clearly within your responsibility, knowledge, and experience, act boldly and make the call. If, from a political, expertise, or experience perspective, someone else is in a better position to make the decision, confidently delegate the issue to that person.

Diplomacy

Diplomacy is fundamentally working with people, bringing people together to deal with difficult issues.
                    —*John Roos, American businessman and diplomat*[8]

The concept of leadership diplomacy relates to sound judgment in action. This represents the mature, developed characteristic of having a wise, ethical, and emotionally intelligent outlook on yourself, your organization, and its internal and external activities. Operating from that perspective, you must have a culture of integrity, high corporate core values, effective communications, honest negotiations, and superior standards of business conduct. Then, employ that mature emotional intelligence and ethical judgment in the context of a discussion, interaction, or negotiation.

Otto von Bismarck, the first chancellor of Germany, defined diplomacy as: "the never-ending negotiation of reciprocal concessions between states."[29] What does all this mean? First, without reverting to an academic textbook approach for day-to-day corporate life, diplomacy lays out a professional code of conduct that intrinsically governs our actions, politics, communications, negotiations, and decision-making. Considering other related leadership characteristics, such as integrity, reliability, and commitment, diplomacy creates an organizational modus operandi or ethos that engenders a highly effective leadership culture. Finally, without straying into the topic of personal branding, it also creates an overarching perception of your character and organizational culture.

I recall a personal example of delicate diplomacy that dramatically resolved a significant contract dispute. We were attempting to mobilize a major project, but the initial multimillion-euro contract was experiencing substantial delays over a relatively minor contract technicality. After a robust but lengthy RFP, everyone was anxious to begin, but negotiations were bogged down for weeks with the lawyers.

We had selected the supplier carefully, had done our due diligence, and they had assembled an excellent team that we desperately needed to launch this critical project. It was indisputable that we would proceed with this project, with virtually zero chance of either party changing their minds. In the contract, we had agreed upon a 10 percent signing bonus to mobilize an initial sixty consultants. In order to break the dead-lock and kick off the project, I suggested we advance the supplier an unrequested 5 percent "Bridging Contract" signature payment to get the project rolling.

The unanticipated 500,000-euro advance payment delighted the supplier's headquarters senior management, who recognized the good-will gesture and immediately threw active support and commitment behind the project. This accelerated the contract dispute resolution, and we immediately mobilized the team. It also helped catalyze a highly successful partner relationship throughout the yearlong project and for many years afterward.

Recognize that diplomacy is the fine art of working together polit-ically and civilly to find the best possible solution to any situation. It is not about one-sided negotiations or winning at any cost. It is about astute strategy, influencing decisions, and managing relationships to ensure successful long-term partnering for effective operations.

Leadership diplomacy is developed through experience, training, and coaching and is a measure of an effective leader's professional matu-rity. Enhancing and maturing your leadership diplomacy skills reinforces your relationships and thus contributes to the effective functioning of your team and organization. It also significantly affects your success working throughout your organization and with partners, suppliers, and even customers. Finally, good diplomacy as a modus operandi generally results in a more pleasant and agreeable working context for everyone involved.

Takeaway: Diplomacy is perhaps the one attribute most represen-tative of a mature executive leader, as it comprises elements of wis-dom, integrity, and negotiation skills. When dealing with senior management or complex issues, pause to ponder strategically and holistically about all aspects of the issue and its ramifications for stakeholders. This will enhance your perception as a deep and stra-tegic thinker.

Decisiveness

Companies rarely die from moving too fast, but they frequently die from moving too slowly.
        —*Reed Hastings, chairman and co-CEO, Netflix*[30]

Decisiveness is a formidable leadership quality that distinguishes a top-rated effective leader from an ineffective one. It couples professional confidence and resolute action to realize timely decision-making and operational efficiency. The ability to make appropriately accurate and rapid decisions and set direction inspires confidence, accelerates an organization's pace, and creates a competitive advantage. Procrastination, indecisiveness, and protracted decision-making are regarded as highly negative relative to leadership competency. Decisive and rapid decision-making is essential for any high-performance, fast-moving organization to meet new market demand and ensure rapid cycle time for new product development and service delivery. Further, it inspires confidence in your coworkers and establishes your credibility as an effective leader.

We have all been confronted with large, complex, and important decisions. However, lapsing into analysis paralysis through too much research, endless futile debates, the creation of excessive alternatives, or involving nonessential decision-makers all run the risk of either a convoluted or flawed decision or, at the least, exacerbating the problem further by excessive delay.

A strong, decisive leader needs to have the experience, courage, and self-confidence to focus rapidly on fundamental issues, filter out extraneous data, swiftly review relevant research, confer with the essential experts, prioritize, analyze, and synthesize the issues, be comfortable with uncertainty and risk, and then make a sound judgment and take a decisive decision. A mature and experienced leader exercising robust and rapid decision-making will generally make a high percentage of correct choices, thus offsetting any small portion of errors by accelerating the overall organization's speed and efficiency.

Again, I refer you to Daniel Kahneman's book *Thinking, Fast and Slow,* which points out an experienced leader's ability to make rapid and sound judgments and decisions in areas where they have extensive

familiarity and knowledge. Here, they are drawing on years of learning, experience, mental maps, and models of similar prior circumstances.
Thus, they can clearly and quickly recognize similar patterns of effective
or flawed thinking. Conversely, he cautions of cases where, when confronted with entirely new and complex problems, additional research,
in-depth analysis, and perhaps tapping external experts are required to
make a sound assessment. The critical issue is knowing yourself and recognizing when you have the requisite expertise in the relevant arena and
then having the confidence to know when you have enough information
to make a decisive and rapid decision without an unnecessary and costly
delay.[31]

From the organization and team's perspective, decisiveness is one of
the most critical characteristics of a successful, high-performance leader.
Thus, decisiveness is a fundamental measure of a leader's effectiveness
and credibility and is essential in the hyperefficient, rapidly moving marketplace we work in today.

Remember, no decision or a slow decision is generally the wrong
decision.

Takeaway: Decisiveness is a mark of a senior, experienced, and confident leader. When you have sufficient knowledge and experience
to inform a decision or action, don't lapse into analysis paralysis or
procrastinate; make a rapid and decisive decision, as time to market
and organizational speed are critical competitive advantages.

Perseverance

I'm convinced that about half of what separates successful entrepreneurs from the non-successful ones is pure perseverance.
       —*Steve Jobs, former Chairman and CEO, Apple Inc.*[32]

Topmost leaders do not give up when confronted with obstacles or facing unexpected difficulties and will persevere even when the going is rough and morale is low. In popular business language, we often refer to this as having grit, as popularized by the classic bestselling book *Grit* by Angela Duckworth. The oft-repeated witticism has never been truer: "When the going gets tough, the tough get going."[33]

I'm also reminded of Jesse Itzler's book recounting the Navy SEAL 40 percent rule.[34] The rule is basic: When you're totally exhausted, think you're completely finished, and can't give any more, you're only 40 percent done; you've got 60 percent of your capacity left. This assures us that, with the proper motivation, we can always draw on untapped reserves of willpower and energy.

Where does this deep drive and passionate persistence derive? It wells up from a combination of personal courage and self-confidence, coupled with a conscious belief in the mission or goal, plus an emotional commitment and determination to overcome all obstacles, no matter what! That same stubborn and steadfast personal tenacity is critical in our role as team leaders. If things were always easy, then we wouldn't need leaders. However, it is when we have significant challenges, tremendous obstacles, and unexpected difficulties that we need a genuine leader, not just for their insights and wisdom but to inspire, support, and motivate the team to persevere.

This is why a leader must articulate an inspiring vision linked to a convincing purpose to ensure the team has the emotional commitment to buy into that vision to tap into the "wellspring of motivation" necessary to prevail in the long run. When the team is struggling, morale is low, and the way forward is unclear, the leader must step in with confidence, commitment, and tenacity to encourage the team and motivate them to persist until a breakthrough is achieved and the task accomplished. Or if, unfortunately, a stumble occurs and failure results, the leader must pick the team up, rally them, put things in perspective, reassure them, and give them confidence that they can overcome, be successful, and win in the future.

This is particularly important for tangible and concrete projects with clear objectives, definable challenges, and people-related "soft skill" issues. Among the most difficult challenges we have as leaders are implementing broad, sweeping organizational and transformation changes. With these programs, you may have significant challenges with entrenched thinking and recalcitrant incumbents who are not motivated to change.

In major long-term initiatives where the outcome's success is uncertain, the leader must endure, maintain the vision, and marshal the troops forward, perhaps even for years, against seemingly insurmountable odds. Likewise, indefatigable perseverance is undoubtedly a leader's most critical asset in major transformations to increase the odds of eventual success. As Jim Collins reminds us in *Great by Choice*: "Any person can seem great when luck and circumstances are going their way. It's when the challenges hit that people and companies reveal their true grit."[35]

It has oft been told that when Thomas Edison was asked if he was discouraged after trying over one thousand filaments to create the light bulb, he responded, "No, I now know thousands of things that won't work!"[36] That is exceptional positive perseverance!

Takeaway: Life and work, in particular, are constantly confronted with challenges. A significant part of success in both comes down to indefatigable perseverance. The critical thing for a leader is to sustain their persistence in the face of difficulty and model the same determination to give your teams hope, confidence, and courage.

Reliability

Reliability is the precondition for trust.
    —*Wolfgang Schauble, president of the German Bundestag*[37]

Finally, I include reliability as the last intellectual characteristic, as it comprises an amalgam of various attributes mentioned above, comprising elements of trust, commitment, and perseverance. But it is unique in its own right as it results in a behavioral profile, norm, and ethos where you establish leadership credibility and an enduring reputation for achieving what you commit to.

Reliability in this context relates to a conscious commitment plus an ingrained drive to deliver on what you promise to others and yourself. This is crucial for a leader's integrity and trust in the eyes of colleagues and staff. From others' perspectives, if you can't trust what someone says or commits to doing, it throws into doubt their word on further promises, commitments to staff, or even expectations as to whether they will deliver on actions or responsibilities. It also raises questions about the leader's commitment or loyalty when there are compromises, problems, or challenges.

Some cultures, including corporate cultures, occasionally have serious reliability issues. They sometimes exhibit behaviors such as delaying tactics to put people off or discourage them, not responding at all, or even saying, "I'll get back to you on that," and never doing so. These appalling behaviors exhibit a lack of integrity and honesty and erode trust in the prevaricator. If one's motivation is not entirely malevolent, however, making a commitment, overcommitting, and then missing a deadline or forgetting the issue demonstrates flakiness or a lack of discipline. In these cases, the unfortunate recipient or observer of these behaviors will suffer, at best, a disappointment and, at worst, a loss of respect for and confidence in the leader.

Conversely, a cautious leader who thinks before they commit, understands the ramifications, makes an appropriate decision, and then makes commitments and delivers consistently on them gains respect and esteem in the staff's and organization's eyes. If colleagues recognize that your reliability is judicious and consistent, they will trust you, believe what you say, and act accordingly.

If you are not consistent and reliable, colleagues and staff may ignore or undermine your actions or promises. Even worse, this lack of reliability can cause staff and colleagues to adopt this same aberrant behavior. They can then conclude that one does not have to be honest and truthful in their communications or reliably deliver on their commitments in your organization! Behavior of this type erodes personal integrity and trust in what people say and exhibits a lack of dedication and discipline for project deliverables. This results in a deterioration of cultural norms and unpredictable outcomes and fosters a culture of mediocrity. Extend this to its logical conclusion, and you have a company whose potential customers do not have faith or trust in that company or its products and services.

I vividly recall having a highly intelligent and visionary boss who consistently misconstrued the facts and could rarely be trusted to follow through on commitments. This resulted in him suffering virtually a total loss of credibility throughout his entire tier of senior direct reports. It was a complete nightmare working for him. By a great stroke of luck, my next boss was completely the opposite. He said exactly what he thought and always did what he promised. What a contrast and blessing it was to work for the second leader.

One of my bywords for life and work is a Tom Peters motto: "Always under-promise and over-deliver. Never over-promise and under-deliver."[38]

Takeaway: Reliability lies at the core of your leadership credibility. It relates to trust, honesty, and integrity and demonstrates how dependable your word is and whether you keep your promises and deliver on commitments. If you are true to yourself and scrupulously honest with others, you will build a reputation of reliability. Credibility takes time to build but can be undermined easily with a careless comment.

The Fourth Five: Learned Leadership Traits

Courage, confidence, commitment, communicative, and creativity are high-performing learned behaviors that start with an innate solid leadership character and evolve over time with learning, experience, and maturity. This knowledge and capability development develops into mastery of these essential characteristics, which are fundamental to all strong and successful leaders.[39]

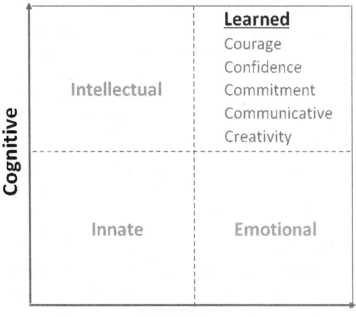

Leadership Characteristics Matrix—Learned Characteristics

Courage

If you don't risk anything you risk everything.
—*Mark Zuckerberg, Chairman and CEO, Facebook*[40]

Aspiring leaders must unquestionably have or develop a significant measure of courage to achieve maximum effectiveness and mastery.

While I don't view courage as an exclusively innate characteristic, a leader certainly benefits from a strong character and can develop exceptional strength that develops into courage through formative character-building challenges. You will recall my comments from Warren Bennis, who discusses how dramatic "crucibles" can transform into formidable leadership character in people's lives. That particular combination of inner strength, coupled with assertive conduct, converts into courage. It has been said that courage is "passionate purposefulness."

Additionally, I believe it also emerges further through developing self-confidence and commitment. Courage is a characteristic that enables a person to confront obstacles confidently and assertively, and although courage doesn't eliminate fear, it transcends it. From that foundation of confidence, commitment, and conduct, courage can manifest itself in many different ways, physically, socially, intellectually, or emotionally.

As we have all experienced or observed courage, perhaps an additional essential elaboration required is how to develop and harness courage. We come on to confidence next, but courage requires confidence, resulting in part from experience coupled with successful coping behaviors. It is akin to athleticism in that you strengthen and refine your skills with practice. With that skill development and mastery of the activity, you become more confident, and with confidence, you develop courage.

In my diverse career internationally and across industries, I perceived my own building of courage based on increasing experience, positive reinforcement, and confidence. This growing confidence resulted in a reduction of risk aversion and thus a greater ability to cope with adversity and risk, thus also increasing courage. Along with this experience, confidence and acceptance of risk are elements of will and determination that strengthen courage. I can recall situations during my career when confronted with significant change and challenges; there was no other alternative than to steel myself and muster the courage to proceed! No doubt, this tolerance for risk and courage to explore the unknown was one of the positive factors in my ability to initiate, accept, and be successful in many diverse international assignments. In particular, in entirely new roles and industries.

This reminds me of my initial interview lunch with Reuters in San Francisco in the late 1980s regarding a role in Hong Kong. The Reuters British executive from Hong Kong bluntly stated that he was surprised that, with two young children of three and six years, I would uproot myself from a comfortable job at American Express to go to what was frankly a highly risky new role in Asia. I recall a thoughtful pause as I considered my response. Then I metaphorically girded my loins, mustered my courage, and stated that, yes, I had a cushy job at AMEX in San Francisco, but that was what made their role so appealing. It was the uncertainty and element of the unknown, plus the opportunity to explore new horizons and learn new things, that made the role so appealing. So, I took the Hong Kong job, which kicked off thirty-five fascinating years of expatriate life.

Takeaway: All senior leadership roles entail significant challenges and an element of risk. To confront and overcome risk requires courage. While we all have differing levels of inherent courage, personal growth and experience help to develop confidence and, thus, courage. Remember the old saying that the biggest risk is not taking enough risk, so bolster your courage to embrace the challenge.

Confidence

Confidence isn't optimism or pessimism; it's the expectation of a positive outcome.

—Rosabeth Moss Kanter, professor of business,
Harvard University[41]

The second high-performing behavior is confidence, which can be a learned behavior besides being an intrinsic, innate characteristic. Even with intelligence, experience, and skills, any aspiring leader would be ineffective without a substantial measure of confidence. Some unique natural-born leaders possess positive innate and nurtured behaviors, imbuing them with "natural" self-confidence. However, business leaders can also learn and develop "contextual" confidence, which can be cultivated further, matured, and optimized. Let's explore various aspects of self-confidence and how they are acquired.

On a personal level, one aspect of confidence equates to self-esteem as an inward-facing internal sense of self relative to individual worth and value. Undoubtedly, this is a composite learned behavior resulting from a healthy familial upbringing where the person felt loved and valued and further from the lifelong experience of positive feedback resulting in self-respect, self-worth, and personal value.

At a social and behavioral level, we can think of self-confidence as an outward-facing self-assurance of one's ability and capability to accomplish a task or succeed in specific situations. This self-confidence is gained through experience and developed capabilities, coupled with positive feedback and reinforcement resulting from successes and achievements over time.

Recognize that confidence is a combination of expertise and experience. Therefore, in addition to personal self-esteem and capability, building new or transferring prior related experience within a new activity or role is necessary to become fully confident in that position. Depending on how much prior experience one can bring to a new situation in terms of transferrable skills, it can take some or even many months to become fully competent in all the intricacies of the new role.

Once you have mastered the knowledge and skills required for the role, your newly acquired experience, coupled with personal self-esteem and expertise, will help develop and reinforce your self-confidence. Over time, with cumulative transferrable experiences, one will build sufficient self-confidence to undertake virtually any reasonable task. Eventually, this results in a positive attitude, certainty, and self-belief that you will probably succeed when confronting and tackling a wide range of challenges. This is vital in business. It leads to greater confidence in taking on new challenges, setting higher goals, more self-assurance in decision-making, and risk-taking and dealing with people.

Interestingly, these inward and outward behaviors of self-esteem and self-confidence, which comprise confidence, are not identical and don't automatically operate in sync. When a leader has high self-esteem as well as solid self-confidence, you have a mature, emotionally stable, highly skilled, and capable individual. This person has the simultaneous ability to be a strong leader and be confident enough to delegate and empower staff and share recognition and rewards. This, in turn, brings out the best in everyone, ultimately strengthening the entire team's effort.

However, this is not always the case. Make a quick survey of celebrities, musicians, and politicians, and you do not have to go far to find insecure individuals with low self-esteem who are immensely capable and self-confident, or even overconfident in a particular skill or talent. This is exceedingly unfortunate but not uncommon as one sees the alcohol abuse, drug addiction, and levels of suicides among talented and famous but emotionally insecure individuals. These individuals possess a distinctly unstable confidence profile.

Conversely, you can also observe other individuals with solid self-esteem who lack external self-confidence. Unfortunately, this can stifle their ability to self-actualize or even achieve success because of their inability to maximize their potential socially. There are also many examples of highly talented but reclusive poets or artists whose works are never or only recognized late in life or even posthumously.

To maximize your potential and be as successful as possible, leaders benefit from both internal self-esteem and external self-confidence for optimum performance. Fortunately, these behaviors and skills can be learned and developed effectively over time through dedicated conscious and courageous effort and recurring successful experiences.

> **Takeaway:** Personal self-esteem and self-confidence provide a solid basis for professional confidence. However, confidence in your leadership role is primarily a function of relevant expertise or prior transferable experience.
>
> A major promotion or an entirely new role or domain may take some months to acclimate to. However, remember even tangential prior experience can bring new insights and value to a new responsibility.

Commitment

The kind of commitment I find among the best performers across virtually every field is a single-minded passion for what they do, an unwavering desire for excellence in the way they think and the way they work.

—Jim Collins, business leader, author, and consultant [42]

Commitment is the firm and unwavering dedication to a particular belief, cause, activity, project, team, or organization that is apparent intellectually, emotionally, and physically.

Commitment is again one of those behaviors where there is an internal framework and an external modus operandi. Commitment operates both as an internal set of standards or principles, as well as how you represent and act on them in your objectives and interactions with colleagues and staff.

We have discussed building staff loyalty and commitment to your vision and purpose on numerous occasions. But, as a prerequisite to winning that employee's allegiance, the team must also have unquestionable confidence in your commitment to them and the cause.

Where does that confidence in the leader and commitment to the vision arise? As we have stressed, it starts with the leader's intrinsic integrity and honesty, creating a trust relationship. But beyond that, it also comes from the explicit recognition of the leader's deep conviction and belief in the mission by the staff. This conviction and commitment are beyond slogans, speeches, and platitudes, which the team will intuitively sense and instinctively recognize and respect. Without that authentic assurance of the leader's commitment to the staff, developing reciprocal team commitment and loyalty to the leader or mission will be inadequate or almost impossible.

The following event from my TUI and Accenture days immediately came to mind when considering commitment. Once, while I was at TUI in Spain, we had a particularly intractable problem which I needed Accenture's urgent help to resolve. Despite it being Saturday morning, I felt confident enough in my relationship with Jordi Paris, the Accenture Account Director in Barcelona, to call him. So, I called saying: "Jordi, my sincere apologies for calling you on Saturday, but I urgently need your help. Can you talk for ten minutes?" First, Jordi did answer and then responded. "Of course, Greg, please give me two minutes; I'm leading a bicycle excursion of thirty Boy Scouts. Let me get them safely to a stoplight, and then we can talk!" Incredibly, he was leading thirty children on bikes that he guided to a safe stop, and then we talked, setting up the required solution. That, for me, is an example of profoundly dedicated and unshakeable commitment!

When I recounted this story to a friend regarding this example of commitment, she challenged, "Surely his commitment should have been to the children?" I replied yes, and it was; first, he safely stopped the children, and then we talked!

I believe commitment is a cohesive glue that binds people, teams, and organizations together to achieve remarkable things. Unquestionably, the leader's commitment is an essential activator in that alchemy of creating the right vision, climate, and corporate culture to bring it all together productively and sustainably. You and your colleagues will also discover that impassioned personal commitment and its associated satisfaction are primary contributors to job satisfaction and personal self-actualization.

Takeaway: Your leadership commitment to staff and the mission is essential to your team's confidence and loyalty. Ensure your organizational vision and mission are sufficiently aligned with your value system, as your employees will instinctively sense your internal level of commitment and react accordingly.

Communicative

Communication is the most important skill any leader can possess.
     —*Richard Branson, English business magnate*[43]

Effective communication must assuredly be added to our list of essential Leadership skills. No leader leads in isolation; highly developed communications skills enhance everything you do, from staff conversations, meetings, and presentations to emails, memos, and reports. However, for the purpose of this leadership study, let's focus primarily on verbal communication.

As a general rule, overcommunicating, almost to a fault, is preferable to under-communicating. To maintain trust and team collaboration, the benefits of overcommunication far outweigh the downsides and risks of not sharing enough. Staff want to be involved, enjoy generating ideas, and feel valued and valuable when actively participating in setting direction, brainstorming, or solving problems. Further, involving staff and specialists in the conversations will always add invaluable input and ideas to the issue.

As a foundation for this communications discussion, let's explore the leadership behavioral attributes that will enhance your communications and bring them to life.

- Ensure you create and share your compelling vision expansively using vivid analogies to infuse it with a sense of *purpose* to gain staff buy-in.
- *Communicate* energetically, colorfully, and effectively using executive storytelling, analogy, and metaphors.
- *Inspire* the team with *enthusiasm* and emotional *passion* through animated communications to bring the vision to life.
- Lead with *integrity* by centering yourself within your value framework and applying your ethical modus operandi.
- Build *trust* through proactive staff engagement, continuous communications, and reciprocal social exchange.
- Verbally exhibit and express sincere *empathy* toward your colleagues and staff.

- Challenge yourself constantly to ensure your communications exude genuine *authenticity.*
- Ensure your communications are suitably *diplomatic* and have a *decisive* call to action.
- Finally, fundamentally, communications must inherently be a two-way dialogue. Therefore, attentive and active *listening* is equally important as effective speaking.

Therefore, infuse your communications with the best of your leadership style and skills to ensure you engage your teams regularly, solicit their input and participation, involve them in decision-making, and empower them through delegation. The tangible benefits of actively involving employees in these discussions will enhance idea generation and solution identification from knowledgeable staff, increase staff trust, and improve staff morale and motivation.

As I've said, overcommunicating is far better than under-communicating, and I've followed that axiom, perhaps almost to a fault. However, one vivid example of the value of intense, continuous communication comes to mind. In the yearlong, three-company carve-out in forty-five countries we have discussed, with over one hundred staff members tackling over four thousand separate tasks, the complexity and challenges would have been overwhelming without continuous collaborative communications.

One of the critical success factors during this highly successful project was the daily stand-up involving all workstream heads and functional specialists. Many of you will have experienced the value of agile development stand-ups, for which this was a very intense and essential example. In this case, I cannot overstate the importance of the constant daily contributions of the twenty staff members who regularly participated. This comprised the leadership, project managers, workstream heads, and critically, more junior but experienced specialists. The involvement of these knowledgeable functional workers ensured all plans and actions were grounded in the reality of how the business and systems operated. Without this constant top-to-bottom leadership, project, and cross-functional collaboration, it would have been virtually inconceivable to achieve our objectives, let alone realize the on-time, on-budget, zero-defect result that was accomplished.

The overarching critical success factor in this program was continuous, robust, team-wide communications. This was reinforced and enabled by complete team trust, full acceptance of cross-functional specialists' views, honesty, no sugarcoating of the facts, and an objective and pragmatic positioning of the daily status reports of all workstreams.

Good communication, by definition, implies that it must be two-way, honest, holistic, coherent, trustful, tolerant, objective, and immediate. Any communications lacking these fundamental underpinnings may potentially be flawed or faulty.

Takeaway: As a substantial amount of traditional team-based management communications is nonverbal, you must significantly increase the frequency, quality, and methodology of your leadership interactions in the new hybrid on-site and virtual working environments.

Creativity

There is no doubt that creativity is the most important human resource of all. Without creativity, there would be no progress, and we would be forever repeating the same patterns.
—*Edward de Bono, author, inventor, and consultant*[44]

Creativity is a vital recurring theme for leadership and organizations. Our discussion here focuses on developing and cultivating creativity as an intrinsic leadership characteristic.

Whereas innovation explicitly commercializes a new concept into a commercial success, creativity is a broader concept permeating virtually every aspect of a leader's work. I view creativity as a pervasive personal characteristic, similar to when I say you should apply sound judgment or attention to quality to any issue or activity.

Therefore, I contend that anything that a leader says, writes, and does should purposefully consider a creative intent or aspect. Even such seemingly mundane issues as a budget spreadsheet or an employee's appraisal can and should be fashioned creatively. To be the best and most effective leader possible, one should make a deliberate attempt in everything they do to make it better, more interesting, more attractive, more effective, or cheaper. This is not to waste unnecessary effort on whitewashing organizational cosmetics or rearranging the deckchairs on the *Titanic*, but to keep creativity continuously in mind as an ethos of how to conduct yourself, lead your team, and run your business. Further, this creative focus helps make even the most ordinary or routine task just a little bit more interesting.

This encouragement to emphasize creativity is about much more than saying: "Just Do It!" It is about making a conscious commitment and developing a discipline of creativity and continuous improvement throughout your professional and personal life. You will undoubtedly find that the quality of your thought, imagination, communications, work, and actions will improve based on your conscious and constant attempt to improve creatively on whatever you encounter.

There are a number of practical yet highly effective ways to foster and engender creativity in your role and daily work. Perhaps the most important thing is to think intentionally about doing it. Then, consciously stepping back from your issue, product, or problem and considering how it can be extended and expanded and how it is similar or different to related or completely unrelated things can dramatically enhance your perception and perspective on those products, issues, or problems. Edward de Bono, whose quote I used to introduce this section, has numerous books and online resources on lateral thinking and thinking outside the box to help develop effective methods and patterns for creative thinking.

Following this creative ethos, you will perceive the world differently, make new connections and deeper associations between unrelated topics and phenomena, and generate new solutions. As a result, you will have more originality in problem-solving, people management, organizational design, product concepts, and invaluable new connections and associations. The immediate result is that your imagination will flourish, and you will find yourself generating new ideas and alternatives across virtually every domain you touch.

Being creative means solving problems in new and original ways. It means intentionally thinking about changing your perspective to originate novel approaches. It also means taking risks, breaking with routine, and doing something different and unique to improve or enhance your work. Ultimately, this mindful intention to inject creativity into your work will generate additional tangible benefits for you, your colleagues, and across the business.

Creativity and creative thinking are also highly contagious, as they are collectively thought-provoking, stimulating, and enjoyable. By intentionally encouraging and developing this attitude in your work, you will discover that you are consciously and even unconsciously modeling and mentoring your colleagues and teams to be more creative. The net result will be that your entire organization will realize increased value creation from new and original approaches to creative thinking.

Not only will you become a better leader, but your teams will also become more effective. You will solve problems more effectively, improve your overall operations, create significant new value, and you and your team will be more creative, have more fun, and enjoy an improved work-life balance. Finally, expanding your creative juices will result in you and your team dramatically amplifying your self-esteem and realizing greater career and life self-actualization.

Takeaway: Crafting a creative organizational culture where you infuse and integrate creativity into virtually everything you do will foster significant value creation and make your work life more interesting, enjoyable, and successful.

This completes the Leadership Skills Model and the 20 essential Leadership Characteristics Matrix.

Each individual is unique. Regardless of your experience, age, or seniority, this model provides a robust, memorable, and comprehensive framework of leadership characteristics for any aspiring leader's career advancement and skill development plan.

We will return to these characteristics as a foundation for leadership assessment, growth, and development.[45]

Hudson – Garrison
Leadership Characteristics Matrix

Cognitive	**Intellectual**	**Learned**
	Judgment	Courage
	Diplomacy	Confidence
	Decisiveness	Commitment
	Perseverance	Communicative
	Reliability	Creativity
	Innate	**Emotional**
	Integrity	Purpose
	Empathy	Passion
	Visionary	Enthusiasm
	Authenticity	Inspirational
	Trust	Optimism

Behavioural

Leadership Characteristics Matrix—Full populated Matrix

The Leadership Characteristics Model can also be employed as a simple, easy-to-use tool for leadership character profiling for recruitment, role placement, or succession planning.

By comparing a candidate against your desired characteristics for a particular role, you get a sense of the candidate's fit against your specific position and company.[46]

Hudson Garrison Leadership Characteristics Profile Tool

Leadership Characteristics	Standardized Equal Rating Score	Sample Role & Organizational Requirement
Integrity	5	7
Empathy	5	5
Visionary	5	6
Authenticity	5	5
Trust	5	5
Purpose	5	6
Passion	5	7
Enthusiasm	5	4
Inspirational	5	5
Optimism	5	5
Judgment	5	5
Diplomacy	5	4
Decisiveness	5	4
Perseverance	5	4
Reliability	5	5
Courage	5	3
Confidence	5	5
Commitment	5	5
Communicative	5	4
Creativity	5	6
Total	100	100

Leadership Characteristics Profile.

For corporations and individuals requiring a formal, widely tri-aled, and extensively validated instrument, I refer you to the following resources in the upcoming Leadership Models and Assessment Tools chapter.

- The Myers–Briggs Personality Type Indicator (MBTI)
- The Birkman Method
- Korn Ferry Leadership Assessment Tool and Process
- Leadership Architect Tool kit
- Thomas International Personal Profile Analysis (PPA)
- The Insights Discovery Tool

Key Takeaways—Leadership Character

- Leadership is a composite of the following qualities; however, it all distills down to the fact that exceptional leaders have Character.
- Integrity is the foundational cornerstone of character underpinning every interaction you have and each decision you make, to be guided by the highest possible level of ethical, honest, and moral behavior.
- If you allow your humanity to shine through your professional behavior, especially with authentic Empathy, you will create and strengthen the relationship bond with your team and colleagues.
- Mutual Trust is cultivated through integrity, sincerity, and authenticity and is at the heart of the "Social Exchange Theory" reciprocal relationship between the leader and the team.
- Topmost leaders do not give up when confronted with obstacles and will Persevere to motivate and inspire the team, even when the going is rough and morale is low. We often refer to this as "having Grit!"
- Reliability relates to an ingrained drive, plus a conscious commitment to deliver what you promise, where you establish leadership credibility and an enduring reputation to achieve what you commit to.

CHAPTER 5

Know Thyself: Deciphering and Interpreting Others

Leadership Models and Assessment Tools

Having explored leadership character and the twenty paramount leadership characteristics matrix comprising successful leaders' crucial attributes and behaviors, let's dig deeper into the psychology and assessment of leadership models and behaviors.

This next section surveys the leadership field's most prominent and respected leadership models and assessment tools. Perhaps again, the phrase "know thyself" is highly relevant here. Psychometric tests or assessments are studies or tests conducted to measure a person's cognitive abilities, personality profiles, abilities, skills, or behaviors. These tools are one of the best ways to objectively, analytically, and scientifically analyze and understand yourself and your teams individually and collectively. This can be fascinating and invaluable for recruitment, career planning, mentoring, capability development, and team building.

This chapter on leadership models and assessment tools is one of my personal favorites, as I've always been intrigued by psychology and psychometric testing. My interest in psychology, in part, led me to major in neurology during my medical studies internship. This, along with a technology inclination and analytical orientation, stimulated my interest in psychometric testing. All this evolved naturally as a logical extension and physical expression of psychological interests within the business context.

Shortly after becoming the training manager for American Express in San Francisco in the mid-1980s, I took a weeklong residential course on psychometric testing at the University of San Francisco. Among the program's highlights were keynote lectures by several leaders in the field, including Will Schutz presenting FIRO-B, Robert Blake the Managerial Grid, and Ken Thomas the Thomas–Kilmann Conflict Mode Instrument. The conference was enlightening, educational, and thought-provoking, and as a result, I've been an aficionado of business applications of psychometric testing ever since.

This interest took on richer and more direct expression years later when I had the occasion, as interim COO, to run Acumen International, now Human Factors International, a psychometric testing company in the San Francisco Bay Area in 2002–2003.

Throughout my career, I've had the opportunity to take part in and conduct numerous leadership assessment tools, both in my own recruitment processes as well as when assessing candidates for roles. These powerful tools have guided me, educated me, helped me professionally and personally, and, most importantly, led me to be a more insightful and effective team leader over the years.

Following is a review of my favorite assessments and tests. A number of these authoritative and valuable psychometric leadership assessment tools warrant inclusion for your consideration, depending on your specific requirements. Further, there is an extended list of assessments appended in the Appendix.

I provide brief introductions of each to pique your appetite for more in-depth individual study or to tap professional external expert support as required. Professional psychometric assessment tools frequently benefit from considerable research and facilitator administration.

I've grouped the leadership model Instruments and psychometric assessment Tools into five categories for convenience and concept reinforcement. Recognize the boundaries between these categories are often fuzzy, with significant overlap between the areas. Hence, the instrument category groupings are for learning convenience rather than hard and fast, precise definitions.

- Leadership models
- Management models
- Recruitment/placement tools
- Team building
- Psychology and personality types

Leadership Models

- LPI®: Leadership Practices Inventory®
- Emotional Intelligence EQ-i 2.0.
- Situational Leadership

Leadership Models included in the Appendix

- Lewin's 3 Core Leadership Styles Framework
- Tannenbaum-Schmidt Leadership Continuum
- Dunham and Pierce's Leadership Process Model

Leadership Practices Inventory®

Our first leadership assessment tool is the Leadership Practices Inventory® (LPI®), one of the world's most extensively used, rigorously validated, and longest-in-use leadership psychometric assessment tools.

It's also an assessment tool that I particularly like, as it is highly aligned with both my own leadership philosophies and predilection toward supporting and validating theory with tangible qualitative and quantitative evidence.

The LPI evolved out of numerous workshops, extensive research, in-depth interviews, and analysis of case studies conducted by Jim Kouzes and Barry Posner for their trailblazing book *The Leadership Challenge*.

In *The Leadership Challenge*, which we reviewed in the leadership gurus chapter, Kouzes and Posner present the Five Practices of Exemplary Leadership: model the way, inspire a shared vision, challenge the process, enable others to act, and encourage the heart.[1]

The Five Practices of Exemplary Leadership®

The Leadership Challenge—The Five Practices.

The Exemplary Leadership framework's practices and disciplines provide a comprehensive and pragmatic overview of the leadership function. Further, these five practices constitute the conceptual foundation of the LPI Leadership Psychometric assessment tools. The Five Practices framework was conceived and developed by examining and codifying an extensive collection of case studies of "personal-best" leadership experiences.

The LPI provides leaders with a comprehensive and validated tool kit for assessing an individual's leadership behavior. The LPI: Leadership Practices Inventory measures how often individuals, colleagues, and teams exercise The Five Practices of Exemplary Leadership, which have been documented and shown to produce optimal leadership behaviors and results. The inventory provides feedback and reports identifying when the learner performs well and where they need to concentrate to improve as a best-of-class leader. In addition, the LPI offers targeted recommendations for developing and enhancing leadership capabilities with specific guidance and practical actions for strengthening leadership skills.

The LPI correlates The Five Practices of Exemplary Leadership® with six essential behaviors comprising thirty leadership criteria. The accompanying Personal-Best Leadership Experience questionnaire asks a total of thirty-eight open-ended questions to compare and assess a leader's experience against an extensive historical database of prior respondents' personal-best experiences.[2]

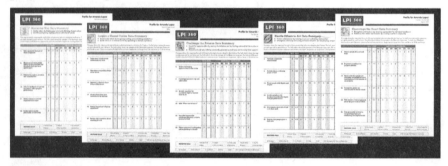

LPI Leadership Psychometric assessment—LPI: Practices Inventory.

The LPI benefits from thirty-five years of data collection from five thousand case studies and more than five million survey respondents. Further, over seven hundred external related research studies, peer reviews, and extensive reliability and validity testing have been conducted.

Continuing peer reviews and research corroborate findings that the Five Practices and the LPI assessment correlate leader effectiveness with staff morale, motivation, and loyalty.[3]

For a detailed study of the Five Practices of Exemplary Leadership, please review Jim Kouzes's and Barry Posner's book *The Leadership Challenge*[4] in the leadership gurus chapter.

Takeaway: If you are a senior leader or people manager in a larger organization, The Leadership Practices Inventory is an excellent tool to consider for a baseline survey of your leadership team's leadership maturity and capabilities. For the most effective results, ensure you have an experienced internal or external facilitator.

Emotional Intelligence EQ-i 2.0®

We have extensively discussed the value and increasing importance of emotional intelligence for leaders in today's work culture. It is also directly correlated to the related topics of servant leadership and authenticity.

For these reasons, it is often helpful for leaders to understand it more deeply and further how to assess and measure it. Excellent emotional intelligence assessment tools are available, building on the ground-breaking work of Professor Reuven Bar-On, an American-Israeli clinical and organizational psychologist who developed the Bar-On Emotional Quotient Inventory™ (the EQ-i™).[5]

Built upon the original insights and foundation of Dr. BarOn's EQ-i®, Multi-Health Systems Inc. of Toronto, Canada, perfected the Emotional Quotient Inventory (EQ-i 2.0®),[6] which is among the most robustly scientifically validated and employed emotional intelligence tools globally.

In addition to the emotional intelligence explanations we reviewed conceptually, EQ-i 2.0 provides a comprehensive analysis and assessment of emotional intelligence capabilities. The tool places a strong emphasis on workplace performance relative to leadership effectiveness, assessing five EQ capabilities: self-perception, self-expression, interpersonal, decision-making, and stress management, and fifteen EQ competencies:

1. Self-regard	9. Impulse control
2. Emotional self-awareness	10. Reality-testing
3. Emotional self-expression	11. Flexibility
4. Independence	12. Problem-solving
5. Empathy	13. Self-actualization
6. Social responsibility	14. Optimism
7. Interpersonal relationship	15. Happiness/well-being
8. Stress tolerance	

As per the criteria above, the EQ effectiveness report can provide a detailed analysis of a leader's current capabilities and identify potential areas for improvement for themselves, staff, or colleagues.[7]

Fortunately, emotional intelligence is a clear concept and cluster of capabilities that develop with experience and can be taught, learned, coached, and developed over time. It is particularly valuable for leadership recruitment/placement or staff coaching and skill development. It has also been proven constructive for improving the awareness and performance of senior executives who have risen to be captains of industry but can benefit from enhanced social soft skills. Successful implementation and development of EQ through the professional facilitated assessment can improve leadership performance and communications, including interpersonal relationships.[8]

Emotional Intelligence EQ-i 2.0.

Takeaway: As a critical new leadership dimension, the Bar-On Emotional Quotient Inventory™ has spawned virtually an entirely new industry of EQ assessments. There are numerous easy-to-use online inventories for your own assessment, or contact your HR department or people manager to engage a training consultancy to conduct a team-based survey.

Situational Leadership®

Spending time in start-ups, dot-coms, SMEs, and multinationals has taught me the benefits of both disciplined management and the necessity of "agile, adaptable management." Further, I've hired maintenance workers and graduates, PhDs and retirees, and everything in between, in dozens of countries across the Americas, Middle East, Asia, and Europe. As a result, I can confidently attest to the fact that there is no such thing as one size (or style) fits all in people management situations. Instead, leadership demands are almost as diverse as the members of the staff themselves.

A leader needs to be prepared, capable, and adaptable to deal with whatever work situation life throws at them. This includes different contexts where leaders may need to modify their behavior to suit the type of organization, whether a start-up or a mature company. Further, we also talked about the difference between transactional and transformational leaders and situations. However, as you appreciate, not all challenges are at these macro levels. A leader needs to be responsive and adaptable to the needs and demands of managing different types of individuals, for example, veterans and new hires, enthusiastic and motivated employees, as well as occasionally cynical, jaded, or discouraged staffers. Consequently, we need the awareness and skill sets to identify and differentiate these circumstances in order to effectively manage and motivate all types of individuals.

There are many approaches to setting employee objectives and managing distinct staff types. Moreover, one must be pragmatic in rapidly and effectively managing staff. One particularly effective methodology I learned during my training days and have used throughout my management experience is the Situational Leadership model created by Dr. Paul Hersey and Dr. Ken Blanchard. This model provides an easy-to-use and effective staff management model that correlates different leadership styles to individual and team performance readiness levels.

The high-level principle is that leaders must adapt their leadership style according to their staff's willingness (psychological commitment) and ability (task capability). Simplified in my own words is that employee behavior can be broken down into motivation and ability at a high level. In other words, is the employee willing and able or lacking in either?

Based on this, the leader must adjust their management style to ensure the most effective approach for managing those particular employees.

Applying these two metrics positively and negatively identifies the followers' readiness level for the task you are asking them to perform, plus an operative leadership model for effectively managing them.[9]

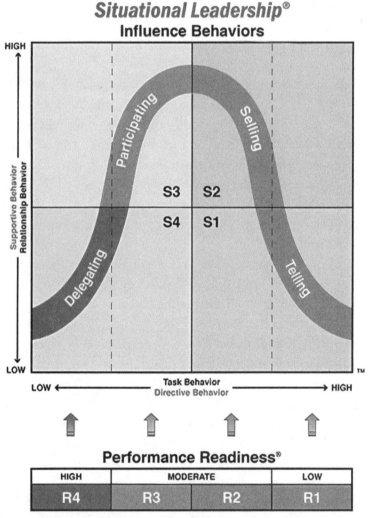

Situational Leadership.

The Situational Leadership model comprises the following classification of individuals:

R1: The individual is unable and insecure or unwilling to perform the task. In this case, the S1 leadership "telling" style, where the leader gives precise instructions and monitors closely, is the most effective.

R2: The individual is unable (lacks skills) but confident or willing to perform the task. The S2 leadership style, "selling," is the most effective, as the leader explains how to complete the task, sets goals, and gives guidance and support.

R3: The individual is able but insecure or unwilling to perform the task. The S3 leadership style, "participating," is appropriate when the leader initiates a two-way conversation with the follower, mentoring, encouraging efforts, and praising success.

R4: The individual is able and willing to perform the task. The S4 leadership style, "delegating," is when the leader can delegate to capable individuals for planning and execution and checks in periodically if needed.[10]

Understanding the model and approach at a high level and keeping it always in the back of your mind will help guide you in efficiently planning and executing objectives. It is also useful when you are in the heat of the moment to recognize the optimal approach for each task you ask the individual to perform. For example, when dealing with individuals with a low level of performance readiness for completing the task, one has to be "task-oriented," precise, and directing (however, not aggressive), or "telling and selling" in the classic model. Conversely, in dealing with staff with a higher level of performance readiness for performing the task, you can be more "relationship-oriented" using supportive and delegating approaches.

Additionally, remember that followers' knowledge and capabilities will change over time and are contextually sensitive. Hence, we as leaders need to recognize these changes and adjust our styles accordingly. For example, staff will gain knowledge and skill over time and become capable and confident, requiring less guidance and supervision. Further, a long-term employee who is motivated and competent in a role with tasks they have performed many times in the past might be anxious or resistant to an entirely new and challenging assignment. Over the years, as a technologist grappling with evolving technological changes, I've had to deal with staff retraining or resistance to change on numerous occasions.

The digital transformation agenda most of us have been through in recent years is a typical example of a situation in which some staff may have been thrust uncomfortably into a disruptive transformational change. As always, with a major shift in processes and technologies, some people adapt easily and rapidly, some staff need extra guidance and training, others resist but eventually make the transition, and perhaps some cannot adapt. These types of changes in any industry are as challenging for leadership as they are for the employees. The Situational Leadership model is an essential tool in our leadership repertoire to identify rapidly at a high level the individual employee situation and the associated management style that may be most appropriate and effective.

Recognize that whenever you have an issue with a staff member, ask yourself, is your employee willing and able? Then, adjust your style accordingly. This straightforward and easy-to-apply model has popped into my head countless times when dealing with staff to provide a quick sense check of the situation. This ensured that I understood what was happening, was not placing unrealistic demands on a new or struggling employee, or if I needed to shift gears and tactics to get someone back on track. This quick check of the situation will also help ensure you don't micromanage and constrain an experienced and capable employee. You will probably need to use multiple approaches and techniques simultaneously across a large and varied team. This tool helps clarify who requires what help and when.

A quick study of the Situational Leadership model can provide you with a practical tool kit of staff management tools. I suggest you take an online assessment initially to get a sense of the instrument and then take advantage of or contract for a professionally facilitated Situational Leadership program.

Takeaway: Whenever you have a staff problem or a performance issue, ask yourself the simple but insightful question: "Is the employee willing and able?" This will immediately identify if your problem is a motivational or capability issue, and you can address the matter according to appropriate task- or relationship-oriented leadership skills.

Management Models
- Martin M. Broadwell: Four stages of competence
- Myers–Briggs Type Indicator
- Insights Discovery

Management Models included in the Appendix
- The Birkman Method
- Blake and Mouton's Managerial Grid

Martin M. Broadwell: Four stages of competence

Martin Broadwell's four stages of competence,[11] described originally for training purposes, is now more broadly applied as an insightful and invaluable tool for identifying and managing staff skills and capabilities.[12]

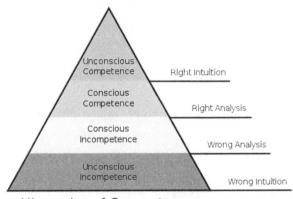

Hierarchy of Competence

Martin M. Broadwell—Four stages of competence.

This model primarily focuses on acquiring knowledge or skills rather than including the additional specification of motivation as in the Situational Leadership model. Still, naturally, motivation is an essential driver as a catalyst for skill acquisition.

The concept begins with unconscious incompetence, where one is unaware of or has not been exposed to a new body of knowledge. For example, this could consider a youth, a new educational challenge, or the development of a new skill. For example, during their education, a child might not be aware of calculus, or an adult might not be familiar with quantum physics. Further, a recent graduate might not know your market or products. They are, initially, therefore, unconsciously incompetent.

Once the individual becomes aware of a body of knowledge, they then progress to the stage of conscious incompetence. Here, they understand their lack of knowledge or skill. Therefore, they should be given an opportunity and resources to apply themselves to retrain and reskill to close that gap or deficit of knowledge or skills.

With effort, training, and practice, the individual or employee can develop the abilities or skills to become proficient in the new area to the extent that they eventually become consciously competent in this newly acquired body of knowledge (calculus or quantum physics) or skill (skiing or programming).

Over time, with continuous practice, one becomes so experienced and adept at an activity it becomes second nature. Instead of consciously performing the task, it can be performed efficiently and fluidly without thinking about completing it. At this point, we become unconsciously competent in this skill or task.[13]

We will all have experienced unconscious competence in one endeavor or another, such as after we learned to drive or became experienced in skiing. The same applies to most work activities after perhaps six months or so when we are fully trained and no longer uncomfortable with our tasks. Examples might be when learning Excel, becoming competent with coding in a new language, operating a new machine, or developing a business case. Once a task is mastered, we perform it virtually automatically without consciously thinking about it or considering how to perform it.

This process of becoming consciously and unconsciously competent reminds me of German philosopher Martin Heidegger's discussion of the modes of consciousness. He refers to being asleep or unaware, becoming awake or conscious, and the highest state of becoming asleep again when you achieve unconscious competence. At the final level, you shift your attention away from the task; it becomes second nature and you no longer need conscious attention to perform the task. As athletes will tell you, once you have achieved mastery of an activity, the top-level performance requires a shift from conscious attention to achieving a highly focused optimal mental state where you are in the zone or in the groove. We pick up this theme again with Mihaly Csikszentmihalyi's concept of flow.

I have found this model useful personally and professionally as it is easy to learn and apply and clearly crystallizes the process of knowledge acquisition, building toward mastery. I particularly like combining this model with the situational leadership "willing and able" model.

First, consider the Situational Leadership model of whether a person is "willing and able." In this context, being able is the same as competence. Then, add the Broadwell construct of conscious awareness, and you have a rich understanding of their motivation and capability, as well as their conscious awareness of the situation. Therefore, ask yourself, is a staff member willing and able, as well as unconscious or conscious of their skill or performance? This may seem complicated at first, so start with considering both models separately until you are comfortable with each, and then you will naturally begin to consider them simultaneously (i.e., conscious competence).

Takeaway: Combine this competence model with the Situational Leadership tool for immediate but powerful insights into staff behavior. Ask yourself, is your staff member willing and able, as well as unconscious or conscious of their skill or performance? This identifies employee attitude and capabilities issues as well as their self-awareness of the situation and professional maturity.

Myers–Briggs Type Indicator™ [14]

One of the most widely used leadership assessment tools is the Myers-Briggs Type Indicator (MBTI), with two million assessments conducted annually. This psychometric tool can be a leader-conducted or self-administered questionnaire that profiles psychological differences in how people see the world and make decisions.

The Myers–Briggs Type Indicator is a personal assessment tool for identifying a person's personality type, strengths, and preferences. Myers-Briggs was initially based on Carl Jung's psychological types theories. Jung's theories state that people's interests, motivations, and values differ; however, their behaviors, perceptions, and judgments are internally consistent.

By systematically assessing, clustering, and classifying these behaviors, you can identify how people tend to perceive situations and how they are likely to respond. Comprehending these individual differences can help people understand themselves better and help them adapt their occupations and careers to align with their personal preferences, styles, and skills. Further, recognizing these capabilities and propensities according to strengths and weaknesses can help leaders balance teams' skills and optimize project delivery capabilities.

Jung's personality types theory describes how people behave and operate according to characteristic patterns in diverse situations. Myers–Briggs uses these types to create eight behavioral patterns across four scales.[15] (See chart on page 247.)

The first extraversion (E)–introversion (I) scale describes how people behave in social settings and interactions relative to external versus internal-facing tendencies or preferences. Most of us have both behaviors to some extent but have a tendency toward one or the other.

The second scale of sensing (S)–intuition (N) deals with how people experience and learn from the world. Some people prefer to experience things firsthand and learn directly from their senses. Others intuit and interpret situations using imagination, conceptual thinking, and abstract reasoning.

Next, we have thinking (T)–feeling (F), which addresses how people manage information and make decisions. Some people are objective and make considered decisions based on known and objective facts and figures. Others sense and feel emotions using their gut instinct to assess situations and make observations.

Finally, the last scale, judging (J)–perceiving (P), considers how people behave when making decisions and taking action. Some people prefer a tangible, concrete structure and factual information from which to make a thoughtful decision. In contrast, others are more intuitive, fluid, and flexible when interpreting a situation and arriving at a conclusion.[16]

Remember, we all occasionally use most of these skills and behaviors; Myers–Briggs assesses our predominant style and typical tendencies toward the distinct personality types and associated behaviors. Clearly understanding these types and identifying your and your team's preferences can be helpful in interacting with individuals and crafting well-balanced and effective teams. One of the key benefits of Myers–Briggs is the broad-based acceptance and extensive coverage of this tool. It is not unusual at all at work or socially to have a discussion where others will be familiar with the Myers–Briggs and be interested in your "type." Having taken the tool multiple times over many years, I've seen some interesting evolution in my experience and behaviors. However, now I seem to have settled down to being primarily an ENTJ.

Takeaway: Whether out of personal interest or professional application, I recommend starting out with an online Myers–Briggs assessment. Then, with a high-level understanding of the four scales of extraversion/introversion, sensing/intuition, thinking/feeling, and judging/perceiving, you will have a more conscious awareness and insight into why staff act and react the way they do.

What's Your Personality Type?

Use the questions on the outside of the chart to determine the four letters of your Myers-Briggs type.
For each pair of letters, choose the side that seems most natural to you, even if you don't agree with every description.

1. Are you outwardly or inwardly focused? If you:

- Could be described as talkative, outgoing
- Like to be in a fast-paced environment
- Tend to work out ideas with others, think out loud
- Enjoy being the center of attention

then you prefer

E
Extraversion

- Could be described as reserved, private
- Prefer a slower pace with time for contemplation
- Tend to think things through inside your head
- Would rather observe than be the center of attention

then you prefer

I
Introversion

2. How do you prefer to take in information? If you:

- Focus on the reality of how things are
- Pay attention to concrete facts and details
- Prefer ideas that have practical applications
- Like to describe things in a specific, literal way

then you prefer

S
Sensing

- Imagine the possibilities of how things could be
- Notice the big picture, see how everything connects
- Enjoy ideas and concepts for their own sake
- Like to describe things in a figurative, poetic way

then you prefer

N
Intuition

3. How do you prefer to make decisions? If you:

- Make decisions in an impersonal way, using logical reasoning
- Value justice, fairness
- Enjoy finding the flaws in an argument
- Could be described as reasonable, level-headed

then you prefer

T
Thinking

- Base your decisions on personal values and how your actions affect others
- Value harmony, forgiveness
- Like to please others and point out the best in people
- Could be described as warm, empathetic

then you prefer

F
Feeling

4. How do you prefer to live your outer life? If you:

- Prefer to have matters settled
- Think rules and deadlines should be respected
- Prefer to have detailed, step-by-step instructions
- Make plans, want to know what you're getting into

then you prefer

J
Judging

- Prefer to leave your options open
- See rules and deadlines as flexible
- Like to improvise and make things up as you go
- Are spontaneous, enjoy surprises and new situations

then you prefer

P
Perceiving

Myers–Briggs Type Indicator.

Insights Discovery

The Insights Discovery[17] tool is a modern, widely used, and comprehensively validated personality profile assessment also based on Carl Jung's research. It is frequently employed for recruitment, placement, and team building. I've used this tool extensively in recent years and found it robust, insightful, and engaging for individuals and teams. It's always been a highly popular, captivating, and motivating workshop activity for my teams.

Besides its invaluable assessment insights, participants can rapidly relate to and use the clear and concise color charts, models, and descriptions to distinguish behavioral types. The Insights Discovery model uses these comprehensible and memorable charts to help people understand their behavioral style, strengths, and value to teams as follows.

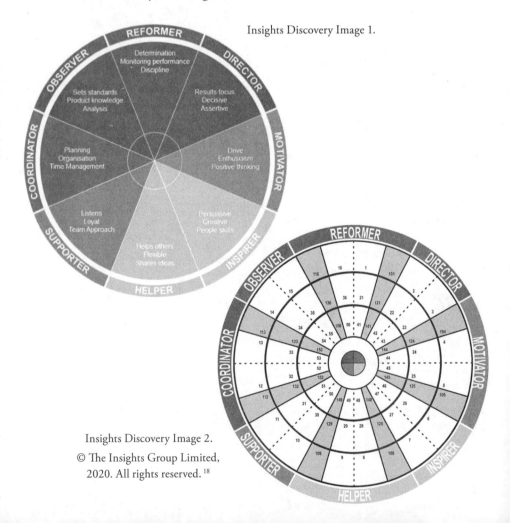

Insights Discovery Image 1.

Insights Discovery Image 2.

The "cool blue" upper left quadrant represents introverted and cautious individuals; these are thinking people who are thoughtful, objective, and task-oriented.

The "earth green" lower left quadrant profile is a combination of introverted and feeling individuals who are harmonious, reflective, deep, and consensus-driven.

The "fiery red" upper right quadrant individuals are extroverted, quick-thinking people who are sociable, action- and activity-oriented, and logical.

The "sunshine yellow" lower right quadrant people are extroverted and feeling individuals who are sociable, considerate, engaging, and idea- and action-oriented.[19]

While the color charts are engaging and interesting, good facilitation is beneficial to delve beneath the surface of "I'm a cool blue" or "I'm a sunshine yellow" to more substantial and meaningful issues. The Insights Discovery is a professional and insightful assessment; thus, a good certified facilitator will help address issues such as identifying, respecting, balancing, and valuing team members and getting the best out of everyone in a collaborative team working environment. You can find more information by visiting https://www.insights.com/products/insights-discovery/.

Takeaway: The Insights Discovery is one of the more recent and creative Jungian personality profiles. Because of participants' frequent, enthusiastic engagement with the tool, it is an outstanding choice for an insightful and thought-provoking but lively and enjoyable off-site team-building conference.

Recruitment / Placement

- Korn Ferry Leadership Assessment
- The Leadership Architect Lominger International

A European Recruitment Tool in the Appendix

- Thomas International Personality Profile

Korn Ferry Leadership Assessment

The Korn Ferry Leadership Assessment tool and process is a highly respected leadership Assessment tool with a reported fifty years of historical analytics and 69 million professional assessments. That is a great deal of valuable data and feedback with which to refine their assessment metrics! Learn more at:

https://www.kornferry.com/solutions/assessment-and-succession /leadership-assessment.[20]

Beyond this industry recommendation, I can attest to this tool's professionalism and associated in-person assessments, having been through the tool assessment and interview process on three occasions in my career. Learn more at:

https://www.kornferry.com/content/dam/kornferry/docs/article -migration//KFALP_Technical_Manual_final.pdf.[21]

At TUI Group, at one point, we worked with Korn Ferry to produce a Global CIO Capability Model and Assessment tool, which we used successfully as a CIO recruitment and skills development tool.

Takeaway: Korn Ferry, with strong recruitment, interim management, training, and organizational design capabilities, is an excellent choice for a wide range of leadership assessment and recruitment needs. Otherwise, for a free, flexible, and easy-to-use tool, you can adapt the leadership characteristics list at the end of the Leadership: Constructs of Character chapter to suit your company, culture, and role requirements.

Leadership Architect Lominger International—Korn Ferry

As mentioned, circa 2014, our IT organization engaged Korn Ferry to develop a global IT leadership framework and capability maturity model. This comprised multiple criteria: strategic skills, operating skills, and personal and interpersonal Skills. As a result, Korn Ferry created our leadership framework using these four lenses to assess our IT leadership performance, potential, and capabilities. This ultimately comprised learning styles, learning ability, leadership framework, and IT skills and experience.

The leadership framework and capability model were derived from a Korn Ferry company, Lominger International, which developed the respected Leadership Architect Framework. The Leadership Architect[22] is a comprehensive suite of assessment and development tools, including a leadership library and tool kit derived from competency work conducted with the Center for Creative Leadership-CCL.

The Leadership Architect tool kit provides extensive resources for leadership competency modeling, organizational effectiveness assessment, corporate strategy and talent frameworks, 360-degree assessment tools, and training and learning frameworks.[23]

Leadership Architect Lominger Intl. Korn/Ferry.

Team Building
- Belbin Team Roles Model
- Johari Window
- Tuckman's Stages of Group Development

Team Building Tools included in the Appendix
- FIRO and Element B Theory: The Human Element
- Thomas-Kilmann: Conflict Mode Instrument

Belbin® Team Roles Model

Dr. Meredith Belbin developed the Belbin® Team Roles Model[24] in the 1980s. It has been used extensively, particularly in Britain and Europe, as well as internationally as a team-building assessment and team-development tool.

I have participated in Belbin Team-Building programs on two separate occasions and used it as a team-building assessment tool for my own teams two additional times. I have found it an excellent tool for team role style assessment, discussion, improving communications, and team restructuring in each case. People may be under the impression that everyone understands each other within the team. However, reviewing the assessment and identifying the individual's behavioral styles provides significant insight into how differently people work. You will actually see people's surprise and revelation when their and others' behaviors are identified. It is common to hear people around the table exclaim, "Oh, now I understand why you are like that, and now I get it, because you are a resource investigator or a completer finisher or plant." These will become clear later, but each of the roles is unique. Identifying each person's primary and secondary roles is fascinating and highly valuable for team building and optimizing team effectiveness.

The research is, and I can personally attest to it, that each decent size, effective team requires most of the skills identified in the Belbin Model. If a particular skill is missing or too heavily weighted toward a specific role, your team can be hindered by missing that skill or, conversely, can be unbalanced by having too much of one skill. For example, too many creative "plants" and too few "completer finishers" can result in a great deal of fun and plenty of creative ideas but little follow-on action or reliable execution.

Belbin describes the roles as tendencies to behave and interrelate within the team in specific ways. First, there are three action-oriented roles (shaper, implementer, and completer-finisher), then three people-oriented roles (co-ordinator, team-worker, resource-investigator), and finally, three cerebral roles (plant, monitor-evaluator, and specialist).[25]

Here are the Belbin Team Roles; I strongly recommend you take the time to study each role carefully:[26]

Belbin® Team Role Summary Descriptions

Resource Investigator

Contribution: Outgoing, enthusiastic. Explores opportunities and develops contacts.

Allowable Weaknesses: Might be over-optimistic, and can lose interest once the initial enthusiasm has passed.

Teamworker

Contribution: Co-operative, perceptive and diplomatic. Listens and averts friction.

Allowable Weaknesses: Can be indecisive in crunch situations and tends to avoid confrontation.

Co-ordinator

Contribution: Mature, confident, identifies talent. Clarifies goals. Delegates effectively.

Allowable Weaknesses: Can be seen as manipulative and might offload their own share of the work.

Plant

Contribution: Creative, imaginative, free-thinking. Generates ideas and solves difficult problems.

Allowable Weaknesses: Might ignore incidentals, and may be too pre-occupied to communicate effectively.

Monitor Evaluator

Contribution: Sober, strategic and discerning. Sees all options and judges accurately.

Allowable Weaknesses: Sometimes lacks the drive and ability to inspire others and can be overly critical.

Specialist

Contribution: Single-minded, self-starting and dedicated. They provide specialist knowledge and skills.

Allowable Weaknesses: Can only contribute on a narrow front and tends to dwell on the technicalities.

Shaper

Contribution: Challenging, dynamic, thrives on pressure. Has the drive and courage to overcome obstacles.

Allowable Weaknesses: Can be prone to provocation, and may sometimes offend people's feelings.

Implementer

Contribution: Practical, reliable, efficient. Turns ideas into actions and organises work that needs to be done.

Allowable Weaknesses: Can be a bit inflexible and slow to respond to new possibilities.

Completer Finisher

Contribution: Painstaking, conscientious, anxious. Searches out errors. Polishes and perfects.

Allowable Weaknesses: Can be inclined to worry unduly, and reluctant to delegate.

Belbin Team Roles Model.

Belbin Team Role behavioral based assessments and reports for individuals & teams, for both the workplace & educational use, can be purchased directly from our website/office/global representatives and is the only sanctioned method available.

Ideally, a team would have each of the nine roles, but not every team is that fortunate or comprises that many people. You will probably find that different individuals will have a couple of role capabilities or can provide those additional functions for the team. For example, my natural style is that of a plant, but I'm also a shaper, often a co-ordinator, and secondarily a resource investigator. However, I'm likely atypical as I'm frequently the leader, but it does point out that even a team of four or five people can realize and comprise the requisite crucial skills. However, to avoid someone being a one-person band and melting down, you will need to balance the team's roles and efforts. Therefore, you need to identify if any essential skills are missing and ensure you can add or compensate for those skills to ensure overall team effectiveness. Given my skills, I'm conscious of my need to be complemented with completer finishers, specialists, and implementers to ensure we can execute and get the job done effectively.

The Belbin Roles and other similar team roles assessments can be extremely valuable for improving team interpersonal relationships, helping make your team much more effective, engaging, motivating, and even fun. However, a caution: deep analysis during team-building sessions can also surface the underlying causes of long-term resentment or conflict among team members. Therefore, I recommend a trained facilitator to surface, deal with, and resolve these issues. Following and in the Appendix are a couple of additional effective team assessment tools I've used, although not as frequently, and thus, the Belbin Roles Model is still my preferred assessment tool.

Takeaway: At the simplest level, a review of the nine Belbin Team Roles—shaper, implementer, completer-finisher, co-ordinator, team-worker, resource-investigator, plant, monitor-evaluator, and specialist—is an excellent model for creating an effective team. Further, with a competent facilitator, the Belbin Assessment tool provides for an outstanding off-site team-building process.

Johari Window

I ran across the Johari Window at a workshop in the Bay Area years ago. I found it an insightful and revelatory concept and model, which I have discussed with staff many times over the years. It's interesting, invaluable, and fun, especially as fewer people are familiar with it.

The Johari Window is a psychological model developed by Joseph Luft and Harrington Ingham, which analyzes the relationship and understanding between people or group members. It is designed to elicit self-insight to encourage people to communicate openly and to improve their awareness of each other. This helps increase an individual's understanding of themselves and the perception of others. The model is based on the idea that trust can be mutually enhanced by revealing information about yourself to others. Conversely, learning for yourself is derived from their feedback and insights.

The four quadrants of the Johari Window panes represent a person's communications profile or model. The graphic below communicates the concept, but in the real world, the shape and size of the windowpanes vary dramatically.[27]

Johari Window.

Johari Quadrant 1: "Open area" or "public area."
Quadrant 1 is the shared information area. This is information about
the person, their knowledge, experience, skills, behaviors, and emo-
tions that are known by the person and known by the group.
Johari Quadrant 2: "Blind area" or "blind spot."
Quadrant 2 is what others know about a person that is not known
to the person themselves. By seeking feedback from others, the exer-
cise's objective is to reduce this area and increase the size of the Open
Area windowpane above.
Johari Quadrant 3: "Hidden area" or "facade."
Quadrant 3 is what we know but keep hidden from others. This hidden self comprises information and views people know about themselves but are unknown to others. In business, there may occasionally
be a need for a bit of this, but it is usually advantageous to reduce the
Hidden Area.
Johari Quadrant 4: "Unknown area" or "unknown self."
Quadrant 4 may contain experiences, information, and feelings that
are unknown to the person themselves and are unknown to others. In
this case, hopefully, and ideally, this area is relatively small. However,
this unknown area represents a potential risk based on possible blind
spots or missed opportunities to share information and benefit from
a richer relationship with others.[28]

The assessment and feedback tool's objectives are to identify and model
the size and shape of the individual quadrants and increase the size of
Quadrant 1, the Open Area, through discussion and feedback, thus
improving communications. This is especially relevant within a group to
increase the Open Area with all team members simultaneously, thereby
expanding the team's collective understanding, open communications,
and increasing trust.

Takeaway: This simple but powerful and insightful concept is a great
metaphor to keep in your regular repertoire of management communications concepts. A hand-drawn Johari Window model and explanation is often a revelation for staff in performance discussions.

Tuckman's Stages of Group Development

Dr. Bruce Tuckman[29] created an exceedingly useful project mobilization and group development model, which I have used regularly over the years. His four-stage model (forming, storming, norming, performing) can be used formally for group self-analysis, team building, problem-solving, and conflict resolution. However, you can also keep it in mind and use it informally to help understand where a group or team might be in their development. I can attest to the model's effectiveness and usefulness for both teams and projects.[30,31]

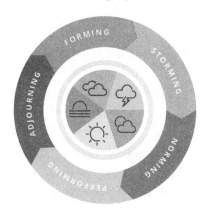

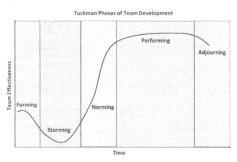

Tuckman's Stages of Group Development—2.

Tuckman's Stages of Group Development—1.

Forming

The model theory asserts that teams take time to form and become productive and that teams typically develop over time through predictable stages during their development. When a team is set up and begins to form, there are always multiple different individual reactions and challenges. Some people will be excited and optimistic, others may be unclear or confused, and some may even be anxious and perhaps reticent. Recognize that each individual's reaction may differ based on their confidence, ability, and experience.

As the team forms, getting acquainted, establishing mutual understanding, and developing trust will all take time. Your challenge as a leader is to set the vision and communicate clearly regarding the objectives, expectations, outcomes, and individual roles and responsibilities. Then, endeavor to catalyze and build trust. Finally, ensure you actively address and manage any individual or collective issues.

Storming

Once the team has formed and people have gotten to know each other, some of the initial excitement of the initiative may wear off. That is when you will begin to get into the details and experience some of the challenges and issues confronting the task or project. People may also become anxious, frustrated, or competitive. This is when individual styles and personal agendas surface to add complexity or challenges to the collaborative working environment. Frustration and conflict are likely to crop up, putting the project or initiative at risk.

This stage can be a real challenge and presents a risk for the leader and the project. Now is when your soft skills and emotional intelligence must kick in to identify and manage conflict, reset expectations, reestablish trust, and realign the team. The model is also invaluable to reassure you and the team that most groups go through this stage and that you should anticipate it, watch for it, not be put off by it, and plan to manage it when it occurs.

Norming

Through the process of storming, issues are raised and generally are eventually resolved, either through the process of team socialization or by leadership intervention. As team members start socializing and getting to know each other better, they will begin communicating and collaborating to resolve work-based issues. Through those team interactions, they will learn to resolve differences, appreciate each other, develop personal relationships, and perhaps even start socializing internally and externally.

Teams will eventually settle down, develop mutual respect, leverage each other's strengths, move beyond the anxious and conflictive storming, and begin to normalize. Interactions become more stable and fluid, trust is established, and the team focuses on the tasks.

The leader's responsibility will be to help guide this socialization process with a deft rather than heavy hand. Their role is to enable, but not force, this process by creating nonthreatening, constructive, and even enjoyable activities to ease the anxiety, release the tension, and create opportunities for positive socialization. The leader can then use this constructive platform to develop positive ways of working, create a favorable work culture, and eventually support the team to maximize their work efforts and support the project.

Performing

Once the team has begun norming, they will gradually shift to the performing state. This is when they have developed open and efficient communications, increased collaboration, and know how to work well together. They will leverage each other's strengths and compensate for their limitations. Eventually, they will become comfortable with their role and colleagues and how to conduct their work optimally, ultimately developing into a high-performing team.

The leader can now shift from more active tactical management of the team activities to a more supportive role, motivating and empowering the team members to take more responsibility for the day-to-day operation and delivery of the objectives. Accordingly, the leader's focus can move on to managing the interdepartmental and organizational activities beyond the self-guided, high-performing team.

Adjourning

Adjourning is a valuable, relatively recent addition by Tuckman. It proposes that a good leader should prepare the teams for change and transition when projects or groups have completed their journey together. There will be practical organizational design topics to address and further staff career and emotional issues for the affected individuals. In the cases of long-term, high-performing teams, there may be some significant stress, perhaps resentment, and even separation anxiety. For example, after the five-year Reuters Usability Lab transformation, multiple strong work and personal relationships were forged. However, after the project competition, several individuals struggled to reorient themselves when the project was finally wrapped up and shut down. Many rewarding and enduring relationships were built, and some individuals are still in touch some twenty years later. There is a detailed case study of this program in the penultimate chapter of Book 2.

Therefore, the leader's role is to anticipate the change and its knock-on social and organizational implications and prepare to guide the team through the transition. One practical approach is to have a closing celebration of successes, recounting challenges and how they were overcome and recognizing individual accomplishments. Finally, consider planning a meal, awarding prizes, and preparing a photo of the team and a token memento of the effort, all of which will be greatly appreciated. An effective closure to the project can leave a lasting positive glow regarding the experience, providing encouragement and confidence for team members during and post the transition.[32, 33]

Takeaway: The Tuckman Stages of Group Development (forming, storming, norming, performing, adjourning) is a model to keep in mind for kicking off virtually every project and new team. Understanding that almost every project and team goes through this cycle is very reassuring, and it provides a helpful tool for communicating and addressing the growth challenges that all groups go through.

Psychology and Personality Styles
- Maslow's Hierarchy of Needs
- Frederick Herzberg: Motivation-Hygiene Theory
- Ned Herrmann: The Creative Brain
- Mihaly Csikszentmihalyi: Flow

Psychological study included in the Appendix
- Hawthorne Effect: Observer Effects

Maslow's Hierarchy of Needs

As we look at the issue of leadership and motivation, there is significant merit in exploring human needs and staff motivation in greater detail. Abraham Maslow's hierarchy of needs is a useful and almost universally accepted model for understanding human needs at a high level. One doesn't have to dissect and challenge it ad infinitum. Therefore, a general appreciation of the model is very worthwhile and practical for a quick litmus test of your staff motivation.

Maslow's hierarchy of needs and the associated pyramid describe a motivation theory that originally comprised a five-tier model of needs. First, you have the two basic physiological and safety needs starting at the base or foundation. Then, the middle two tiers are psychological needs of belonging, love, and self-esteem. Finally, you have the top tier, which is self-actualization.

Physiological needs are the basic needs like food, water, clothing, and shelter. Safety needs relate to personal safety, emotional security, health, and necessary physical resources. Belonging and love deal with family, emotional attachment, friendship, and community. Self-esteem considers perceptions of self-worth, status, recognition, and respect. Self-actualization is when one achieves what they intended and set out to do, including accomplishing goals and mastering skills.

Maslow describes a few fundamental principles through this model and pyramid. First, human motivation starts with a natural and basic need to satisfy the essential requirements of safety and security. Once these basic foundational needs are met, there is a psychological tendency to move on to the emotional and social needs of belonging and love. Next, there is an inherent natural desire to maximize personal self-esteem. Finally, having satisfied the fundamental and psychological needs, instinctive human nature endeavors to self-fulfill, ideally ultimately reaching self-actualization.[34] Self-actualization is the process or state of mastery, accomplishment, or fulfillment of your abilities, goals, or dreams. Self-actualization goes beyond ego-based self-esteem to the state where you accomplish your objectives, feel self-satisfaction in fulfilling your potential, and realize personal acceptance of yourself.[35]

Maslow's Hierarchy of Needs.

There are a couple of further important nuances and variables that occur within the pyramid of needs that warrant elaboration:

- Lack of satisfaction of needs at any level encourages an instinctive drive to fulfill those needs, producing stress if they are not satisfied. Further, the longer the deficit of any need, the greater the motivation to address that need.
- Needs must be primarily, but not entirely, satisfied to move on to subsequent motivational needs at higher levels in the hierarchy.
- There is a natural propensity or tendency to move up through the pyramid; however, one may be at different levels at different times for different situations and circumstances. For example, one might be at different levels, personally, financially, or professionally. Think of, for example, a brilliant artist before they have become recognized by the marketplace. They may be artistically self-actualized but still suffer stress because of financial struggles. This is because their personal, economic, and professional status have not been aligned.
- Also, life and career circumstances may disrupt the natural upward evolution, causing one to fluctuate between levels or drop down to a lower level if threatened. For example, a lost job, death, or divorce could destabilize a person's self-esteem or

threaten their safety or security, causing them to drop to a lower level until they can recover and satisfy that need again.[36]

I recall when I had just jumped from AOL to join Worldsport Networks as CIO/CTO when we were immediately toppled by the dot-com collapse in 2000. While I still felt professionally competent and confident, the pipeline of potential senior roles dried up dramatically due to the oversaturation of multiple dot-com CIOs/CTOs on the market simultaneously. This caused my family and me considerable financial and personal anxiety until I secured the PwC Menlo Park role. Virtually overnight, I had crashed from level 4, with confident self-esteem, to levels 1 and 2, with financial, career, and security concerns.

In business, leaders must understand where individuals and teams *are relative to their motivational and emotional needs.* This directly relates to the previous discussions of staff maturity and management strategies with the Situational Leadership model and the maturity capability matrix. Therefore, you will need to modify your leadership and management style according to the individual's capabilities, motivation, and state of mind.

Further, when you detect a behavioral change, perhaps where a top performer suddenly becomes distracted or creates errors, don't automatically leap to conclusions and jump all over them. It is best to reflect for a moment to assess what else might be happening: a staff conflict, personal problem, family illness, a child's harassment at school, or a marital issue. Try to identify why a staff member has dropped down the hierarchy from esteem to love and belonging or from belonging to safety and security. This will aid in determining the root cause and help identify your best approach to support and guide the employee back on track.

This hierarchy of needs psychological model is highly valuable, as it is simple, easy to remember, and beneficial in the course of your day-to-day leadership. I studied Maslow in college, and it has stuck with me ever since and frequently surfaces at the right moment when pondering staff behavior. More detailed research is beneficial but not absolutely necessary once you understand it and know how to apply the basic principles above.

In recent years, psychology theorists and researchers have concluded that before he died, Maslow had identified an additional sixth tier of need—self-transcendence. These transcended individuals who reach the top of Maslow's revised hierarchy typically seek a cause and benefit beyond their personal agenda. They identify with something more significant than purely individual issues, often engaging in selfless service to others.[37]

Maslow characterized a person aspiring to self-transcendence as a person who has accepted who they are (self-esteem), who further has achieved and mastered their mission, purpose, or craft (self-actualization), and then refocuses their purpose and attention externally to contribute constructively to society beyond their individual needs and concerns.[38]

One can readily envision this perspective and identify esteemed current and historical individuals who have risen to the top of their field, accomplished virtually everything they could within their organization, and gained money and resources well beyond their needs. Subsequently, that accomplished individual begins to look beyond themselves to explore how they might contribute to improving or enhancing society beyond themselves.

Notable examples are Yvon Chouinard, the founder of outdoor outfitter Patagonia. He recently gave away ownership of his company, transferring it to nonprofit organizations pledged to fight climate change. Another extraordinary example is Douglas Tompkins, the founder of North Face and Esprit, who acquired and conserved vast wilderness properties in South America, which he subsequently donated to Argentina and Chile to become protected national parks.

Despite being a controversial figure and beyond any ego drivers, Bill Gates stepping down from Microsoft and starting the Gates Foundation is a further example of a person attempting to achieve self-transcendence.

Understanding the models for personal drivers and emotional needs throughout Maslow's hierarchy of needs, the concept of self-transcendence is an entirely logical and natural evolution of human psychological yearning, needs, and desires. Thus, we can now represent Maslow's hierarchy with this additional sixth layer.[39]

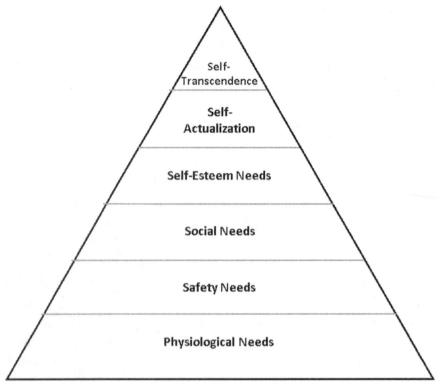

Maslow's Self-Transcendence.

Takeaway: As a senior leader, you will be expected to understand and manage people effectively. A basic understanding of Maslow is a great place to start understanding some fundamental elements of human nature and how events can cause individuals to shift up and down the hierarchy of needs. Further, your leadership responsibility is to help your people develop, grow, and eventually self-actualize.

Frederick Herzberg: Motivation-Hygiene Theory

Herzberg's Two-Factor Motivation-Hygiene Theory[40] is related to, and often aligned to, or incorporated into Maslow's hierarchy of needs.

Herzberg theorized that there are work characteristics or attributes that are motivational factors that, if present, result in job satisfaction. Further, other contrasting work characteristics he termed hygiene factors can cause dissatisfaction if missing or perceived as unsatisfactory.

Motivational factors are intrinsic issues that internally motivate employees, such as achievement, advancement, recognition, opportunities, promotions, and personal development. These aspects of the job provide job satisfaction and inspire and encourage the employee.

Hygiene factors are extrinsic issues that are external to the job tasks. These factors do not motivate the employee, but their absence can be serious demotivators. These include working conditions, job security, satisfactory salary and remuneration, status, and relationships. Therefore, rectifying or at least mitigating these demotivators is essential for eliminating dissatisfaction.[41]

Along with Maslow, this simple but powerful idea is invaluable to keep in the back of your mind when considering motivating and inspiring staff. Further, remember that hygiene factors are also crucial, particularly as their deficit can be a significant demotivator. These two factors are not mutually exclusive and must be addressed individually for full job satisfaction to be present.

Following is a diagram depicting how Herzberg's Two-Factor Motivation-Hygiene Theory can be aligned with Maslow's hierarchy of needs:[42]

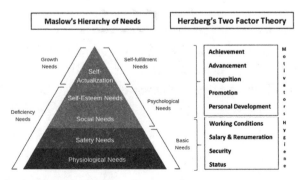

Frederick Herzberg Motivation-Hygiene Theory.

As a straightforward and relevant personal example, I have always attempted to achieve my very best in every role (achievement and self-development are important personal motivators) throughout my career. But I've never considered the associated annual salary bonus (a hygiene factor) as a target or aspiration when performing my work. However, I was also cognizant of the bonus as an important compensation factor (a potential hygiene demotivator). So, while the bonus was not a motivator, I would have been highly disappointed if it had not been offered or delivered.

Again, Herzberg's Two-Factor Motivation-Hygiene Theory is not complicated but is very important when considering what motivates (and demotivates) employees and how to construct job opportunities, objectives, compensation, and rewards to address the particular needs of individuals and the overall team. Don't confuse motivators and hygiene factors, or you may have some unpleasant surprises while trying to inspire, manage, and support your staff. The classic mistake is offering and substituting hygiene factor–type benefits instead of the more powerful motivation-style benefits.

I'll remind you of my decision to accept the travel industry role instead of the gambling/gaming job, which offered a significantly higher salary. The travel industry role was, for me, a significant motivator, yet the higher salary for the gaming role, which was only a hygiene factor, could not trump the more attractive opportunity for me.

Takeaway: Herzberg is a salient follow-up to Maslow's pyramid of needs. Understanding what motivates staff versus things that are hygiene factors, which are basic expectations or core requirements, is essential. A common mistake leaders make is trying to motivate people with things they take for granted or don't value. However, remember, a lack of a hygiene factor can be a demotivator!

Ned Herrmann: The Creative Brain

Ned Herrmann, the creator of Whole Brain® Thinking, conceived the analysis of the brain relative to business contexts and applications while working in training and development at General Electric's Corporate University.

At a high level, you will all be familiar with the concept of right and left brain people, as it has entered popular culture rudimentarily as right brain people are the creatives, and left brain the analytics. However, Whole Brain® Thinking is much more profound than that, and an entire body of training/development and management thinking has developed around these concepts. The extensively studied and validated research has proved interesting and beneficial for individuals in their personal lives and has many valuable applications in corporate life.

Ned Herrmann was a prominent businessperson, trainer, and scientist, as well as a musician, singer, and artist. These perceived diametrically opposed abilities and skills fascinated him and led him to research and analyze various brain functions.

Ned was initially intrigued by Roger Sperry's research into patients with epilepsy whose corpus callosum, the neural pathway between the brain's hemispheres, had been severed. This research proved that each hemisphere provides distinctly discrete functions.[43] This differentiation led to the early concepts of the conventional idea of left-brain- and right-brain-dominant people. This fascinating left-brain and right-brain model of the brain's functions became a trendy meme that spread like wildfire during the human potential development movement in the 1970s and 1980s and still exists today.

Intrigued by the initial Sperry research, Herrmann expanded his investigations and findings further, including the triune brain theory of Paul MacLean.[44] This evolutionary development model of the brain proposes that the brain comprises an original reptilian brain at the base of the skull, which manages motor and sensory functions (i.e., the cerebellum). Then, just above the cerebellum is the limbic brain, which is responsible for behavior, emotions, and memory. Finally, the highest level, which is the most recent and most highly developed layer in humans, is the cerebral cortex or thinking brain (the neocortex), which is responsible for perception, thinking, reasoning, and language. While current neuropsychology proves the brain is far more complex, at a high level, this model has practical value.

These explorations eventually led to Herrmann's insights into Whole Brain Thinking® and his conception of the Whole Brain Thinking® model. His Whole Brain® architectural model representing brain processes comprises two axes, the left (convergent thinking) and right (divergent thinking), and the vertical axes' upper (abstract thinking) and lower (concrete thinking). This resulted in four quadrants categorized into upper left, lower left, lower right, and upper right.

This fascinating model opened up a great deal of additional brain science research, resulting in the realization that the brain is much more complex and challenging than the oversimplification of a physiological architecture. Dr. Herrmann's research identified that while the hemispheres process information differently, most brain functions regularly employ vast integrated neurocircuits that use both hemispheres simultaneously. He cites the example of language where the left hemisphere recognizes words, sentences, and grammar; however, the right hemisphere processes the cognitive and emotional language elements of sense, meaning, and nuance. Clearly, effective communication requires a holistic, complex, and seamless interplay between both hemispheres.

These insights led Herrmann to evolve beyond the discrete neuroscientific physical manifestations of function to create a powerful new concept of a metaphor of thinking styles. This important shift from brain structure and utility to thinking modes developed into a metaphoric model of four interconnected clusters of specialized mental processes that interoperate harmoniously, comprising the Whole Brain®.

Ned Herrmann crystallized and distilled these complex brain functions into a practical and valuable metaphorical model of how we think, feel, and react. He refers to the "upper mode" thinking processes for thinking that are more cognitive, abstract, and conceptual. The "lower mode" thinking processes are more concrete, grounded, and emotional in nature. The left mode thinking processes are more logical, analytical, and quantitative, while the right mode thinking processes are more intuitive, conceptual, and abstract. At a high level, this comprises the four quadrants of Herrmann's Whole Brain® Model with the left and right upper mode processes and the left and right lower mode processes.[45]

Delving deeper into these quadrants' highly specialized functioning provides a fascinating metaphoric thinking landscape of how the brain functions at a high level. Ned Herrmann's Whole Brain® Model below depicts a four-quadrant metaphoric model as we have come to recognize it today, representing our thinking preference.[46]

The Whole Brain® Model

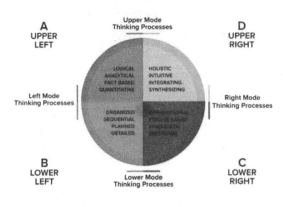

Confidential – Intended for licensed professional and academic use only

Ned Herrmann—Whole Brain Model.

The four-color, four-quadrant graphic and Whole Brain® are trademarks of Herrmann Global © 2018.

- *Quadrant A, the upper left*, is where a person prefers complex analytical and quantitative details and manages logical and rational thinking.
- *Quadrant B, the lower left*, is where the brain handles details, structure, organizing, planning, and systematic preferences.
- *Quadrant C, the lower right*, is where our senses, feelings, emotions, and kinesthetic preferences occur.
- *Quadrant D, the upper right*, is where our synthesizing, integrating, imagination, and creative preferences reside.[47]

As you can see, this metaphorical thinking model is more comprehensive, robust, validated, and insightful than the simplistic physiological model and the flawed early right-brain versus left-brain people hypothesis.

What does this mean for us as leaders and our teams? First, we all possess all four quadrants and can tap the resources of each of the modes. Further, we have different profiles and combinations of thinking preferences through our nature, nurture, education, and development efforts.

Therein lie the personal and professional opportunities and perhaps occasionally challenges. In any team, the composition of the actors or participants with their own characteristics will influence and impact the efficiency and effectiveness of the interpersonal relationships and productive operation of projects and teams.

The implications are vast. Individual capabilities relative to skills and abilities deriving from preferences across the four quadrants may significantly impact one's satisfaction and success in particular roles.

Specific attention to one's thinking preferences should be considered for roles that demand high interest and capabilities in refined analytic skills, creativity, and imagination, planning and organizing, or coaching and mentoring. There are obvious significant implications for effective organizational communications (or conflict) between individuals with different thinking models. Further, when building a team or structuring a project, pay careful attention to the balance of team preferences and skills and ensure the composition of the team members effectively covers specific specialty requirements.

Takeaway: Remembering the specifics of the Herrmann Whole Brain® Model is less important than understanding and recognizing that people are unique in their thinking and behavioral styles and playing to each individual's strengths. Ensure people are in the appropriate roles and balance everyone's skills to achieve the greatest value out of their collective knowledge and capabilities.

Herrmann Platform for Management Development[48]

Building on the Ned Herrmann Thinking Model, Herrmann International has worked for forty years with companies and individuals to bring thinking-style insights to people and teams.

How people think guides their behavior, and people comprise teams and deliver the work. Therefore, logically, the effectiveness of people and teams makes or breaks the success of organizations.

Herrmann International's research, applications, and assessment tools are used to bring awareness to thinking styles and biases, identify and manage stress, build collaboration, improve communication, and enhance problem-solving and decision-making.

The Whole Brain® Thinking Model, HBDI®, and an array of other assessments and practical tools are now available on an application platform that allows everyone to define easily, measure, and share their cognitive diversity and take action to improve processes and productivity anywhere, anytime.

The Herrmann International Whole Brain® Thinking Platform provides application suites for individual awareness, interpersonal collaboration, team effectiveness, and organizational agility.

Herrmann's Inclusive Culture Suite
For diagnosing, designing, and maximizing cognitive diversity
Herrmann's Effective Manager Suite
Improving communications and collaboration, reducing conflict, and optimizing cognitive talent
Herrmann's Innovation Suite
Building an innovation culture and catalyzing and accelerating innovation
Herrmann's Change Suite
Managing change and transformations, mobilizing and integrating teams, managing and delivering synergies.

Mihaly Csikszentmihalyi: Flow[49]

The renowned Hungarian American psychologist Mihaly Csikszentmihalyi has extensively researched the optimal experience phenomenon he calls "flow."[50]

We often refer to the flow state as "being in the groove" or "being in the zone." Flow is an intense, integrated mental and physical state where a person is fully immersed in an activity and has a heightened state of attention and focus, full involvement, and often pleasure in performing or implementing an action. It is characterized by total absorption in the activity to the extent that the person is often almost wholly unaware of the passage of time or even conscious of external events around them.

No doubt you will all have experienced flow at one time or another. Whether in mastering an instrument, being immersed in a work of art, painting, or pottery, writing a poem, or participating in a particularly focused sports activity such as skiing. You become so absorbed in the action that you experience a moment of unconscious competence, performing the feat exceptionally well and virtually without trying. These special moments often remain fond memories that we can instantly recall and visualize to give us strength, confidence, or encouragement, even in dissimilar endeavors. By extension, there are major implications for maximizing our leadership and business work environment as well.

Essential to the achievement of flow is that one must be mentally and physically capable of the task, thoroughly trained, and exceptionally experienced. Once these requisite criteria are achieved, mastery of the activity or task can be accomplished. One is then prepared to immerse themselves in that task and occasionally achieve that unique experience of flow.

Often, you only become aware of the flow experience after the fact and immediately recognize you were fully immersed in the activity and experienced it as an exhilarating, high-performance activity or occurrence. Those moments are precious, invaluable, and memorable. An additional challenge for us as leaders is to create the environment and opportunity within which our capable, creative, and skilled employees can thrive, perform, and perhaps even experience flow in the context of our organization. High-performing teams achieving flow can realize profoundly creative and valuable business value.

Perhaps in my professional career, the best example of flow, or lack thereof, is in public speaking. In my early career, public speaking was always challenging and nerve-racking for me. However, over the years, by constantly working at it and continuing to develop experience and skill, it ceased to be a liability and eventually became a skill and asset. Ultimately, I recall in recent years thoroughly enjoying it, slipping into the groove, and experiencing times when the words, sentences, examples, and even humor flowed automatically without planning or thinking. Some of these moments were genuinely memorable peak experiences for me. But reflecting back, initially, public speaking was not natural for me; it took those years of practice and experience to master it to the extent that I could cast off the nerves, focus on the topic and audience, and immerse myself in the moment. Those events are highly rewarding, but they don't come for free.

I've found Csikszentmihalyi's research and writing enlightening and inspiring. He is a prolific writer; I have read and highly recommend these three titles:

1. *Optimal Experience: Psychological Studies of Flow in Consciousness*[51]
2. *Flow: The Psychology of Optimal Experience*
3. *Creativity: Flow and the Psychology of Discovery and Invention*[52]

To the extent we as leaders can also achieve mastery of our work and foster the same with colleagues and staff, we may also experience flow in our efforts and, as a result, realize exceptional accomplishment, heightened satisfaction, and value creation.

Takeaway: Managing high-performing staff is somewhat akin to being a sports coach in that you need to encourage, develop, and support your talent to achieve their utmost and shine. There are times when, once you have established the optimal conditions for them to perform, you need to stand back and gently guide them, if necessary, but then let them run!

A final comment regarding assessments and psychometric testing: Having studied this area extensively off and on for some thirty-five years and worked in this field, I can attest to the fact that no psychometric tool is perfect and 100 percent accurate. This is because we are dealing with complex human nature and even more complicated team interworking relationships.

However, these tools are profoundly thought-provoking, personally enlightening, and professionally inspirational. Further, when used carefully and judiciously with a trained facilitator, they can be incredibly insightful and hugely valuable in providing self-reflective behavioral assessments as a starting point and catalyst for improving interpersonal relationships and optimizing team working.

There is an additional extended list of business assessment tools included in the appendix.

Key Takeaways—Leadership Models & Assessment Tools

- Emotional Intelligence EQ-i 2.0. The Emotional Quotient report provides an analysis of the leader's capabilities to assist in identifying areas of potential skill development for the leader or staff.
- Situational Leadership – This tool analyzes employee behavior by motivation and ability. Leaders must adapt their management style according to staff Task Capability and Psychological Commitment.
- Myers–Briggs Type Indicator is a highly rated Jungian-based personality type assessment tool. Identifying these styles helps leaders balance skills within teams and optimize capabilities for projects.
- Belbin Team Roles Model describes specific required capabilities for effective teams. The Belbin Model can be valuable for improving team relationships and helping your team be much more effective.
- Maslow's Hierarchy of Needs Pyramid is a motivation theory comprising two basic physiological and safety needs, two psychological needs of belonging and esteem and self-actualization.

CHAPTER 6

Venerable Oaks and Your Legacy: Making It All Count

Hearkening all the way back to the beginning of our journey, like the stonemason whose labors may only come to fruition with the cathedral's competition in perhaps another hundred years, let's conclude with a long-view perspective. I'll close with one more favorite story,[1] which the anthropologist and philosopher Gregory Bateson[2] often told.

New (!) College Oxford, founded in 1379, is one of the oldest of the renowned Oxford University colleges in England. This historic old college has a magnificent great dining hall eighty feet by forty feet (24 m × 12 m), with enormous arched oak beams two feet square and forty-five feet long gracing the ceiling.[3]

The Dining Hall of Balliol College, Oxford University. Photo by David Iliff

Over a hundred years ago, upon examining the dining hall roof, workers found it riddled with beetles. As a result, the centuries-old beams would have to be replaced. The College Council greeted this distressing news with dismay and great concern as beams this large would have to come from oaks hundreds of years old, which would be virtually impossible to source.

One of the junior fellows suggested that perhaps there might be some old oaks on the vast forested college grounds. So, they contacted the college forester to see if there were any such appropriate venerable old oaks. The forester responded with a knowing smile: "Well, sirs, we was wonderin' when you'd be askin'."

As it turns out, when the college was built hundreds of years ago, a grove of oaks was planted by some forward-thinking planners to replace the dining hall beams, as oak beams were habitually attacked by beetles and invariably eventually always need replacement. This knowledge had been passed down from each Forester to the next for five hundred years, saying don't cut those oaks; they are for the dining hall!

This type of long-range vision and pay-it-forward thinking[4] is a type of generous, altruistic legacy that each of us can aspire to leave, even if in a small way, just as the stonemasons selflessly provided the cathedral for the benefit of future generations.

I leave you with a quick round-up survey to remind you of some of the key takeaways we have explored for your leadership journey.

- To make work meaningful in order to inspire and motivate staff, leaders must create a compelling vision infused with a profound sense of purpose.
- In order to lead people authentically, you must discover your own "North Star" beacon that defines the essence of who you are as a leader.
- Once you have set an inspiring vision (what) and passionate purpose (why), ensure that the way you act and work (how) is conducted with integrity and virtue.

- When leaders "Lead with the Heart," they radiate ethical and empathetic conduct that reinforces a trust-based relationship with co-workers.
- The Alchemy of Leadership manifests when the leader initiates benevolent behaviors toward staff that create a positive, reciprocal social exchange relationship.
- A Servant Leader is a leader who, through their natural authentic and altruistic instincts and intent, has genuine care and concern to nurture and serve their staff.
- To be most effective today's leaders must have strong Emotional Intelligence and highly developed people skills alongside their cognitive and technical skills.
- Leadership is a composite of qualities: integrity, trust, empathy, optimism, and perseverance. However, it all distills down to that exceptional leaders have Character.

These takeaways and messages, along with all the other topics relating to leadership traits and attributes, readers can refer to and model their behavior on. Besides enhancing productivity, many of these practices can help perpetuate healthy and happy work relationships and foster the integration of positive values and benevolent principles throughout our work, with colleagues, and in our personal lives.

As Aristotle taught, everyone has a different path to a good life based on discovering and constructively fulfilling their unique potential. To achieve a full life, we must infuse our actions with virtue and constantly better ourselves by developing our abilities to the fullest.

Similarly, as Aristotle counsels us to discover our discrete path to a good life, we can find and develop our own unique leadership identity. The deep knowledge, best practices, and effective tools in this anthology of leadership can guide you to analyze, develop, and refine your personal leadership identity.

Starting with recognizing your own talents and skills, you can begin building a robust leadership foundation and framework to construct your overarching leadership persona based on the principles found in chapter 2,

The Alchemy of Leadership. Identifying the foundational pillars and principles of leading with the heart, servant leadership, business ethics and values, and transactional or transformational leadership will help you establish a solid leadership framework that will guide and support your overall leadership philosophy and modus operandi for the future.

Having set the philosophical scope of your leadership style, next we study the foundational, as well as the latest and greatest thinking of the top leadership gurus and academics in chapter 3, Standing on the Shoulders of Giants. Examining towering figures like Drucker, Bennis, and Porter, as well as groundbreaking thinkers such as Senge, Hamel, and Goleman, will provide rich and invaluable principles and perspectives for effectively leading, motivating, and managing teams.

With the foundation, pillars, and the latest thinking on leadership laid down, review in detail the twenty critical constructs of leadership character in chapter 4. Again, we are all different, and all organizational demands are distinct; however, identifying your leadership strengths and areas for development within these key leadership attributes will assist in road-mapping your journey from an aspiring to exceptional leader. Studying and mastering leadership characteristics such as integrity, empathy, trust, vision, judgment, optimism, communication, and creativity will provide you with a robust composite of the crucial components and behaviors of your leadership identity.

Now that you have built the foundation, pillars, thought leadership, and critical components of leadership character, we further analyzed the preeminent leadership models and tools, including an exhaustive study of leadership psychometric assessments. Reviewing and understanding models and tools, like Situational Leadership, emotional intelligence, Myers–Briggs, team building, stages of competence, Maslow, Herzberg, and Csikszentmihalyi give you the tools and techniques to understand and manage the complexities and nuances of people in teams today.

A thoughtful and thorough study of all these elements throughout this book, from the fundamental foundation through to the critical competencies of exceptional leaders, will give you virtually all the deep knowledge, thought leadership, best practices, assessments, and essential tools needed to find and refine your exceptional leadership identity.

Aristotle concludes that genuine happiness emerges through personal development and dedication to a virtuous life through work and study. Seeking happiness should not be a goal in itself, as our challenge is to pursue a life of self-fulfillment, and success and happiness will follow naturally.

How we choose what we do, and how we approach it . . . will deter-mine whether the sum of our days adds up to a formless blur or to something resembling a work of art.

—Mihaly Csikszentmihalyi[5]

Appendix I

Following is an additional list of Corporate Storytelling Analogies and Metaphors continuing from those listed in Chapter 1, Corporate Storytelling, Metaphor, and Analogy:

- Trying to construct the roof of the house before laying the proper foundation can mean that the system, tool, or project will be, at best, unstable or, worse, unusable and collapse altogether.
- When confronted with trying to fix or patch up a problematic or failing system that desperately needs replacement, ask: "Do you really want to replace your kitchen or bathroom when the foundation is subsiding, walls are crumbling, and the roof needs replacing? Wouldn't you be better off replacing the house entirely or moving?"
- A classic, simple, and valuable analogy is: "Asking to reengineer a system while simultaneously operating and maintaining it is like attempting to change the race car's tires on the track during the race!"
- By continuously building workaround solutions without a master plan and cobbling things together, you create defects, resulting in technical debt that will make the system suboptimal or dysfunctional, requiring a complete replacement in the future.
- Sometimes, during mergers or systems centralization, you have complexity challenges. Caution: "If we cobble together a system from existing diverse components from all across the company, we are going to end up with a 'Frankenstein's monster' that will be ugly and dysfunctional, and will take longer and ultimately be more expensive."

- When confronted with a flawed but cheap solution to a significant problem, where there is a more appropriate but expensive solution, comment: "You're trying to replace a Mercedes engine with that of a Chevy; it is simply not going to fit." An integrated solution cannot be easily replaced with inappropriate and inconsistent components.
- If people are chipping away at a problem and missing the big picture, caution them: "You are approaching this problem like cooking hors d'oeuvres or tapas when we need to prepare a whole Sunday dinner."
- We are all occasionally confronted with constraints: "Sorry, but times are tough, budgets are constrained, and what you have is 'Champagne taste on a beer budget.' Can't you be a bit more realistic?"
- If something is a complete mess, and you are warning that the approach is likely to fail, you can use the old proverb: "You can't make a silk purse out of a sow's ear."
- If people make an illogical or inaccurate comparison as a proof statement, apply: "You're not comparing apples to apples; you're comparing apples to oranges." You need to compare like items to discover an appropriate solution.
- Regarding the challenge of aligning parts of the organization within a major program to ensure all functions, the business, management, finance, and IT are aligned. I've used the example of building a skyscraper, where architects have to consider the foundations, elevators, electrical systems, and plumbing to ensure that everything fits the blueprint and can be built to function and interoperate correctly.
- In crisis contingency planning or before a solution can be implemented, reassure staff or colleagues that even a leaky rowboat during a storm in the middle of the ocean is better than none at all!
- When team building or negotiating a short-term collaboration with disparate actors or groups, you can remind them: "We are all in this boat together, and we'd better learn to work together if we expect to achieve an appropriate solution."

Appendix II

In addition to my favorite leadership assessment tools, psychometric tests, and business psychology research findings found in chapter 5, the following are a number of additional foundational and historical tools. Each of these is important and valuable in its own right. Nevertheless, I append them in the Appendix as some are more esoteric in their use or are specialty assessments requiring professional monitors.

Leadership Models

- Lewin's Three Core Leadership Styles Framework
- Tannenbaum-Schmidt Leadership Continuum
- Dunham and Pierce's Leadership Process Model

For further information and extensive study, also explore:
(Not included due to overlap with instruments in the main text)

- Fiedler's Contingency Model
- French and Raven's Six Forms of Power
- Path-Goal Theory
- Trait Theory
- Zenger and Folkman's Ten Fatal Leadership Flaws

Lewin's 3 Core Leadership Styles

Kurt Lewin, the founder of modern social psychology, developed the three styles of leadership behavior, which is perhaps the earliest of the situational leadership models. This was also the first leadership model I studied while at American Express when my astute work colleague and friend Ernie Lopez provided me with an article on Lewin's leadership styles.[1]

Lewin's three different leadership styles are authoritarian, participative, and delegative. He theorized that effective leaders have a primary preference for one particular type but should be adaptable enough to employ all three styles depending on the organizational situation. Meanwhile, inexperienced or mediocre leaders may rely on one specific default style regardless of the organizational structure or issue. Based on their leadership style, leaders' ideal situation and clear objective is to be "paired" with an appropriate workplace situation.[2]

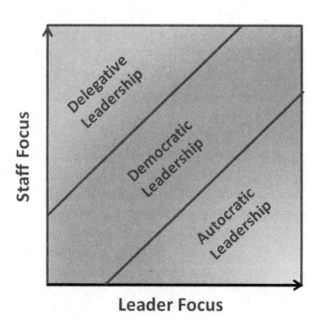

Lewin's 3 Core Leadership Styles Framework.

Authoritarian Leadership involves a "command and control" style leader delivering tasks, assignments, and objectives to the team, with specific and directive instructions for doing the job or completing a task. Managers with an authoritarian leadership style often make decisions without consultation with the team.

As the name implies, *Participative Leadership* is a leader who will involve team members and work as a part of the team to accomplish tasks. They are still in charge and lead the team, but they are far more collaborative and cooperative. Staff are involved and encouraged to contribute ideas, and everyone will participate in evaluating ideas and solutions to achieve the best result for the team.

Delegative Leadership designates a leader who has complete confidence and trust in the team's abilities and thus can delegate extensively to team members. This presumes that the team is knowledgeable, experienced, and capable of managing the team's day-to-day operations with minimal monitoring and supervision. This allows the leader to step back and be more hands-off, allowing them to concentrate on other external organizational challenges and issues. This can be particularly useful when there is a requirement for the leader to "manage upward" in the organization or focus on overseeing external partners or suppliers.[3]

Takeaway: Each of these three leadership styles can be successful if employed in the appropriate context with the relevant team and corporate culture. Ensure you are adaptable enough to employ the right style at the right time and in the proper context.

Tannenbaum-Schmidt Leadership Continuum[4]

The Tannenbaum Leadership model builds on the idea that it is difficult to pigeonhole leaders into one discrete style or another. Therefore, Tannenbaum came up with the concept of a continuum that provides a range of leadership skills mapping a continuous evolution of leader styles and employee participation from autocratic to participative.

This model's beauty is its flexibility in recognizing that leadership is not a binary, either/or situation, but rather a natural flow of interactions between the leader and the staff. Further, depending on the organization, activity, and staff capability, a leader, as in the previous models, may need to adjust their style based on the situation to take more control or cede more responsibility.

While this model is conceived as a continuous fluid continuum, Tannenbaum and Schmidt map seven styles to reflect various high-level leadership styles that depict typical leadership behaviors. One moves from the far-left autocratic side, where a leader tells the employees what to do, to the far right, where the leader can delegate or even completely abdicate authority to capable team members based on their adequately developed competencies.

Interestingly, over the years, I've noticed that in managing multiple teams in various countries globally, I have often had to use many of these styles simultaneously, depending on the diverse capabilities and cultures of disparate teams.[5]

Tannenbaum and Schmidt's - Leadership Continuum

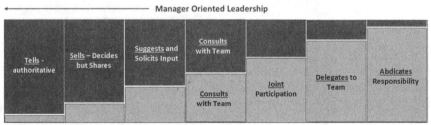

Tannenbaum-Schmidt Leadership Continuum.

The leadership styles presented on the scale are representative, simple, and self-evident but not necessarily all-inclusive.

Tannenbaum and Schmidt's high-level categories are:

- The *Tells* style comprises a directive leader who gives explicit instructions to the team.
- The *Sells* style involves a dialogue where a leader suggests and then agrees on the direction with staff.
- The *Suggests* style is where the leader recommends ideas and solutions and solicits team input and ideas.
- The *Consults* style is when the leader recognizes the team is sufficiently capable of participating in decisions.
- The *Joint* style means that the leader becomes an active participant within the team.
- The *Delegates* style is when the leader has a high degree of trust in the team and can delegate to them.
- The *Abdicates* style means that a leader allocates full responsibility to a responsible and capable team.[6]

Takeaway: Remember, these are indicative representative styles on a continuum. Therefore, leaders must shift styles up and down the scale depending on the organizational context and team members' maturity and capabilities.

Dunham and Pierce®'s Leadership Process Model[7]

The Dunham and Pierce leadership process model is a recent model presenting a holistic or overarching systems-thinking approach to leadership within the organization's overall context.

This interactive model considers inclusively the leader, the staff, the organizational context, and how the dynamic processes of each relate to objectives and impact outcomes.

Dunham and Pierce's Leadership Process Model[8]

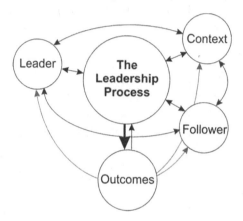

Dunham and Pierce's Leadership Process Model.

As we've seen in the prior models, leadership effectiveness depends on the leader's leadership style, maturity, and experience. The leader's style must be appropriate to the organizational culture and context and the staff's knowledge, experience, and motivation. As a result, the staff morale and teams' overall effectiveness depend on the leader and their style. Further, the organizational context, working environment, and corporate culture heavily influence the leader and the staff. Then, leadership direction and staff activities must align with the organizational modus operandi and business processes. Finally, collectively, the leader, the staff, the processes, and the organizational context are all integral dependencies for a successful outcome.

The model and design reinforce the fact that each of these actors and activities are dynamically interrelated, with each one affecting and, in turn, being influenced by each of the others. The extent to which each of these elements can be collaboratively and constructively harmonized with the others is the extent to which the ecosystem will be fluid, frictionless, and optimized.

This dynamic and flexible model can be used in organizational design, mobilizing projects, and supporting team development. Key outcomes include assigning objectives and providing feedback, building relationships and consensus, improving communications and collaboration, and empowering staff.[9]

An analog for this model's use is Porter's Five Forces, with which you can visualize, identify, and manage the various actors, contexts, and forces to consider optimizing the team, department, or overall organization.

Takeaway: As a conceptual model, Dunham and Pierce's leadership process model is valuable for structuring and planning organizational designs, teams, and project-based activities.

Management Models
- The Birkman Method
- Blake and Mouton's Managerial Grid

RECRUITMENT/PLACEMENT
- Thomas International Personality Recruitment Profile

The Birkman Method

If you've been in business for a while, you will probably have taken part in various personality profile tests for recruitment, career development, or team building. Despite the many flavors of these profiles, if you received a "color chart" assessment at the end, you likely have taken a test that has its foundations in work done by Roger Birkman when he was an occupational psychologist for the U.S. Army Air Corps. The Birkman Method is a powerful, insightful, and reliable assessment.

The Birkman test and Map Symbols[10] derive from the assessment and measurement of multiple factors, including interests, behaviors, and needs. The output provides a personality profile for your standard approach to situations, behavioral style, and motivation areas. Birkman is noteworthy because it is a trait-based instrument based on empirical research versus other psychology-based systems.

It is an extensive and somewhat lengthy and, therefore, time-consuming instrument; however, therein lies one of its strengths, as it is comprehensive, quite flexible, and highly reliable. It has a smaller but highly loyal community of practitioners and benefits from the historical experience of millions of test validations.

Birkman is useful for specific role-based assessments such as hiring, placement, conflict resolution, and team building, where mission-critical determinations regarding the selection or realignment of people or roles are vital.

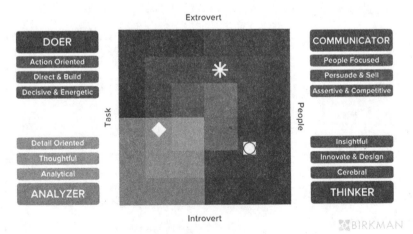

Birkman International Image 1.

Red represents a climate of action, energy, and practicality.
THE LAND OF DOING.

Green represents a climate of socializing and responsiveness.
THE LAND OF COMMUNICATING

 Yellow represents a climate of planning, fairness, and objectivity.
THE LAND OF ANALYZING

Blue represents a climate of reflecting, sensing, and expressing.
THE LAND OF THINKING

Birkman International Image 2.

Graphics courtesy of Birkman International, Inc[11]

One of the Birkman Report's key summary outputs is the Birkman Map below, which provides a personality overview of two dimensions. The vertical dimension measures extroversion versus introversion, and the horizontal dimension maps task and people orientation. These two dimensions create the four quadrants of the map.

- *The upper left quadrant represents the Doers.* Doers are action-oriented, assertive, adept at problem-solving and decision-making, and thrive in activity-oriented roles like team or project management.
- *The upper right quadrant depicts the Communicators.* Communicators, as the name implies, are extroverted and good with people. They are often good at business development, sales, presenting, teaching, and coaching.
- *The lower left quadrant represents the Analyzers* who are more introverted and task-oriented rather than people-oriented. This profile often indicates people who are analytical and technical and are good at and enjoy research and analysis.
- *The lower right quadrant represents the Thinkers,* who are your idea people and creative, innovative, conceptual thinkers who are invaluable assets in new product development, emerging technology, product design, or innovation labs.[12]

I have taken the Birkman assessment a couple of times. A number of other companies have recently developed several additional popular assessments primarily based on the same concept; however, Birkman was one of the originals and is still highly respected and relevant.[13]

Takeaway: While these dimensions and quadrants do not map directly against the Herrmann Whole Brain® model, reviewing both together provides significant insights into human nature in the business context. A deep understanding of how people think and work is invaluable to building and managing staff in teams.

Blake and Mouton's Managerial Grid

Related to McGregor's Theories X and Y, task management and relationship orientation, Robert Blake and Jane Mouton[14] developed the leadership styles grid or managerial grid. This model extended McGregor's theories, placing more flesh on that skeleton by elaborating various leadership styles against the task and relationship axes.

The managerial grid represents two dimensions of leader behavior: concern for people and accomplishment of company objectives. Concern for people is addressed on the y-axis, and concern for the company results, emphasizing production and productivity, is represented on the x-axis.[15]

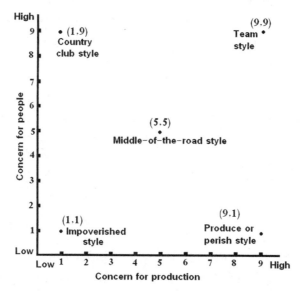

Blake and Mouton's Managerial Grid.

Blake and Mouton embellish the grid by defining the leader's style within each of the corresponding quadrants as per the following styles:

Impoverished Management: Managers with this style are low on both people and production dimensions; therefore, they have minimal concern for the team and are also ambivalent about company productivity. As a result, they are ineffective overall and solely concerned with personal issues such as job security and tenure.

Authority / Compliance Management: Produce or perish in the diagram above. These managers are Theory X task-oriented, autocratic, or dictatorial managers. They are primarily concerned about production and have little concern for people. Employee needs are disregarded, and objectives revolve around organizational productivity.

Middle-of-the-Road: This management style is a compromising style where the leader tries to maintain a balance between the company's goals and people's needs. Employee morale is marginal, and productivity is average in performance. Overall, this style is a mediocre compromise for both the staff and the company.

Country Club: This leadership style is collegial and characterized by low task and high people orientation. The leader gives careful attention to staff needs, providing them with a comfortable environment. As a result, morale will be good, but productivity will probably be just above average, given the relative inattention to corporate objectives.

Team Management: These leaders have both high people and task focus. According to Blake and Mouton, the Theory Y management style is deemed the most effective. Leaders are empowered, motivated, and confident, with a strong team commitment and delivery orientation that results in high employee morale and operational productivity.[16]

Takeaway: This leadership styles grid provides a different view on Theories X and Y and situational leadership and creates some memorable styles as a metaphor for remembering these types in context.

Recruitment / Placement

Thomas International Personality Recruitment Profile

I have taken the Thomas International PPA assessment twice and found it insightful and accurate. While I've not applied it in my teams, my direct personal experience leads me to recommend the PPA assessments for recruitment and placement.

The Thomas International Personal Profile Analysis[17] is an extensively validated and highly respected psychometric behavioral profile assessment that has been used as a recruitment and placement tool for over forty years.

The PPA assessment provides analysis and insights relative to specific identified roles and potential candidate fit and evaluation tools to understand behavior styles to predict performance.

One crucial difference with the PPA approach is that it assesses behavior styles relative to company culture and functional role context. This results in a valuable customized report mapped against a specific role instead of providing a one-size-fits-all generic personality profile.

The PPA analyzes how individuals react to work situations that are positive or negative and assesses whether the leader's reactions to those situations are proactive or reactive. It measures four primary role-specific profiles relating to:

Dominance: This examines the candidate's profile for leadership assertiveness, dominance, and authority.

Influence: This profile deals with sociability and the candidate's ability to exercise persuasion and influence management to achieve results.

Steadiness: Being stable, reliable, and exhibiting demonstrable self-control are vital criteria for leadership, even in a dynamic, fast-moving environment.

Compliance: This is an increasingly critical requirement for responsible senior management, as well as financial and reporting roles.

Relative to these four areas, candidates are further scored on their comparative value for the specific role based on individual strengths, weaknesses, motivations, communications, and behaviors.[18] Based on my positive personal experience, I'm also comfortable recommending Thomas International.

https://www.thomas.co/assessments/psychometric-aptitude-assessments.

Takeaway: The PPA is a highly effective and validated tool for recruitment. However, you can also use it as a self-assessment tool to help you prepare for an interview or to develop a personal career development plan.

Team Building
- FIRO and Element B Theory: The Human Element
- Thomas-Kilmann: Conflict Mode Instrument

For further information and study, also explore:
(Not included due to overlap with instruments in the main text)
- Process Communication Model®

FIRO and Element B Theory: The Human Element

As mentioned, I once attended a course at the University of San Francisco by American psychologist Dr. Will Schutz, who developed the FIRO-B psychometric instrument. He mentioned being influenced by Freud, Fromm, Adler, and Jung. For decades, the FIRO theory has been one of the gold standards in scientifically validated tools for interpersonal relations and organizational design applications.

The tool was initially developed for research purposes for the U.S. Navy to determine which members of a team were most likely to work together effectively. This assessment is based on the universal human desire for inclusion, control, and affection and the theory that continuous fulfillment of these desires drives people's motivation in interpersonal interactions.

Subsequently, Dr. Schutz updated and expanded the FIRO theory and created the current FIRO instruments, the Elements of Awareness. These form the basis of his subsequent work, a transformational process called The Human Element.® For those of you who may be familiar with and loyal to the original FIRO-B, it will be helpful to understand the evolution of The Human Element and its enhancements to the FIRO-B Instrument. These "Elements of Awareness" provide information to enhance self-awareness to help individuals understand why people behave and interact as they do and the consequences of those behaviors. The new instruments are Element B: Behavior, Element F: Feelings, and Element S: Self-Concept. The following graphic depicts the full suite of assessments.[19]

The enhanced FIRO Element B instrument and model consider the dimensions of Inclusion, Control, and Openness dimensions.

- *Inclusion*: The aspect of optimizing contact and interaction with people. This dimension recognizes that people vary dramatically relative to the amount of interpersonal interaction they express and desire. Some people are naturally extroverted, and others are introverted. Further, while people tend to exhibit clear preferences that are statistically stable over different situations, this measure is contextually sensitive relative to different situations, relationships, and events. People often believe that

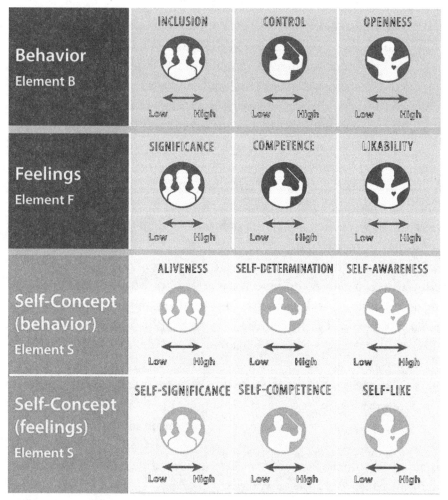

	INCLUSION	CONTROL	OPENNESS
Behavior Element B	Low ↔ High	Low ↔ High	Low ↔ High
	SIGNIFICANCE	COMPETENCE	LIKABILITY
Feelings Element F	Low ↔ High	Low ↔ High	Low ↔ High
	ALIVENESS	SELF-DETERMINATION	SELF-AWARENESS
Self-Concept (behavior) Element S	Low ↔ High	Low ↔ High	Low ↔ High
	SELF-SIGNIFICANCE	SELF-COMPETENCE	SELF-LIKE
Self-Concept (feelings) Element S	Low ↔ High	Low ↔ High	Low ↔ High

©2021 Business Consultants, Inc. From the Human Element workbook, reprinted with permission.

they are "different" in various situations, but according to FIRO, their preferences remain largely the same, although they may flex their behavior for a period of time.

- ***Control***: This relates to achieving desired control over people. Individuals vary relative to the amount of control they exhibit or experience. Again, this is contextually sensitive; however, some people want to be in charge, others are collaborative and cooperative, and finally, some prefer others to take responsibility and control.

- *Openness*: Considers the level of personal openness with people. As we will see next in the Johari Window, depending on emotional intelligence, social comfort, and professional confidence, some people are highly self-aware and are comfortable sharing and discussing personal feelings and interactions with others. On the other hand, other people may be more private and guarded and, therefore, less open.[20]

As you consider these three criteria, you will appreciate the contextual aspect of these dimensions. For example, your behavior as a leader may dictate a slightly different balance of behaviors than that you exhibit with family or intimate friends.

The Element B instrument asks you a number of questions to describe things you experience and perceive relative to these three dimensions of inclusion, control, and openness. First, you explore the aspects of how you act and express and then receive or respond to others. This is abbreviated to the characteristics of what you *do* and *get*.

- What you *do*—in other words, how you act and express yourself toward others.
- What you *get*—what you receive back from others.

Then, for each behavior, you can examine the difference between what you perceive or *see* and what you desire or *want*.

- What you *see*—what you perceive relative to the three dimensions and what you do, get, or receive.
- What you *want*—what you desire in each of the dimensions relative to what you do and receive.

Element B then delves into depth with the corresponding analysis in these areas, providing invaluable personal insight and professional guidance for individuals and teams to improve communications and collaboration. Finally, the overall matrix of the dimensions and the resulting analysis are spread out along the entire spectrum according to the following twelve measures.[21,22]

		See	Want
Inclusion	Do	xxx	xxx
	Get	xxx	xxx
Control	Do	xxx	xxx
	Get	xxx	xxx
Openness	Do	xxx	xxx
	Get	xxx	xxx

Element B instrument.

This analysis and the resulting feedback mechanisms will highlight gaps or disconnects between your or your colleagues or team's actual or perceived and desired state.

A trained FIRO facilitator will derive valuable insights from this matrix and its implications and add significant value to the assessment feedback sessions. Subsequently, corrective team-building activities will be designed to address individual conflicts or any team-based dissonance.

These instruments were developed and proven in demanding military circumstances and have been validated extensively for corporate communications and team-building activities.

To initially familiarize yourself with these tools, you may find it interesting to trial an online FIRO—Element Behavior assessment from the Schutz Company.

Takeaway: I suggest you start with an online FIRO—Element Behavior assessment from the Schutz Company to get a brief introduction and gain a basic functional understanding. However, to conduct a team development exercise, you should engage a trained facilitator to yield the best results from the team-building activity.

Thomas-Kilmann Conflict Mode

The Thomas-Kilmann Conflict Mode Instrument[23] is a valuable psychometric tool to assess individual communication styles within a team setting. It highlights team composition challenges in communicating and managing conflict to find constructive solutions to difficulties with relationship interactions.[24]

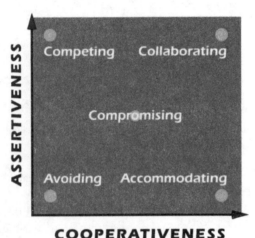

Thomas-Kilmann Conflict Mode Instrument.

In the Thomas-Kilmann Conflict Mode Instrument Profile and Interpretive Report, there are five modes as follows:

Competing: Here, a team member is assertive, competitive, and uncooperative.
An individual with this style will often operate independently to satisfy their own concerns at the expense of others within the team.
Collaborating: This team member is assertive but also cooperative at the same time.
This individual will try to find a win/win solution to satisfy both their and their colleagues' concerns.
Compromising: Here, the team member is balanced in assertiveness and cooperativeness. This member is willing to compromise to find an intermediate solution that partially satisfies all team members' needs.

Avoiding: This person is unassertive and uncooperative. This team member will avoid confronting the situation and likely avoid contact, interactions, or discussions relating to the issue under debate.

Accommodating: Unassertive and cooperative. This individual will sacrifice and suppress their own concerns to cooperate with colleagues.[25]

I have used this instrument and found it interesting and valuable. However, each behavior, except for collaborating, has some dysfunctional downside, even accommodating. You must also be careful with the slightly evocative titles to ensure no one takes offense. Also, be cautious with avoiding behavior to ensure no unrelated personal circumstances are driving this aberrant behavior.

Diplomatic and professional facilitation can often yield significant value in calling out and correcting inappropriate behavior. As interpersonal challenges frequently carry some history and emotional baggage, an objective and independent facilitator may be more effective in broaching sensitive subjects and delicately delivering corrective feedback.

Takeaway: This assessment is valuable to surface minor dysfunction within the team. If there are significant issues, unless you are comfortable with performance improvement discussions, you should engage a professional consultant to conduct the assessment. The further benefit of an external consultant is that they are neutral and not their direct supervisor; thus, discussions may be more objective.

Psychology and Personality Styles

Hawthorne: Observer Effect

The Hawthorne experiments are a fascinating and insightful classic organization study to tuck away in your management stories and leadership tool kit.[26] It is an old study, but as it relates to fundamental human nature, it is, therefore, timeless.

Management of the Western Electric factory near Chicago commissioned Fritz Roethlisberger, a professor of industrial research at Harvard Business School, to conduct a study to determine if changes in lighting in the production line area would affect worker productivity.

As the study started, a careful baseline of productivity was done. The first experiment began with replacing the lights in the assembly line to improve the lighting. Fortunately, worker productivity increased measurably. Encouraged by the results, modifications were made to the lights to provide additional work area visibility, and again, productivity improved. Next, they further refined the lighting, and worker productivity continued to improve. Intrigued, they experimented for years. Curiously, each time they made a change, productivity improved.

They then decided to reverse the experiment to determine the relevant factors for productivity improvement, so they lowered the lights, and counterintuitively, surprisingly, the productivity improved again. They then reduced and dimmed the lights even more to revert back to where they started, and again, productivity improved. Finally, when they concluded the experiments, employee productivity declined!

This study has been analyzed endlessly, and multiple variations have been re-created. The supposition from the experiments was that it was not the changes in lighting that were the root cause of the employee productivity improvement. Instead, it was the management's attention given to the staff and their active participation in this organizational design experiment. The conclusion ultimately drawn from the studies was that productivity improvements resulted from the motivational impact on employees because of the interest and attention directed toward them![27]

Therefore, the net takeaway from the "Hawthorne effect" is that staff and teams enjoy and thrive through leadership and management attention. Also, morale and motivation are further increased through employee participation. In psychology, the Hawthorne effect has now become known as the observer effect, where people's behavior changes because of being watched or observed.

An additional fascinating study relating to the observer effect was done in the psychology department at Newcastle University in the UK. Melissa Bateson and researchers were interested in the honesty and compliance of payments through an unmonitored honor system in the departmental coffee room. Over ten weeks, they alternated images of flowers and pairs of eyes posted over the payment honesty box for coffee, tea, and milk.[28]

Intriguingly, voluntary payments for a liter of milk almost tripled from ten to thirty cents when the flowers were posted over the payment box. Then, the average donation skyrocketed to nearly seventy cents when the eyes were substituted. Subconsciously, the images of the eyes over the donation box piqued the conscience of the coffee and tea drinkers.[29]

In my experience, while I didn't consciously intend to replicate the Hawthorne experiments, I recall the many smiles and positive feedback I received over the years from the simple act of greeting everyone on the team briefly each morning. A moment of personal courtesy and individual attention each day helped to continually maintain the connection and bond with a large number of people and perhaps also made me more approachable.

Imagine a simple cost/benefit analysis of a simple and easy momentary act of authentic management attention contributing to an already motivated team. These acts should be genuine and conducted out of generosity of spirit, and further, as a leader, it's hard to deny the economic and operational leverage of a highly motivated team.

Takeaway: Never underestimate the positive impact of an approving nod, word of encouragement, or public acknowledgment of a minor success on your staff. Simple words and actions can have a significant encouraging reaction on the part of an employee. Continuous positive reinforcement, especially now with remote employees, can create and maintain strong motivation and loyalty within the team.

Acknowledgments

A special greeting and thank-you to my former colleagues at Accenture Consulting Europe, TUI Group, Hotelbeds, PricewaterhouseCoopers London, Worldsport Networks, AOL Europe, Reuters Usability Labs—London, Reuters Asia Training—Hong Kong and Singapore, and American Express Travel USA, who gave me their friendship, encouragement, and support over the years. There are too many friends to name, but I cherish all our memories. Thank you!

It would be remiss of me not also to acknowledge the leadership thinkers, academics, authors, and practitioners who inspired me, educated me, and provided me guidance throughout my career:

Tom Peters, Clayton Christensen, Charles Handy, Robert Pirsig, David Whyte, Mihaly Csikszentmihalyi, Frans Johansson, Warren G. Bennis, Peter Drucker, Michael Porter, Daniel Goleman, Reuven Bar-On, Rosabeth Moss Kanter, Jim Collins, Daniel Kahneman, Michael Hammer, James Champy, John Kotter, James Kouzes, Barry Posner, Stephen R. Covey, Peter Senge, Alvin and Heidi Toffler, Gary Hamel, C.K. Prahalad, Henry Chesbrough, Will Schutz, Ken Blanchard, Meredith Belbin, Edward De Bono, Frederick Taylor, W. Edwards Deming, Joseph Juran, Bill George, Douglas McGregor, Katharine Cook Briggs, William Ouchi, Joseph Badaracco, David O. Ulrich, Isabel Briggs Myers, Ned Herrmann, Roger Birkman, Kenneth Thomas, Ralph Kilmann, Joseph Luft, Harrington Ingham, Frederick Herzberg, Robert Townsend, Kurt Lewin, Paul Hersey, Abraham Maslow, Fritz Roethlisberger, Benjamin Tregoe, Charles Kepner, Robert Blake, Jane Mouton, Martin Broadwell, Genrich Altshuller, Robert Tannenbaum, Warren Schmidt, Randall B. Dunham, Philip Crosby, Jon Pierce, Bruce Tuckman, Richard Bandler, John Grinder, Vilfredo Pareto.

Endnotes

Preface

1   TUI Group. 2021. Accessed January 14, 2021. https://www.tuigroup.com/en-en.
2   Peters, Tom. "Virtual Teams: Here Today, Gone Tomorrow." *On Achieving Excellence*, 1–7. 1994. Approval Holly Bauer, Tom Peters Group 19/10/2021.
3   *Pay It Forward*. 2000. Box Office Mojo n.d. Accessed April 21, 2021. http://www.boxofficemojo.com/release/rl896042497/weekend.
4   Catherine Ryan Hyde. 2021. Accessed March 04, 2021. http://www.catherineryanhyde.com/.
5   Snelling, Steve. January 2015. "15 Career Planning Steps." IIE Annual conference. Proceedings, Institute of Industrial and Systems Engineers (IISE) 1.

Chapter 1

1   Saint-Exupéry, Antoine de. 1948. Goodreads 01 April. https://www.goodreads.com/quotes/121975-a-rock-pile-ceases-to-be-a-rock-pile-the.
2   Thoreau, Henry David. *Walden*. 1854. Boston: Ticknor and Fields.
3   Fritz, Robert. *The Fifth Discipline* by Peter Senge, 194. 2006. New York: Random House Business.
4   Bill George. August 10, 2015. BillGeorge.Org. https://www.billgeorge.org/page/category/true-north/.
5   Leahy, Terry. *Management in Ten Words*. 2013. New York: Random House Business.
6   Butler-Bowdon, Tom. *50 Business Classics*. 2018. London, UK: Nicholas Brealey Publishing.
7   Bennis, Warren. August 4, 2014. "The Remarkable Legacy of Warren Bennis." Accessed January 3, 2021.
8   Wojcicki, Ms. Esther. April 26, 2019. "I Raised Two CEOs and a Doctor. These Are My Secrets to Parenting Successful Children." *Time*. Accessed November 03, 2023. https://time.com/5578064/esther-wojcicki-raise-successful-kids/.
9   Frankl, Viktor. *Man's Search for Meaning*. 2006. Boston: Beacon Press.

10 International Olympic Committee. "Olympic Games Munich 1972—About the Games." Accessed November 2, 2023. https://olympics.com/en/olympic-games/munich-1972.

11 Lufkin, Bryan. March 14, 2018. "Stephen Hawking's advice for a fulfilling career." BBC Worklife. Accessed April 11, 2020. https://.bbc.com///-stephen-hawkings-advice-for-a-fulfilling-career.

12 Vernon, Jamie L. May. June 2017. "Understanding the Butterfly Effect." *American Scientist* 130. Accessed January 28, 2021. https://www.americanscientist.org/article/understanding-the-butterfly-effect.

13 Barnes, Barry. 2015. "Blending Art with Commerce to Expand Aesthetic Leadership: Insights from Steve Jobs and Jerry Garcia." *Journal of Applied Management and Entrepreneurship* 20, no. 3, 92. Accessed July 4, 2020.

14 Saint-Exupéry, Antoine de. *Citadelle.* 1948. Paris: Éditions Gallimard. Accessed June 20, 2020.

15 Sinek, Simon. *Start with Why: How Great Leaders Inspire Everyone to Take Action.* 2011. London: Portfolio.

16 Sinek, Simon. September 2009. TED Talks. Accessed January 9, 2021. https://www.ted.com/talks/simon_sinek_how_great_leaders_inspire_action?language=en.

17 Nietzsche, Friedrich. "Simple Thing Called Life." Accessed January 9, 2021. http://www.simplethingcalledlife.com/success/live-can-bear-almost/.

18 Frankl, Viktor. *Man's Search for Meaning.* 2006. Boston: Beacon Press.

19 Thomson Reuters. Thomson Reuters Foundation. Accessed December 27, 2020. http://www.trust.org/.

20 Pirsig, Robert. *Zen and the Art of Motorcycle Maintenance: An Inquiry into Values.* 1974. New York: William Morrow and Company.

21 Nooyi, Indra. December 4, 2019. IGN24. "Rags to Riches Story 19. Accessed April 21, 2021. https://industryglobalnews24.com/rags-to-riches-story-19-indra-nooyi-.

22 Jobs, Steve. June 14, 2005. "'You've got to find what you love,'" Jobs says. Accessed April 21, 2021. https://news.stanford.edu/2005/06/14/jobs-061505/.

23 Buckingham, Marcus. September 9, 2019. "What Is a Good Job?" Brighton, Massachusetts: Harvard Business Review.

24 Okri, Ben, Robin Richardson, and Bernice Miles. *Equality Stories: Recognition, Respect and Raising Achievement.* Stoke on Trent, UK: Trentham Books. Accessed August 17, 2020.

25 John Roth and Adrian Shephard. December 1, 2020. "8 Soft Skills That Make You an Even Better Leader." *Entrepreneur.* Accessed December 31, 2020. https://www.entrepreneur.com/article/359834.

26 Smith, Paul. *Lead with a Story.* 2012. New York: AMACOM.

27 Skidmore, Joel. "Encyclopedia of Greek Mythology: Sisyphus." Accessed November 16, 2020. http://www.mythweb.com/encyc/entries/sisyphus.html.

28 Maslow, Abraham H. *The Ultimate Training Workshop Handbook*, 20. 1999. New York: McGraw-Hill.

29 Fred Brooks. *The Mythical Man-Month: Essays on Software Engineering.* 1975. New York: Addison-Wesley.

30 Greek Myths & Greek Mythology. 2012. Accessed Jan. 29, 2021. https://www
    .greekmyths-greekmythology.com/pandoras-box-myth/.
31 Bill Gates. Goodreads. Accessed August 1, 2020.
32 David Whyte. *The Heart Aroused: Poetry and the Preservation of the Soul.* 1994.
    New York: Bantam Doubleday.
33 Holohan, Bill. April 1, 2001. "On Rocket Ships and Horses' Behinds: Where
    Did Content Standards Come From?" Accessed April 1, 1996. https://www
    .precisioncontent.com//on-rocket-ships-and-horses-behinds-where-did-your-content
    -standards-come-from/.
34 Sagan, Carl. November 29, 2018. "You have to know the past to understand the
    present." Hyper Island. Accessed October 17, 2020. https://www.hyperisland.com
    /blog/you-have-to-knowthe-past-to-understand-the-present.

Chapter 2

1   Welton, Kathleen. December 22, 2016. "What Would Eleanor Roosevelt Say?"
    Thrive Global. Accessed April 22, 2021. https://medium.com/thrive-global
    /what-would-eleanor-roosevelt-say-2cc0db184fb6.
2   Mandela, Nelson. December 27, 2020. "Nelson Mandela Famous Quotes."
    https://www.sanews.gov.za/south-africa/nelson-mandela-famousquotes#:~:-
    tex=%22A%20good%20%20and%20a,many%20more%20hills%20to%20
    .%22.
3   Putnam, Robert D. 2020. "Social Capital Primer." Accessed February 06, 2022.
    http://robertd.com/alone/social-capital-primer/.
4   Kissinger, Henry. December 27, 2020. "'Leaders must invoke an alchemy of
    greatvision.'—HenryKissinger."https://www.teambonding.com/great-vision-great
    -leader/.
5   Rath, Tom, and Conchie, Barry. *Strengths Based Leadership: Great Leaders, Teams,
    and Why People Follow.* 2009. Washington, DC: Gallup Press.
6   Lencioni, Patrick. *The Five Dysfunctions of a Team.* 2002. Hoboken, New Jersey:
    John Wiley & Sons.
7   Blanchard, Ken, and Spencer Johnson. *The One Minute Manager.* 2015. New York:
    William Morrow & Co, Inc.
8   Greenleaf, Robert K. *The Servant Leader.* 1970. New York: Paulist Press.
9   Greenleaf, Robert K. *Servant Leadership: A Journey into the Nature of Legitimate
    Power and Greatness.* 1977. Mahwah, NJ: The Paulist Press.
10 Greenleaf, Robert K., and Larry C. Spears. *The Power of Servant-Leadership: Essays
    by Robert K. Greenleaf.* 1998. Oakland: Berrett-Koehler.
11 Snyder, Neil H. *Vision, Values, and Courage: Leadership for Quality Management.*
    1993. New York: Free Press.
12 Patterson, Kathleen. August 2003. "Servant Leadership—A Theoretical Model."
    School of Leadership Studies, Regent University. Accessed January 3, 2021. https:
    //www.regent.edu/wp-content/uploads/2020/12/patterson_servant_leadership.pdf.
13 Goleman, Daniel and Monroe, Deborah R. *Cutting Through to Success* 2nd Edition,
    105. 2012. Indianapolis, Indiana.: Dog Ear Publishing.

14 George, Bill. October 1, 2010. " Mindful Leadership." Accessed April 24, 2021. https://www.billgeorge.org/articles/mindful-leadership-compassionand-meditation-develop-effective-leaders/.

15 Peterson, Russ. 2010. "Motivating Your Team for Success." Accessed April 24, 2021. https://www.ispeak.com/motivating-your-team-for-success/amp/.

16 Ash, Phillip. May 23, 2017. "Fast and Effective Change Management." Accessed April 24, 2021. https://link..com/chapter/10.1007/978–981-10–0983-9_42.

17 Schieltz, Matthew and Bennett, Kristen. "Why Transformational Leadership Is Important." Accessed May 24, 2021. https://smallbusiness.chron.com/transformational-leadership-important-10423.html.

18 Geoffrey, Michael. December 30, 2009. "It Takes Leadership." Entrepreneur.com. Accessed April 24, 2021. https://www.entrepreneur./article/204500.

19 Indeed Editorial Team. April 7, 2021. "Business Ethics Definition and Examples." Indeed Editorial Team. Accessed May 24, 2021. https://www.indeed.com/career-advice/career-development/what-are-business-ethics.

20 Josephson, Michael. January 13, 2015. "12 Ethical Principles for Business Executives." Accessed May 22, 2021. https://www.standardizations.org//?p=133.

21 Einstein, Albert. October 29, 2015. philosiblog. Accessed December 27, 2020. https://philosiblog.com/2015/10/29/try-not-to-become-a-man-of-success-but-rather-try-to-become-a-man-of-value/.

22 Cook, Tim. May 17, 2015. "Apple CEO Tim Cook tells graduates: Values and justice belong in the workplace." Accessed December 27, 2020. https://venturebeat.com/2015/05/17/ceo-tim-cooktells-graduates-values-and-justice-belong-in-the-workplace/.

23 Jobs, Steve. August 2, 2013. "Pixar's John Lasseter on Steve Jobs, Creativity, and Disney Infinity." Accessed December 27, 2020. https://www.fastcompany.com/3014992/pixars-john-lasseter-on-steve-jobs-creativity-and-disney-infinity.

24 Crosby, Philip B. *Quality Is Free.* 1979. New York: McGraw-Hill.

25 Deming, W. Edwards. *Out of the Crisis.* 1982. Cambridge, MA: MIT Press.

26 Prigogine, Ilya. *New Perspectives on Complexity.* 1989. Boston: Springer.

27 Poppe, Rod. 2000. Illinois Athletic Directors Association. IADA Hall of Fame Inductees. Accessed March 23, 2022. https://www.illinoisad.org/page/3417/article/393.

28 Reeves, Ed. February 13, 2016. Hall of Fame Induction: Ed Reeves. Accessed March 26, 2022. https://kipdf.com/hall-of-fameinduction_5aacd1ab1723dd00a5efe45f.html.

Chapter 3

1 Westfall, Richard S. March 27, 2021. Britannica. "Isaac Newton: English physicist and mathematician." Accessed April 29, 2021. https://www.britannica.com/biography/Isaac-Newton.

2 Britannica. April 30, 2020. "Bernard de Chartres." Accessed April 29, 2021. https://www.britannica.com/biography/Bernard-de-Chartres.

3 Chen, Chaomei. 2003. "On the Shoulders of Giants." In: *Mapping Scientific Frontiers: The Quest for Knowledge Visualization.* London: Springer.

4   故宫博物馆出版社. 1994, 清宫殿藏画本. 北京:. 1994. "File:吴司马孙武.jpg." Wikimedia Commons. Accessed December 28, 2020. https://upload.wikimedia. org/wikipedia/commons/c/cf/%E5%90%B4%E5%8F%B8%E9%A9%AC%E5% AD%99%E6%AD%A6.jpg.

5   Tzu, Sun. *The Art of War*. 2007. Minneapolis: Filiquarian.

6   Tzu, Sun, and Lionel Giles. 1910. *The Art of War*. Accessed December 28, 2020. https://suntzusaid.com/book/1.

7   Tzu, Sun, and Lionel Giles. 1910. *The Art of War*. Accessed December 28, 2020. https://suntzusaid.com/book/1.

8   Eliadis, Pete. February 22, 2011. "The Enemy of My Enemy." Accessed March 25, 2022. https://www.officer.com/tactical/article/10232157/the-enemy-of-my-enemy.

9   Levy, Steven B. November 3, 2010. LexisNexis Legal NewsRoom. Accessed March 25, 2022. https://www.lexisnexis.com/legalnewsroom/legal-business/b/the-legal -business-community-blog/posts/no-battle-plan-survives-contact-with-the-enemy.

10 Tzu, Sun. *The Art of War*. 2007. Minneapolis: Filiquarian.

11 Rumely Company. World's Work 21. 1911. Frederick Taylor. Wikimedia Commons. Dec. 28, 2020. https://upload.wikimedia.org/wikipedia/commons/e/ee /Frederick_Taylor_1911.jpg.

12 Taylor, Frederick Winslow. *The Principles of Scientific Management*. 2014. Eastford, CT: Martino Fine Books.

13 Bhagyashree S. "Principles of Scientific Management." Accessed Dec. 28, 2020. https://www.economicsdiscussion.net/scientific-management/principles-of -scientific-management/31953.

14 Taylor, Frederick, and B. Miller. 2010. "Scientific management." Accessed January 4, 2021. https://www.studymode.com/essays/Scientific-Management-54974277.html.

15 Drucker Archives. 2021. "Peter Drucker Photo." Courtesy of the Drucker Institute at Claremont Graduate University. Claremont, Calif. 91711: Dr. Bridget Lawlor, Archivist.

16 Doran, George T. 1981. "There's a S.M.A.R.T. way to write management goals." *Management Review* 70, no. 11: 35–36.

17 Drucker, Peter F. *The Practice of Management*. 2006 - Reissue edition. New York: Harper Business.

18 Drucker, Peter. British Library. Business and Management portal. Accessed August 26, 2021. https://www.bl.uk/people/peter-drucker.

19 Ateitomas. February 27, 2013. "William Edwards Deming." Wikimedia Commons. Accessed Dec. 28, 2020 https://es.m.wikipedia.org/wiki/Archivo:We -deming-1953-sml.jpg.

20 Butler Bowden, Tom. "50 Business Classics." *Out of the Crisis*, W. Edwards Deming, 68–72. 2018. London, UK: Nicolas Brealey Publishing.

21 Deming, W. Edwards. *Out of the Crisis*. 2000 Reprint Edition. Cambridge, MA: The MIT Press.

22 Ibid.

23 Deming, W. Edwards. "Dr. Deming's 14 Points for Management." The W. Edwards Deming Institute. Accessed Dec. 28, 2020. https://deming.org/explore /fourteen-points/.

24 Bennis, Warren G. 2022 "Warren Bennis." Courtesy of the Warren Bennis Leadership Initiative. Approval Jack FitzGerald and Donna Chrobot-Mason: University of Cincinnati, 24 March 2022.

25 Bennis, Warren G. *On Becoming a Leader.* 1989. New York: Basic Books.

26 Bennis, Warren and Tennyson, Logan. November 22, 2016. "What is the Difference Between Leadership and Management?" Accessed December 12, 2020. https://law path.com.au/blog/what-is-the-difference-between-leadership-and-management.

27 Weinfurter D.J. "The Keys to Effective Leadership." In *Second Stage Entrepreneurship*, by D. J. Weinfurter, 171–88. 2013. New York: Palgrave Macmillan.

28 Sudhakar, Jemi. "Leadership Is the Capacity to Translate Vision into Reality!" Accessed May 29, 2021. https://www.linkedin.com/pulse/leadership-capacity -translate-vision-reality-ms-jemi-sudhakar/.

29 Thind, Ranjit Singh. March 17, 2014. "True Leaders Are Born, Not Made." Accessed May 29, 2021. https://www.linkedin.com/pulse/20140317062326-81068665 -true-leaders-are-born-not-made/.

30 De Vita, Emma. April 28, 2009. "On Becoming a Leader." Accessed May 29, 2021. https://www.thirdsector.co.uk/becoming-leader/management/article/90.

31 Bennis' Leadership Qualities. Accessed May 29, 2021. http://changingminds.org /disciplines/leadership/articles/bennis_qualities.htm.

32 Bennis, Warren G. *On Becoming a Leader.* 1989. New York: Basic Books.

33 McGregor, Douglas. 2022. "Douglas McGregor Photo." Photo approved by William Groves, Chancellor Antioch University. Photo Courtesy of Antioch University, February 22, 2022.

34 McGregor, Douglas. *The Human Side of Enterprise.* 2006. New York: McGraw Hill.

35 Cunningham, Robert. Ivy Business Journal. Sept/Oct 2011. Accessed April 30, 2021 https://ivybusinessjournal.com/publication/douglas-mcgregor-a-lasting -impression/.

36 McGregor, Douglas. 50 Business Classics. Tom Butler-Bowdon, 218–24. 2018. London: Nicholas Brealey.

37 Garrison, Gregory. August 29, 2021. "Theory X & Theory Y." London, UK.

38 Ouchi, William. June 23, 2021. "William Ouchi." Courtesy of William Ouchi. Accessed January 7, 2021.

39 Kotter, John. 2022. "File: John Kotter.JPG." Photo approved by John Kotter & Sari Gibson, February 18, 2022.

40 Kotter, John. 2022. "John Kotter—8 Steps for Leading Change." Graphic approved by John Kotter and Sari Gibson, 18 February 2022.

41 Kotter, John. Leading Change: An Action Plan from the World's Foremost Expert on Business Leadership. 1996. Brighton, Massachusetts: Harvard Business Review Press.

42 Rosabeth. 2021 orig. jpg. Boston: May 6, 2021.

43 Kouzes, James. 2022. "James Kouzes Photo." Photo Credit: Scott McCue Photography, Orinda, CA.

44 Posner, Barry. photo by Bret Simmons, 2014. TEDx University of Nevada https://search.creativecommons.org/photos/9058da17-9850-4dbe-8e4d-6183c9e35463. TEDx_UniversityofNevada is licensed under CC BY-ND 2.0, 23 January.

45 James M. and Posner, Barry Z. 2021. "This Is What It Means to Lead." Accessed June 3, 2021. https://www.leadershipchallenge.com/Research/Five-Practices.aspx.

46 Kouzes, James M. and Posner, Barry Z. "Great Leaders Create Great Workplaces." https://www.leadershipchallenge.com/. Accessed February 27, 2022. https://www.leadershipchallenge.com/landingpages/Great-Leaders-Create-Great-Workplaces.aspx.

47 Kouzes, James M. and Posner, Barry Z. *Leadership Challenge*. 2017. San Francisco: Jossey-Bass.

48 Handy, Elizabeth. 2015. "Charles Handy, photo." Claremont Colleges Library. https://ccdl.claremont.edu/digital/collection/p15831coll12/id/2515/rec/1, 18 August 2015. Accessed January 7, 2021.

49 Handy, Charles. *Gods of Management*. 2009. London, UK: Souvenir Press.

50 Klatt, Bruce, original Maslow, Abraham H. 1999 *Toward a Psychology of Being*. New York: D. Van Nostrand Company.

51 Handy, Charles. *The Age of Unreason*. 1991. Boston: Harvard Business Review.

52 Covey, Stephen. FMI Show, Palestrante. June 22, 2010. Accessed May 3, 2021. https://commons.wikimedia.org/w/index.php?curid=11080756.https://creativecommons.org/licenses/by/3.0/deed.en.

53 Chen, James. March 3, 2021. "Nash Equilibrium." Accessed November 1, 2021. https://www.investopedia.com/terms/n/nash-equilibrium.asp.

54 Lathrap, Mary T. 1999–2022. "Walk a Mile in His Moccasins." Access Feb. 17, 2022. https://www.aaanativearts.com/walk-mile-in-his-moccasins.

55 Covey, Stephen. *7 Habits Of Highly Effective People*. 2004. New York: Simon & Schuster

56 Americans4Arts. June 19, 2009. "Day Two: Dr. Peter M. Senge" licensed under CC BY 2.0." Creative Commons. Accessed May 3, 2021. https://search.creative-commons.org/photos/7f4aaceb-b285-42b6-9591-83d73663c181.

57 Senge, Peter M. *The Fifth Discipline: The Art & Practice of the Learning Organization*. 2006. New York: Doubleday.

58 Ibid.

59 Smith, Mark K. 2001. "The learning organization," The Encyclopedia of Pedagogy and Informal Education. Accessed May 3, 2021. http://www.infed.org/biblio/learning-organization.htm.

60 Toffler, Alvin. 2006. "Taken at Beverly Hills, California." Wikimedia Commons. Accessed December 28, 2020. https://commons.wikimedia.org/wiki/File:Alvin_Toffler_02.jpg.

61 Bird, Alexander. August 13, 2004. "Thomas Kuhn," The Stanford Encyclopedia of Philosophy (Winter 2018 Edition). Accessed November 2, 2021. https://plato.stanford.edu/archives/win2018/entries/thomas-kuhn/.

62 Toffler, Alvin. *Future Shock*. 1984. New York: Bantam.

63 Toffler, Alvin. *The Third Wave*. 1984. New York: Bantam.

64 Toffler, Alvin. *Powershift: Knowledge, Wealth, and Violence at the Edge of the 21st Century*. 1991. New York: Bantam.

65 Jurvetson. May 29, 2008. "File: Gary Hamel and Eric Schmidt at MLab dinner. jpg." Photo by Steve Jurvetson. Menlo Park: https://creativecommons.org/licenses /by/2.5/deed.en.

66 Prahalad, CK. 2009. WEForum 2009.jpg. Wikimedia Commons. 8 Nov. Accessed Dec. 28, 2020. https://commons.wikimedia.org/wiki/File:CK_Prahalad _WEForum_2009.jpg.

67 Hamel, Gary and Prahalad, C.K. *Competing for the Future*. 1994. Boston: Harvard Business Review.

68 Mielach, David. April 19, 2012. Accessed 1, 2021. https://www.businessinsider .com/we-cant-solve-problems-by-using-the-same-kind-of-thinking-we-used -when-we-created-them-2012-4.

69 Hamel, Gary and Prahalad, C.K. *Competing for the Future*. 1994. Boston: Harvard Business Review.

70 Porter, Michael. September 12, 2017. Wikimedia Commons. Accessed April 12, 2021. https://commons.wikimedia.org/wiki/File:Michael_Porter_2017.jpg.

71 Porter, Michael. *Competitive Strategy*. 1998. New York: Free Press.

72 Competitive Advantage. 2015–2021. "The ability of a company to outperform its competitors." Accessed June 3, 2021. https://corporatefinanceinstitute.com /resources/knowledge/strategy/competitive-advantage/.

73 Porter, Michael. *How Competitive Forces Shape Strategy*. 1979. Boston: Harvard Business Review.

74 Porter, Michael. May 25, 2006. "Illustration of Porters 5 Forces. Illustrates article in: Porter 5 forces analysis." Wikimedia Commons. Accessed December 28, 2020. https://commons.wikimedia.org/wiki/File:Porters_five_forces.PNG.

75 Porter, Michael. *How Competitive Forces Shape Strategy*. 1979. Boston: Harvard Business Review.

76 Porter, Michael and Abhishek, Kritesh. April 19, 2018. Trade Brains. Accessed January 2, 2021. https://tradebrains.in/porters-five-forces-competitive-analysis/.

77 Hammer, Michael. "Michael Martin Hammer." Approval Mrs. Phyllis Hammer, October 17, 2021.

78 Champy, James A. Accessed January 7, 2021. Official permission granted by Jim Champy, May 19, 2021.

79 Hammer, Michael, and James Champy. *Reengineering the Corporation: A Manifesto for Business Revolution*. 2006. New York: Harper Collins.

80 Ibid.

81 Badaracco, Joseph. 2021. Received permission by email from Joe. May 6, 2021.

82 Badaracco, Joseph. *Leading Quietly*. 2002. Boston: Harvard Business Review Press.

83 Ibid.

84 Whyte, David. June 25, 2013. Accessed May 3, 2021. https://commons.wikimedia .org/wiki/File:DavidWhyte2013.jpg.

85 Whyte, David. *The Heart Aroused: Poetry and the Preservation of the Soul*. 1996. New York: Penguin Random House.

86 Ibid.

87 Ibid.

88 Ibid.

89 Ibid.

90 Whyte, David. *Crossing the Unknown Sea: Work as a Pilgrimage of Identity*. 2002. New York: Riverhead Books.

91 Campbell, Joseph. *The Hero with a Thousand Faces*. 1949. New York: Pantheon Books.

92 Mangoed. 2009. Wikimedia Commons. Accessed August 10, 2021. https://commons.wikimedia.org/wiki/File:Jim_Collins.jpg.

93 Collins, James C. *Built to Last: Successful Habits of Visionary Companies*. 1994. New York: HarperCollins Publishers.

94 Butler-Bowdon, Tom. "50 Business Classics." In *The Magic of Thinking Big*, by David Schwartz, 110. 2018. London, UK: Nicolas Brealey Publishing.

95 Collins, James C. 1995. "Building Companies to Last." Accessed August 10, 2021. https://www.jimcollins.com/article_topics/articles/building-companies.html#articletop.

96 Collins, James C. *Good to Great: Why Some Companies Make the Leap . . . And Others Don't*. 2001. New York: Random House Business.

97 Butler-Bowden, Tom. "50 Business Classics." In *Great by Choice*, by Jim Collins, 60. 2018. London: Nicolas Brealey Publishing.

98 Wuertenberg. January 27, 2011. "Daniel Goleman—World Economic Forum Annual Meeting 2011." Wikimedia Commons. Accessed May 06, 2021. https://commons.wikimedia.org/w/index.php?curid=14858288.

99 Goleman, Daniel. *Emotional Intelligence*. 1995. New York: Bantam Books.

100 Ulrich, David. May 15, 2008. Wikimedia Commons. Accessed December 29, 2020. https://en.wikipedia.org/wiki/File:Dave-Ulrich-in-2008.jpg.

101 Ulrich, David. *Leadership Code: Five Rules to Lead By*. 2009. Boston: Harvard Business Review Press.

102 Satara, Alyssa. January 31, 2018. "Sheryl Sandberg Said This About Leadership And It Was Incredibly Insightful." Inc.com. Accessed April 18, 2022. https://www.inc.com/alyssa-satara/sheryl-sandberg-said-this-about-leadership-it-was-incredibly-insightful.html#:~:text=According%20to%20Sheryl%20Sandberg%2C%20%22The,things%20leaders%20should%20be%20doing.

103 Fisk, Peter. 2021. "GameChangers—Leadership Code." Accessed June 03, 2021. https://www.thegeniusworks.com/2018/04/leadership-code-shape-the-future-make-it-happen-engage-people-today-build-the-next-generation-and-invest-in-yourself/.

104 Peters, Tom. Photo—Photo: Allison Shirreffs. tompeters.com. Approval Holly Bauer, Tom Peters Group, October 19, 2021

105 Peters, Thomas J., and Robert H. Waterman. *In Search of Excellence: Lessons from America's Best-Run Companies*. 2006. New York: Harper Business.

106 Ibid.

107 Warhol. February 15, 2021. "15 minutes of fame." Accessed March 01, 2021. https://en.wikipedia.org/wiki/15_minutes_of_fame.

Chapter 4

1   Shackleton, Ernest Henry. *South: The Illustrated Story of Shackleton's Last Expedition*, 148. Reprint edition March 19, 2019 Bristol, UK: Voyageur Press.

2   Garrison, Greg. May 2021. "Hudson-Garrison Leadership Characteristics Matrix." Valldemossa, Mallorca.

3   Ibid.

4   Ibid.

5   Ibid.

6   Ibid.

7   Kiisel, Ty. Forbes.com. "Without It, No Real Success is Possible." 6 February. 2013. Accessed April 24, 2021. https://www.forbes.com/sites/tykiisel/2013/02/05/without-it-no-real-success-is-possible/?sh=a71d83de4914.

8   Sandberg, Sheryl. "5 Reasons Empathy Is Becoming the Number One Leadership Skill." November 7, 2019. Accessed December 27, 2020. https://thriveglobal.com/stories/5-reasons-empathy-is-becoming-the-number-one-leadership-skill/.

9   Jobs, Steve. "Developing Super Leaders." September 1, 2017. Accessed 12/27/2020 https://developingsuperleaders.wordpress.com//09/01/if-you-are-working-on-something-exciting-that-youreally-care-about-you-dont-have-to-pushed-the-vision-pulls-you-steve-jobs/.

10   Sculley, John. October 7, 2011. "John Sculley on Steve Jobs." Bloomberg. Accessed October 13, 2022. https://www.bloomberg.com/news/articles/2011–10-06/john-sculley-on-steve-jobs?leadSource=uverify%20wall.

11   Tichy, Noel and Charan, Ram. "Speed, Simplicity, Self-Confidence: An Interview with Jack Welch." Harvard Business Review. March 2, 2020. Accessed April 24, 2021. https://hbr.org/1989/09/speed-simplicity-self-confidence-an-interview-with-jack-welch.

12   Sandberg, Sheryl. February 2020. "Understanding Your CWB Leadership Study Results." Bentley University. Accessed April 24, 2021. https://www.bentley.edu/academics/research-centers/understanding-cwb-leadership-study-survey-results.

13   Goleman, Daniel. *Emotional Intelligence.* 1995. New York: Bantam Books

14   Santiago, Louise. June 20, 2019. "Trust: The Essential Element in any Community of Practice." Center for Learning Leaders. Accessed April 24, 2021https://centerforlearning.com/leadership-coaching/trust-the-essential-element//

15   Cook, Karen S. December 27, 2020. "Social Exchange Theory." Accessed December 27, 2020. https://www.sciencedirect.com/topics/social-sciences/social-exchange-theory.

16   Bligh, Michelle. 2017. "Leadership and Trust." In *Leadership*, by Joan and Dhiman, Satinder Marques, 24–34. New York and Zurich: Springer International Publishing.

17   Garrison, Greg 2021 "Hudson-Garrison Leadership Characteristics Matrix." 2021. Valldemossa, Mallorca, May.

18   Gallo, Carmine. December 19, 2013. "What Starbucks CEO Howard Schultz Taught Me About Communication and Success." Accessed December 27, 2020. https://www.forbes./sites/carminegallo/2013/12/19/what-starbucks-ceo-howard-schultz-taught-me-about-communication-and-success/?sh=59daf8cb28af.

19 Marques, Joan and Dhiman, Satinder. *Leadership Today.* 2017. Zurich Switzerland and New York: Springer International.

20 Bajaj, Shivani. July 6, 2017. "Learnings from Warren Buffett: 8 Powerful Life Lessons." Medium.com. Accessed April 24, 2021. https://medium.com/@musingfromshivani /learnings-from-warren-buffet-8-powerful-life-lessons-2eaa90690394.

21 Schwab, Charles M. 2021. "Fundamental Techniques In Handling People." Accessed July 02, 2022. https://primarygoals.com/teams/books/win-friends-influence -people/.

22 Peterson, Russ S and Swoboda, Chuck. 2020. "Smart Leaders Purposely Put Themselves at the Bottom of the Org Chart." Forbes.com. May 18, 2020. Accessed April 24, 2021. https://www.forbes.com/sites/chuckswoboda/2020/05/18/smart-leaders -purposely-put-themselves-at-the-bottom-of-the-org-chart/?sh=3554e69141a5.

23 Iger, Robert. "13 Best CEO Books to Read in 2021." Accessed April 28, 2021. Teambuilding. https://teambuilding.com/blog/ceo-books.

24 Redmond, Kevin. February 17, 2018. "Edison's fire." Accessed May 28, 2021. https://usebecause.com//02/17/edisons-fire/

25 Garrison, Greg. May 2021. "Hudson-Garrison Leadership Characteristics Matrix." Valldemossa, Mallorca.

26 Geller, Ben. February 15, 2013. "Best of the Blog: Doing the Right Thing vs. Doing Things Right." Architecture & Governance. Accessed April 28, 2021. https://www.architectureandgovernance.com/elevating-ea/best-blog-right-thing -vs-things-right/.

27 Niebuhr, Reinhold. April 17, 2021. Accessed April 28, 2021. http://www.gutenberg .org/articles/eng/Reinhold_Niebuhr

28 Boudreau. July 15, 2011. "Interview: John Roos United States Ambassador to Japan." *East Bay Times–Mercury News.* Accessed April 28, 2021. https://www.eastbay times.com/2011/07/15/mercury-news-interview-john-roos-united-states-ambassador -to-japan/.

29 Stanzel, Volker. *New Realities in Foreign Affairs: Diplomacy in the 21st Century*, 13. 2019. Baden-Baden, Germany: Nomos Verlag.

30 Thomson, James and Boyd, Tony. December 29, 2020. "The books, films and shows that moved our top CEOs." Financial Review. Accessed April 28, 2021. https://www.afr.com/work-and-careers/leaders/the-books-films-and-shows -that-moved-our-top-ceos-20201222-p56ple.

31 Kahneman, Daniel. *Thinking, Fast and Slow.* 1994. New York: Farrar Straus & Giroux.

32 Haden, Jeff. November 18, 2018. "The 9 Best Steve Jobs Quotes About Business, Success, and Living a Fulfilling Life." Inc.com. Access April 28, 2021.

33 Duckworth, Angela. *Grit: The Power of Passion and Perseverance.* 2016. New York: Scribner.

34 Itzler, Jesse. *Living with a SEAL: 31 Days Training with the Toughest Man on the Planet.* New York: Center Street.

35 Butler-Bowden, Tom. "50 Business Classics." In *Great by Choice*, by Jim Collins, 64. 2018. London: Nicolas Brealey Publishing.

36 Edison. "I Have Gotten a Lot of Results! I Know Several Thousand Things That Won't Work." Accessed May 28, 2021. https://quoteinvestigator.com//07/31 /edison-lot-results/.

37 Schauble, Wolfgang. May 2020. "Why You Need a To-Do List." Hyper Resolute. Accessed April 28, 2021. https://hyper-resolute.com/why-you-need-a-to-do-list/.

38 Peters, Tom. "Under Promise, Over Deliver." Accessed April 29, 2021. https: //tompeters./columns/under-promise-over-deliver/.

39 Garrison, Greg. May 2021. "Hudson-Garrison Leadership Characteristics Matrix." Valldemossa, Mallorca.

40 Pozin, Ilya. February 19, 2018. "Piece of Advice From Mark Zuckerberg That Will Determine Your Success." Inc.com. Accessed December 27, 2020. https://www .inc.com/ilya-pozin/one-piece-of-advice-from-mark-zuckerberg-that-will-determine -your-success-or-failure-in-2018.html.

41 Moss Kanter, Rosabeth. 2021. "Expecting a Positive Outcome—How Confidence Can Help You Cope." Ultimate Academy. Accessed April 29, 2021. https: //ultimate.com/confidence-for-success-courses/confidence-for-success-blog /expecting-a-positive-outcome-how-confidence-can-help-you-cope/.

42 Brackett, Justin. January 7, 2012. "Reasons Why You Will Fail in 2012." Business 2 Community. Accessed April 29, 2021. https://www.business2community.com /2-reasons-why-you-will-fail-in-2012–0114107.

43 Gallo, Carmine. July 7, 2016. "Richard Branson: 'Communication Is The Most Important Skill Any Leader Can Possess.'" *Forbes.* Accessed April 29, 2021. https://www.forbes.com/sites/carminegallo/2015/07/07/richard-branson-commu- nication-is-the-most-important-skill-any-leader-can-possess/?sh=71052bb12e8a.

44 De Bono, Edward. December 27, 2020. "The Science of Creativity." Hubspot. Accessed December 27, 2020. https://blog.hubspot.com/marketing/the-science-of -creativity.

45 Garrison, Greg. May 2021 "Hudson-Garrison Leadership Characteristics Matrix." 2021. Valldemossa, Mallorca.

46 Ibid.

Chapter 5

1 Kouzes, James M., and Barry Z. Posner. *The Leadership Challenge.* 2017. San Francisco, CA: Jossey-Bass.

2 Kouzes, James M., and Barry Z. Posner. 2002. "Great Leaders Create Great Workplaces." Accessed February 27, 2022. https://www.leadershipchallenge.com /landingpages/Great-Leaders-Create-Great-Workplaces.aspx

3 Kouzes, James M., and Barry Z. Posner. "The Leadership Challenge Resources- Whitepapers." Accessed February 27, 2022. https://www.leadershipchallenge.com /Resources.aspx#Whitepapers.

4 Kouzes, James M. and Posner, Barry Z. *The Leadership Challenge.* 2017. San Francisco, CA: Jossey-Bass.

5 Bar-On, Reuven. 2021. "Bar-On Emotional Quotient Inventory." Accessed Feb. 21, 2021. https://www.reuvenbaron.org/wp/reuven-bar-on/about-reuven-bar-on/.

6   Derakhshan, F. February 21, 2015. "Multi-Health Systems Inc. EQ-i 2.0 Leadership Report." Accessed February 21, 2021. https://storefront.mhs.com/collections/eq-i-2-0.

7   Bar-On, Reuven. 2013. "The 15 factors of the Bar-On model." Accessed June 06, 2021. https://www.reuvenbaron.org/wp/the-5-meta-factors-and-15-sub-factors-of-the-bar-on-model/.

8   Derakhshan, F. June 27, 2015. EQi-2.0-Model.jpg. Accessed May 9,2021 https://commons.wikimedia.org/wiki/File:EQi-2.0-Model.jpg.

9   Hersey, Dr. Paul. "Situational Leadership® Model & Performance Readiness® levels." In *Management of Organizational Behavior: Utilizing Human Resources.* 2017. Cary, NC: Center for Leadership Studies.

10 Hersey, Paul, and Ken Blanchard. *Management of Organizational Behavior* 10th Edition. 2012. New York: Pearson Publishing.

11 Broadwell, Martin M. 2020. "Four Stages of Competence." Dec. 2020. https://en.wikipedia.org/wiki/Four_stages_of_competence.

12 Broadwell, Martin M. June 24, 2017. "Stages of Competence." Wikimedia Commons. Accessed December 30, 2020. https://commons.wikimedia.org/wiki/File:Competence_Hierarchy_adapted_from_Noel_Burch_by_Igor_Kokcharov.svg

13 Broadwell, Martin. March 2019. "Four Stages of Competence." Accessed June 10, 2021. https://rider-ed.com/wp-content/uploads/2019/03/Four-Stages-of-Competence.pdf.

14 Myers Briggs. December 29, 2020. "MBTI® Basics." Myers Briggs Foundation. Accessed December 29, 2020. https://www.myersbriggs.org/my-mbti-personality-type/mbti-basics/.

15 Myers Briggs. January 28, 2014. "Chart detailing all Myers-Briggs personality types." Wikimedia Commons. Accessed Dec. 29, 2020. https://commons.wikimedia.org/wiki/File:MyersBriggsTypes .png.

16 Myers Briggs. "MBTI® Basics." Myers Briggs Foundation. Accessed December 29, 2020. https://www.myersbriggs.org/my-mbti-personality-type/mbti-basics/.

17 Insights Discovery. December 30, 2020. "Insights for your people, breakthroughs for your business." Accessed December 30, 2020. https://www.insights.com/products/insights-discovery/.

18 Insights Discovery. 2022. The Insights Group Limited. 2020 Email approval John Beck, 11 March.

19 Insights Discovery. Part 1: The 4 colors 2018 05 July. Accessed June 06, 2021. https://www.mudamasters.com/en/personal-growth-personality/insights-discovery-part-1-4-colors.

20 Korn Ferry. Leadership Assessment. Accessed December 29, 2020. https://www.kornferry.com/solutions/assessment-and-succession/leadership-assessment.

21 Korn Ferry. 2015 "Korn Ferry Assessment of Leadership Potential." Accessed December 29, 2020. https://www.kornferry.com/content/dam/kornferry/docs/article-migration/KFALP_Technical_Manual_final.pdf.

22 Korn Ferry. LDN International 2021 Korn Ferry Leadership Architect™. Accessed May 09, 2021. https://ldninternational.com/korn-ferry-leadership-architect.

23 Paduch. October 1, 2010. "Components of competency based management." May 9, 2021. https://en.wikipedia.org/wiki/File:Competency-circle.jpg.

24 Belbin, Meredith. "The Nine Belbin Team Roles." Belbin.com. Accessed December 30, 2020. https://www.belbin.com/about/belbin-team-roles/.

25 Belbin, Meredith. "What Is a Team Role?" Accessed June 09, 2021. https://www.belbin.com/about/belbin-team-roles.

26 Belbin, Meredith. "The Nine Belbin Team Roles." Belbin.com. Accessed May 13, 2021. https://www.belbin.com/about/belbin-team-roles. Approved Nigel Belbin 13 May, 2021.

27 Spaynton and Luft, Joseph and Ingham. "Johari Window." Wikimedia Commons. Accessed Dec. 30, 2020 https://commons.wikimedia.org/wiki/File:JohariWindow.png.

28 Communication Theory. The Johari Window Model. Accessed June 6, 2021. https://www.communicationtheory.org/the-johari-window-model/.

29 Tuckman, Bruce W. 1965. "Developmental Sequence in Small Groups." *Psychological Bulletin* 63, no. 6: 384–99. Accessed June 20, 2021. http://www.communicationcache.com/uploads/1/0/8/8/10887248/developmental_sequence_in_small_groups_-_reprint.pdf.

30 DovileMi and Tuckman, Bruce. February 11, 2021 "Tuckman's Stages of Group Development." WikiMedia Commons. Licensed under the Creative Commons Attribution-Share Alike 4.0.

31 Garrison, Gregory. Graphic. 1965. "Tuckman Stages of Team Development." Tuckman, B. W. Developmental sequence in small groups. *Psychological Bulletin*, 65(6): 384–399. American Psychological Association.

32 Bruton, John/Lynn. n.d. "Stages of Team Development." Lumen Learning. Accessed June 20, 2021. https://courses.lumenlearning.com/suny-principlesmanagement/chapter/reading-the-five-stages-of-team-development/.

33 Tuckman, Bruce and Stein, Judith. "Using the Stages of Team Development." Accessed Dec. 31, 2020. https://hr.mit.edu/learning-topics/teams/articles/stages-development.

34 Maslow, Abraham. *A Theory of Human Motivation*. 2013. Eastford, CT: Martino Fine Books.

35 Maslow, Abraham. October 25, 2019. "Maslows-Hierarchy-of-Needs-1.png." Wikimedia Commons. Access December 30, 2020. https://commons.wikimedia.org/wiki/File:Maslows-Hierarchy-of-Needs-1.png.

36 Green, Christopher D. and Maslow, Abraham. "Classics in the History of Psychology—A Theory of Human Motivation." Published in *Psychological Review* 50, 370–96. August 2000. Accessed June 09, 2021. http://psychclassics.yorku.ca/Maslow/motivation.htm.

37 Koltko-Rivera, M. E. "Rediscovering the later version of Maslow's hierarchy of needs: Self-transcendence and opportunities for theory, research, and unification." 2006. Review of General Psychology 10(4): 302–17.

38 Venter, Henry J. "Self-Transcendence: Maslow's Answer to Cultural Closeness." 2016. *Journal of Innovation Management* 3–7.

39 Garrison, Gregory—Graphic. "Maslow Hierachy of Needs-Self-Trancendence." Palma Mallorca, September 16, 2022.

40 Herzberg, Frederick. "Motivation to Work." 2017. Abingdon, UK: Routledge.

41 Williams, Linda and Lumen Learning. Herzberg's Two-Factor Theory. Accessed June 9, 2021. https://courses.lumenlearning.com/wmintrobusiness/chapter /reading-two-factor-theory/.

42 Maslow, Abraham. October 25, 2019. "Maslows-Hierarchy-of-Needs-1.png." Wikimedia Commons. Accessed December 30, 2020. https://commons.wikimedia .org/wiki/File:Maslows-Hierarchy-of-Needs-1.png. Herzberg addition to Maslow by Greg Garrison

43 Sperry, Dr. Roger. December 8, 1981. Nobel Lecture. Accessed March 11, 2022. https: //www.nobelprize.org/prizes/medicine/1981/sperry/25059-roger-w-sperry -nobel-lecture-1981/.

44 MacLean, Dr. Paul D. "Science of Psychotherapy—The Triune Brain." October 26, 2016. Accessed March 11, 2022. https://www.thescienceofpsychotherapy .com/the-triune-brain/.

45 Herrmann, Ned. "Whole Brain® Model—Research and Certification Report." Email Approval Virlina Choquette September 3, 2022: Herrmann Global, LLC.

46 Herrmann, Ned. "How It Works." Think Herrmann. Accessed March 11, 2022. https://www.thinkherrmann.com/how-it-works.

47 Herrmann, Ned. "Whole Brain® Model—Research and Certification Report." Email Approval Virlina Choquette September 3, 2022: Herrmann Global, LLC.

48 Herrmann, Ned. 2022. The Herrmann Platform. Accessed March 12, 2022. https://engage.thinkherrmann.com/herrmann-platform.

49 Csikszentmihalyi, Mihaly. 2010. "File:Mihaly Csikszentmihalyi.jpg." https: //commons.wikimedia.org/wiki/File:Mihaly_Csikszentmihalyi.jpg. Ehirsh, 05 June.

50 Csikszentmihalyi, Mihaly. Flow. 2008. New York: Harper Perennial Modern Classics.

51 Csikszentmihalyi, Mihaly, and Isabella Selega Csikszentmihalyi. Optimal Experience: Psychological Studies of Flow in Consciousness. 1992. Cambridge, UK: Cambridge University Press.

52 Csikszentmihalyi, Mihaly. Creativity: Flow and the Psychology of Discovery and Invention. 2013. New York: Harper Perennial.

Chapter 6

1 Bateson, Gregory n.d. Accessed June 22, 2020. https://.atlasobscura.com/places /oak-beams-new-college-oxford.

2 Bateson, Gregory n.d. The International Bateson Institute. Accessed December 31, 2020. https://batesoninstitute.org/gregory-bateson/.

3 Iliff, David. Photo. License: CC BY-SA 3.0 2014 The Dining Hall of Balliol College, Oxford University, UK." Wikimedia Commons. 10 January. Accessed August 30, 2021. https://commons.wikimedia.org/wiki/File:Balliol_College _Dining_Hall,__-_Diliff.jpg.

4 Pay It Forward. February 12, 2000. Box Office Mojo n.d. Accessed March 04, 2021. https://en.wikipedia.org/wiki/Pay_It_Forward_(film).

5   Csikszentmihalyi, Mihaly. *Finding Flow: The Psychology of Engagement with Everyday Life*. 1997. New York: Basic Books.

Appendix

1   Lewin, K., R. Lippit, and R. K. White. 1939. "Patterns of aggressive behavior in experimentally created social climates." *Journal of Social Psychology*, 271–301.
2   Garrison, Greg. July 17, 2021. "Lewin 3 Model." Valldemossa, Spain.
3   Lewin, Kurt & Lippitt, Ronald, & White, Ralph K. 2000. "Patterns of aggressive behavior in experimentally created social climates." Technische Universitat Dresdeen. Accessed June 06, 2021. https://tu-dresden.de/mn/psychologie/ipep /lehrlern/res/dateien/lehre/lehramt/lehrveranstaltungen/Lehrer_Schueler _Interaktion_SS_2011/Lewin_1939_original.pdf?lang=de.
4   Tannenbaum, Robert, and Warren H. Schmidt. *How to Choose a Leadership Pattern*. 2009. Boston, MA: Harvard Business Review Press.
5   Garrison, Gregory. October 20, 2021. "Tannenbaum-Schmidt—Leadership Continuum." Palma, Mallorca.
6   Tannenbaum-Schmidt Leadership Continuum. Accessed June 10, 2021. https://expertprogrammanagement.com//11/tannenbaum-schmidt-leadership -continuum/.
7   Dunham, Randall B., and Jon Pierce. *Managing*. 1989. Northbrook, IL: Scott Foresman & Co.
8   Dunham, Randall and Pierce, Jon. 2012. "Dunham and Pierce's Leadership Process Model." Email approvals Randall B. Dunham, Jon L. Pierce, October 18 and 19.
9   Ospina Avendano, D. 2020. Dunham and Pierce's Leadership Process Model. Accessed June 10, 2021. https://www.toolshero.com//dunham-and-pierces -leadership-process-model/.
10 Birkman, Roger. Birkman Method. Accessed Dec. 30, 2020. https://birkman .com/the-birkman-method/.
11 Birkman, Roger. October 26, 2021. "Birkman Model." Birkman International, Inc. Approved Brittany Buxton.
12 Birkman, Roger W. October 28, 2016. "Birkman Signature Report." ReNewIst. Accessed June 06, 2021. https://re-new-ist.com/pdf/Birkman-Signature-Report .pdf.
13 Birkman, Roger. October 26, 2021. "Birkman Model." Birkman International, Inc. Approved Brittany Buxton.
14 Blake, Robert R., and Jane S. Mouton. *Managerial Grid: Leadership Styles for Achieving Production Through People*. 1966. Houston: Gulf Publishing.
15 Khalid and Blake, Robert R. and Mouton, Jane S. September 23, 2004 WikiMedia Commons-ManagementGrid.PNG. Accessed Dec. 30, 2020. https://en.wikipedia .org/wiki/File:Management_Grid.PNG.
16 Juneja, Prachi. 2018. Blake and Mouton's Managerial Grid. Accessed June10, 2021. https://www.managementstudyguide.com/blake-mouton-managerial-grid .htm.

17 Thomas International. Personal Profile Analysis (PPA) 2002–2021. Accessed June 06, 2021. https://www.thomas.co/personal-profile-analysis-ppa.

18 Thomas International. 2020. Thomas psychometric assessment and aptitude tests. Accessed December 29, 2020. https://www.thomas.co/assessments /psychometric-assessment-aptitude-tests.

19 Schutz, William. 2021. "Fundamental Interpersonal Relations Orientation." ©2021 Business Consultants, Inc. From the Human Element workbook, reprinted with permission. Approval - The Schutz Company, 25 June, 21.

20 Thompson, Henry L. 2000. "An Overview of Element B—A FIRO-Based Instrument." April. Accessed June 06, 2021. https://www..se/files/FIRO -overview_element_b.pdf.

21 Schutz, Dr. Will. 2021. "FIRO Fundamental Interpersonal Relations Orientation." Accessed June 06, 2021. https://www.thehuman.com/firo-theory/.

22 Schutz, William. 2009. "Element B: Behavior." Evolution of FIRO-B. Accessed October 24, 2021. https://www.thehumanelement.com/wp-

23 Thomas, Kenneth W. and Kilmann, Ralph H. 2020. Conflict Mode Instrument. Accessed December 30, 2020. https://kilmann.com/overview -thomas-kilmann-conflict-mode-instrument-tki/.

24 Kilmann, Ralph. 2021. "Thomas-Kilmann Conflict Mode." Overview Thomas Kilmann Conflict Mode Instrument. Accessed May 15, 2021. http://www.kilman-ndiagnostics.com/overview-thomas-kilmann-conflict-mode-instrument-tki.

25 Kilmann, Ralph. 2021. "Thomas-Kilmann Conflict Mode Instrument." Accessed May 15, 2021. http://www.kilmanndiagnostics.com/thomas-kilmann -conflict-mode-instrument-tki.

26 "Hawthorne Effect." Wikipedia. Accessed December 30, 2020. https://en.wikipedia .org/wiki/Hawthorne_effect.

27 Glen, Stephanie. 2021. Hawthorne Effect Definition & History. Accessed June 10, 2021. https://www..com/experimental-design/effect/.

28 Mackenzie, Debora. June 27, 2006. "Big Brother's eyes make us act more honestly." *New Scientist.* Accessed October 27, 2021. https://www.newscientist.com /article/dn9424-big-brother-eyes-make-us-act-more-honestly/.

29 Sample, Ian. June 28, 2006. "The eyes have it for making people behave more honestly." *The Guardian.* Accessed October 27, 2021. https://www.theguardian .com/science/2006//28/psychology.uknews.

Index